REVISION NOTES & QUESTIONS

for New Higher
CHEMISTRY

Eric Allan and John Harris

Hodder & Stoughton

A MEMBER OF THE HODDER HEADLINE GROUP

Orders: please contact Bookpoint Ltd, 130 Milton Park, Abingdon, Oxon OX14 4SB
Telephone: (44) 01235 827720, Fax: (44) 01235 400454. Lines are open from 9.00 -
6.00, Monday to Saturday, with a 24 hour message answering service. Email address:
orders@bookpoint.co.uk

British Library Cataloguing in Publication Data
A catalogue record for this title is available from The British Library

ISBN 0 340 78101 7

Published by Hodder & Stoughton Educational Scotland
First published 2000
Impression number   10 9 8 7 6 5 4 3 2
Year   2006 2005 2004 2003 2002 2001

Cover photo from Beken of Cowes Collection.
Typeset by Wyvern 21 Ltd
Printed in Great Britain for Hodder & Stoughton Educational, a division of Hodder
Headline Plc, 338 Euston Road, London NW1 3BH by
J. W. Arrowsmith Ltd, Bristol

Contents ▪▪▪▪▪▪▪▪▪▪▪▪▪▪▪▪▪▪▪

Unit 1 Energy Matters

Unit 2 The World of Carbon

Unit 3 Chemical Reactions

Preface

These *Revision Notes and Questions for New Higher Chemistry* are intended to be used by candidates who already use our *New Higher Chemistry* textbook, as well as those who use other resources. We have adhered to the same chapter headings as in the textbook and we have used the same layout and method for worked examples although the content is different in the majority of cases.

With regard to the questions, our principal aim has been to provide candidates with a variety of experience of all types of questions encountered in the final exam, namely multiple choice, grid and extended answer questions. Many of the questions are appropriate examples from past exam papers or are slight modifications of them. Past paper questions are denoted by a star (*). We are grateful to SQA for permission to reprint these questions. We make no apology that some questions are harder than strictly necessary for Higher. These are intended to challenge the best candidates.

We owe thanks to our Chemistry colleagues, Mrs J. Blaikie, Mr J.D. Broadfoot and Mr F.I. McGonigal for constructive comments and checking of answers. We are also grateful to Mrs Margaret Lannan for suggestions and checking answers in connection with chapter 13.

Answers are available on a photocopiable sheet from the publishers.

ERA JHH

ENERGY MATTERS

 Reaction Rates

Following the course of a reaction

○ Reactions can be followed by measuring changes in concentration, mass or volume of reactants or products.

A suitable reaction to study is that between marble chips (calcium carbonate) and hydrochloric acid using the apparatus shown in Figure 1.

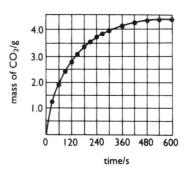

Figure 2 Mass of CO_2 against time

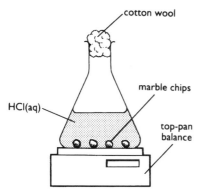

Figure 1

As the reaction proceeds carbon dioxide gas is released and the mass of flask and contents decreases. A cotton wool 'plug' prevents loss of acid spray during effervescence whilst allowing the gas to escape. Equation:

$$CaCO_3(s) + 2HCl(aq) \rightarrow CaCl_2(aq) + CO_2(g) + H_2O(l)$$

Specimen results from an experiment in which 15 g of marble chips, an excess, were added to 50 cm^3 of 4 mol l^{-1} hydrochloric acid are given. The decrease in mass is the mass of carbon dioxide released and this quantity can be plotted against time (Figure 2). From the loss in mass it is also possible, using the equation, to find the concentration of the acid at various times. These calculated results are plotted against time (Figure 3).

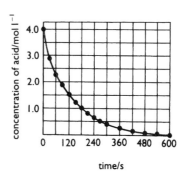

Figure 3 Concentration of acid against time

○ The **rate of reaction** is the change in concentration of reactants or products in unit time.

In Figures 2 and 3, the slope of the graph is steepest at the beginning of the reaction and levels off as time passes, i.e. the rate of reaction is greatest initially and decreases with time.

○ The rate of a reaction is **proportional** to the reciprocal of the time taken.

○ The **average rate** over a certain period of time can be calculated in this experiment from the loss in mass or decrease in acid concentration which occurs in a certain time interval.

Worked Example 1.1

a) Use the data given in Figure 2 to calculate the average rate of reaction during the period from 240 seconds to 300 seconds, in terms of the mass of carbon dioxide produced.

Mass of CO_2 released between 240 s and 300 s $= 4.0 - 3.7 = 0.3$ g

$$\text{Average rate} = \frac{\text{mass of } CO_2}{\text{time interval}}$$

$$= \frac{0.3}{60}$$

$$= 0.005 \text{ g s}^{-1}$$

b) Use the data given in Figure 3 to calculate the average rate of reaction during the period from 120 seconds to 180 seconds, in terms of the decrease in the concentration of hydrochloric acid.

Decrease in concentration of $HCl(aq)$ between 120 s and 180 s
$$= 1.5 - 1.0$$
$$= 0.5 \text{ mol l}^{-1}$$

$$\text{Average rate} = \frac{\text{decrease in acid concentration}}{\text{time interval}}$$

$$= \frac{0.5}{60}$$

$$= 0.0083 \text{ mol l}^{-1} \text{ s}^{-1}$$

Factors affecting the rate of a reaction

○ Reactions, in which one of the reactants is a solid, can be speeded up or slowed down by altering the **particle size** of the solid.

In the reaction discussed in the previous section, using smaller marble chips increases the surface area and speeds up the reaction, as shown by a steeper slope in Figure 4.

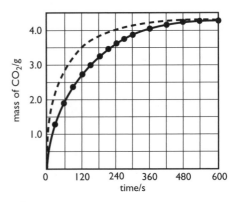

Figure 4

○ **Smaller particle size**, or **larger surface area**, of solid reactants increases reaction rate.

○ Higher **concentration of reactants** in solution increases reaction rate.

The reaction between marble and hydrochloric acid, for example, can be speeded up by increasing the concentration of the acid.

○ Higher **temperature** increases reaction rate.

Prescribed Practical Activity

To investigate the relationship between rate of reaction and concentration of a reactant, a **'clock reaction'** may be used. This is a reaction in which a time lapse occurs before a sudden end-point is reached.

The reaction between hydrogen peroxide and acidified potassium iodide solution is used to show how rate depends on concentration of iodide ions. The equation for the reaction is:

$$H_2O_2(aq) + 2H^+(aq) + 2I^-(aq) \rightarrow 2H_2O(l) + I_2(aq)$$

Starch solution and sodium thiosulphate solution, $Na_2S_2O_3(aq)$, are also in the reaction mixture. Iodine produced in the reaction is immediately changed back into iodide ions by reacting with thiosulphate ions:

$$I_2(aq) + 2S_2O_3^{2-}(aq) \rightarrow 2I^-(aq) + S_4O_6^{2-}(aq)$$

While this is happening the reaction mixture is colourless.

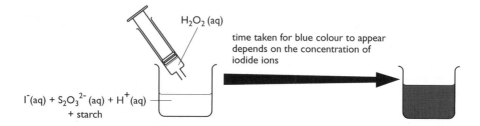

Figure 5

When all of the thiosulphate ions have reacted a blue–black colour suddenly appears as iodine is detected by starch.

As Figure 5 shows potassium iodide solution, starch, sodium thiosulphate solution and dilute sulphuric acid are mixed. Hydrogen peroxide solution is added and the time taken for the mixture to turn blue–black is measured. The experiment is repeated using smaller volumes of the iodide solution but adding water so that the total volume of the reacting mixture is always the same. The concentrations and volumes of all other solutions are kept constant.

The number of moles of thiosulphate ions is the same in each experiment so that when the blue–black colour appears the same extent of reaction has occurred. Since rate is inversely proportional to time, the reciprocal of time (1/t) is taken to be a measure of the rate of the reaction. A graph of rate against volume of KI(aq) is shown in Figure 6.

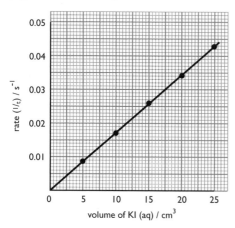

Figure 6

The graph of rate against volume of potassium iodide solution shows a straight line. Since the total volume is always the same, the volume of KI(aq) is a measure of iodide ion concentration.

The straight-line graph means that the rate of this reaction is directly proportional to the concentration of iodide ions.

Prescribed Practical Activity

The effect of temperature on rate can be studied using the following reaction. Acidified potassium permanganate solution, containing purple permanganate ions, MnO_4^-, is decolourised by an aqueous solution of oxalic acid, $(COOH)_2$. This reaction is very slow at room temperature but is almost instantaneous above 80°C. The equation is:

$$5(COOH)_2(aq) + 6H^+(aq) + 2MnO_4^-(aq) \rightarrow$$
$$2Mn^{2+}(aq) + 10CO_2(g) + 8H_2O(l)$$

This experiment is carried out at temperatures ranging from about 40°C to about 70°C.

Volumes and concentrations of all the reactants are kept constant. As shown in Figure 7, the reaction starts when the oxalic acid is added to the permanganate solution, which is acidified with dilute sulphuric acid. The time taken for the solution to become colourless is measured.

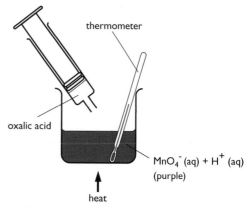

Figure 7

3

As the number of moles of permanganate ions is the same in each experiment, the same amount of reaction has occurred when the end-point has been reached. The reciprocal of the time taken to reach the end-point (1/t) is taken as a measure of the rate of reaction.

A graph of rate against temperature is shown in Figure 8. The rate of reaction increases with rising temperature, but since the graph is a curve the rate is not directly proportional to the temperature.

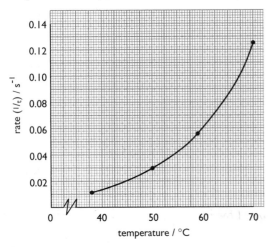

Figure 8

Collision theory

○ All substances are made up of very small particles, which are called atoms, ions or molecules. These particles are continually moving, the speed and extent of the motion is related to whether the substance is a gas, a liquid, a solid or in solution. This description is often referred to as the **'kinetic model of matter'**.

○ For a chemical reaction to occur, the particles of reactants must collide.

○ Any factor which increases the number of collisions per second between the particles of the reactants is likely to increase the rate of reaction.

○ More collisions occur if the particle size of a solid reactant is decreased, since its overall surface area is consequently increased.

○ If the concentration of a reactant is increased, more collisions between particles will take place.

○ Raising the temperature at which the reaction occurs not only increases the number of collisions between particles. Temperature is a measure of the average kinetic energy of the particles in a substance. At a higher temperature the particles have greater kinetic energy and collide with greater force.

○ Reactions occur when reactant particles collide but not all collisions result in a successful reaction.

Activation energy and energy distribution

○ For a reaction to occur the colliding particles must have a minimum amount of kinetic energy, the **activation energy**. This varies from one reaction to another. If the activation energy is high, only a few particles will have enough energy for collisions between them to be successful and hence the reaction will be slow, but a reaction with a low activation energy will be fast.

○ At a given temperature individual molecules of a gas have widely different kinetic energies.

The distribution of kinetic energy values is illustrated in Figure 9. The kinetic energy of individual molecules will continually change due to collisions with other molecules but at constant temperature the overall distribution of energies remains the same.

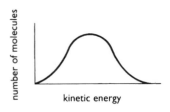

Figure 9 Distribution of energy

Figure 10 also includes the activation energy, E_A. The shaded area represents the number of molecules which have energy greater than the activation energy, i.e. it represents the proportion of molecules which have sufficient energy to react. If the activation energy is greater then the shaded area would be smaller thus representing a smaller proportion of the total number of molecules.

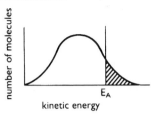

Figure 10 Distribution of energy including activation energy

○ The energy distribution changes when the temperature changes.

The effect of a small rise in temperature, from T_1 to T_2, is shown in Figure 11. The average energy is increased but the most significant feature is the considerable increase in the area that is shaded. This is the real reason why a small change in temperature has such a marked effect on the rate of a reaction.

○ An increase in temperature causes a significant increase in the number of molecules which have energy greater than the activation energy.

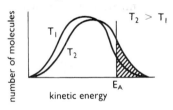

Figure 11 Distribution of energy at different temperatures

Photochemical reactions

○ In some chemical reactions light energy is used to increase the number of molecules which have energy greater than the activation energy.

○ In photosynthesis light energy is absorbed by chlorophyll to convert carbon dioxide and water into glucose and oxygen.

○ In black and white photography when a film is exposed to light silver ions are reduced to silver atoms.

○ Some reactions are 'set off' or initiated by light. A mixture of hydrogen and chlorine

gases explodes when exposed to a light source of high enough energy.

Excess reactant

In previous work balanced equations have enabled the calculation of the mass of a product from the mass of a reactant, or vice versa. In reactions involving two reactants this calculation can only be done if there is more than enough of the other reactant, i.e. it is present in **excess**. An example of a question of this type is, *'4.46 g of lead(II) oxide were reacted with excess dilute nitric acid. Calculate the mass of lead(II) nitrate produced.'*

In the experiment described on page 1 calcium carbonate, in the form of marble chips, was reacted with hydrochloric acid. Worked example 1.2 refers to this reaction.

● Worked Example 1.2 ●

15 g of calcium carbonate were reacted with 50 cm³ of 4 mol l⁻¹ hydrochloric acid.

a) Show by calculation which reactant was present in excess.

b) Calculate the mass of carbon dioxide produced.

$$CaCO_3 + 2HCl \rightarrow CaCl_2 + CO_2 + H_2O$$

1 mol	2 mol		1 mol	
(100 g)			(44 g)	

Answers:

a) Number of moles of $CaCO_3$,

$$n = \frac{m}{gfm} = \frac{15}{100} = 0.15 \text{ mol}$$

where m = mass of substance (in g) and gfm = gram formula mass.

Number of moles of HCl,

$$n = C \times V = 4 \times \frac{50}{1000} = 0.2 \text{ mol}$$

where C = concentration and V = volume.

According to the equation, 1 mol of $CaCO_3$ neutralises 2 mol of HCl.

Hence, 0.1 mol of $CaCO_3$ neutralises 0.2 mol of HCl.

Since there is more than 0.1 mol of $CaCO_3$ present, *this* reactant is in excess.

b) To calculate the mass of carbon dioxide produced we use the quantity of the reactant which is completely reacted (i.e. the acid) and not the one which is present in excess.

According to the equation, 2 mol of HCl produce 1 mol of CO_2.

Hence, 0.2 mol of HCl produce 0.1 mol of CO_2.

$= 0.1 \times 44 = 4.4$ g of CO_2.

Catalysts

○ A catalyst is a substance which alters the rate of a reaction without being used up in the reaction
e.g. manganese(IV) oxide catalyses the decomposition of hydrogen peroxide solution.

$$2H_2O_2(aq) \rightarrow 2H_2O(l) + O_2(g)$$

○ Catalysts play an important part in many industrial processes. Table 1 summarises some of these processes.

○ The catalysts listed in Table 1, along with manganese(IV) oxide in the decomposition of hydrogen peroxide, are said to be **heterogeneous**, since they are in a *different physical state* from the reactants.

○ A catalyst which is in the *same physical state* as the reactants is said to be **homogeneous**.

An example of this is illustrated in Figure 12. The reaction between aqueous solutions of potassium sodium tartrate and hydrogen peroxide is slow, even when the mixture is heated. An aqueous solution containing cobalt(II) ions catalyses it. The immediate colour change to green and the return of the pink colour at the end of the reaction shows that a catalyst may undergo a temporary chemical change during its catalytic activity.

Catalyst	Process	Reaction	Importance
Vanadium(V) oxide	Contact	$2SO_2 + O_2 \rightleftharpoons 2SO_3$	Manufacture of sulphuric acid
Iron	Haber	$N_2 + 3H_2 \rightleftharpoons 2NH_3$	Manufacture of ammonia
Platinum	Catalytic oxidation of ammonia	$4NH_3 + 5O_2 \rightleftharpoons 4NO + 6H_2O$	Manufacture of nitric acid
Nickel	Hydrogenation	Unsaturated oils + $H_2 \rightarrow$ saturated fats	Manufacture of margarine
Aluminium silicate	Catalytic cracking	Breaking down long-chain hydrocarbon molecules	Manufacture of fuels and monomers for the plastics industry

Table 1

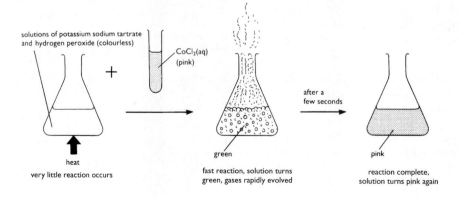

solutions of potassium sodium tartrate and hydrogen peroxide (colourless)

$CoCl_2(aq)$ (pink)

heat
very little reaction occurs

green
fast reaction, solution turns green, gases rapidly evolved

after a few seconds

pink
reaction complete, solution turns pink again

How heterogeneous catalysts work

○ It is an advantage if a heterogeneous catalyst has a large surface area. Catalysis occurs on the surface at certain points called **active sites**. At these sites molecules of at least one of the reactants are **adsorbed**.

○ How a heterogeneous catalyst works can be represented in three stages (Figure 13).

○ A catalyst can become **poisoned** if certain molecules are preferentially adsorbed or even permanently attached to the surface of the catalyst. This reduces the number of active sites available and makes the catalyst ineffective.

Carbon monoxide is a catalyst poison in the Haber Process. In a catalysed industrial process, impurities in reactants can cause additional costs if the catalyst has to be regenerated or renewed.

During the catalytic cracking of long-chain hydrocarbons, carbon is deposited on the surface of the catalyst reducing its efficiency. The catalyst can be regenerated by burning off the carbon in a plentiful supply of air.

Cars with petrol engines have catalytic converters fitted as part of their exhaust systems. The converter contains a ceramic material covered with metals such as platinum and rhodium which catalyse the conversion of carbon monoxide to carbon dioxide and nitrogen oxides to nitrogen. Catalytic converters should only be used in cars which run on unleaded petrol, otherwise the lead compounds will poison the catalyst.

Enzymes

○ Many biochemical reactions in the living cells of plants and animals are catalysed by enzymes. Examples include amylase, which catalyses the hydrolysis of starch, and catalase, present in blood, which catalyses the decomposition of hydrogen peroxide.

○ The molecular shape of an enzyme usually plays a vital role in its function as a catalyst. It operates most effectively at a certain optimum temperature and within a narrow pH range.

○ Enzymes are usually highly **specific**. Maltose and sucrose are disaccharides but are hydrolysed by different enzymes.

○ Industrial applications of enzymes include:

  – yeast to provide enzymes for the fermentation of glucose to ethanol

  – invertase to hydrolyse sucrose to make soft-centred chocolates

  – rennin in cheese production

  – amylase in removing starch from fabrics, a process called desizing.

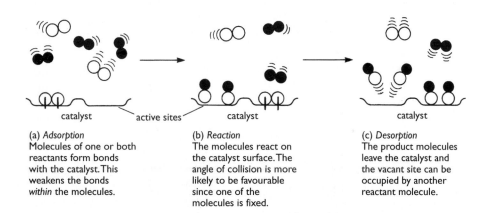

(a) *Adsorption*
Molecules of one or both reactants form bonds with the catalyst. This weakens the bonds *within* the molecules.

(b) *Reaction*
The molecules react on the catalyst surface. The angle of collision is more likely to be favourable since one of the molecules is fixed.

(c) *Desorption*
The product molecules leave the catalyst and the vacant site can be occupied by another reactant molecule.

Figure 13 Heterogeneous catalysis

Questions

Questions 1 and **2** relate to the following graph.

Graph **X** was obtained when 1 g of calcium carbonate powder reacted with excess dilute hydrochloric acid at 20°C.

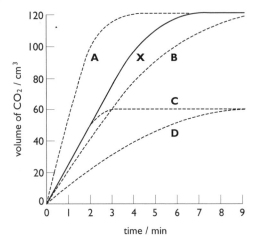

1* Which curve would best represent the reaction of 0.5 g lump calcium carbonate with excess of the same dilute hydrochloric acid?

2 Which curve would best represent the reaction of 1 g of calcium carbonate powder with excess of the same dilute hydrochloric acid at 15°C?

3

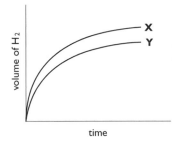

When zinc is reacted with excess dilute sulphuric acid, hydrogen is released. The curves shown above were obtained under different conditions.

The change from **X** to **Y** could be achieved by

A increasing the concentration of the acid
B decreasing the mass of zinc
C decreasing the particle size of the zinc
D adding a catalyst.

4* The graph shows the volume of hydrogen given off against time when an excess of magnesium ribbon is added to 100 cm³ of hydrochloric acid (concentration 1 mol l⁻¹) at 20°C.

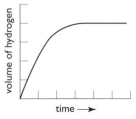

Which graph would show the volume of hydrogen given off when an excess of magnesium ribbon is added to 50 cm³ of hydrochloric acid of the same concentration at 30°C?

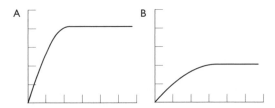

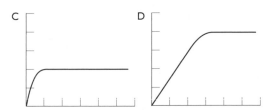

5* For any chemical, the temperature is a measure of

A the average kinetic energy of the particles which react
B the average kinetic energy of all the particles
C the activation energy
D the minimum kinetic energy required before reaction occurs.

6* Two identical samples of zinc were added to an excess of two solutions of sulphuric acid, concentrations 2 mol l⁻¹ and 1 mol l⁻¹ respectively. Which of the following would have been the same for the two samples?

A The total mass lost
B The total time for the reaction
C The initial reaction rate
D The average rate of evolution of gas

7* The relative volumes of hydrogen produced in a given time for three reactions are plotted on the graph.

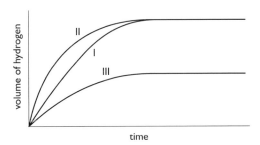

Curve I is for the reaction of excess zinc powder with 100 cm³ of 0.1 mol 1⁻¹ hydrochloric acid.

A	excess magnesium powder	B	50 cm³ of 0.1 mol 1⁻¹ hydrochloric acid	C	50 cm³ of 0.2 mol 1⁻¹ sulphuric acid
D	excess iron powder	E	200 cm³ of 0.1 mol 1⁻¹ hydrochloric acid	F	100 cm³ of 0.05 mol 1⁻¹ sulphuric acid

a) Identify the **two** chemicals which would react to give the results plotted in curve II.
b) Identify the **two** chemicals which would react to give the results plotted in curve III.

8 A pupil added 6.54 g of zinc to 100 cm³ of 0.5 mol 1⁻¹ copper(II) sulphate solution. Identify the correct statement(s) about this experiment.

A	6.54 g of copper is displaced.	B	All of the zinc reacts.	C	0.05 mol of copper is displaced.
D	0.1 mol of zinc sulphate is formed.	E	The solution becomes colourless.	F	Zinc ions are reduced.

9 The reaction between acidified potassium permanganate solution and oxalic acid solution was studied in one of the prescribed practicals.
a) What colour change occurs in this reaction?
b) The reaction was carried out at various temperatures between 40°C and 70°C. It was found that the time taken for this colour change to occur approximately halved for every 10°C rise in temperature.
   i) How would you ensure that a fair comparison was being made in this experiment?
   ii) Draw a graph of rate against temperature to show the results of this experiment.
c) Explain why a small rise in temperature has such a marked effect on the rate of a reaction. Refer to activation energy and include a diagram showing the kinetic energy distribution of reacting particles in your answer.
d) This reaction can be catalysed by $MnSO_4$(aq). Is the catalyst heterogeneous or homogeneous? Explain your choice.

10 A pupil added 10 g of $CaCO_3$ to 100 cm^3 of 1.0 mol l^{-1} HCl. In this experiment

   A all of the $CaCO_3$ dissolved
   B 4.4 g of CO_2 were produced
   C excess acid was used
   D 5 g of $CaCO_3$ did not react.

11 For each of the following reactions indicate whether the catalyst is heterogeneous or homogeneous.

   a) $CH_3CHO(g) \rightarrow CH_4(g) + CO(g)$
      Catalyst: $I_2(g)$

   b) $KClO_3(s) \rightarrow KCl(s) + \frac{3}{2}O_2(g)$
      Catalyst: $MnO_2(s)$

   c) $H_2(g) + I_2(g) \rightarrow 2HI(g)$
      Catalyst: $Au(s)$

12 The following graph shows how the concentration of a dilute acid varies with time during reaction with powdered copper carbonate.

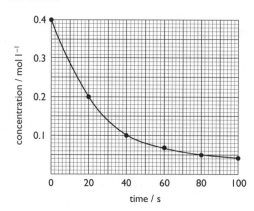

   a) Calculate the average reaction rate during
     i) the first 15 s
     ii) the second 15 s
     iii) the first minute.
   b) The graph levels off after 140 s at a concentration of 0.03 mol l^{-1}. Which reactant is present in excess?

13 a) In an experiment on reaction rate, 2.43 g of magnesium ribbon was added to 100 cm^3 of 2 mol l^{-1} sulphuric acid.
     i) Write the balanced equation for this reaction.
     ii) Show by calculation which reactant was in excess.

b) The following graph was obtained from the experimental results.

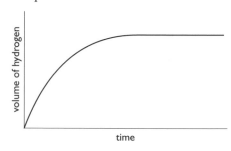

Copy the graph and add lines to show the graphs obtained when the experiment is repeated using
   i) 0.81 g of magnesium powder
   ii) 100 cm^3 of 2 mol l^{-1} hydrochloric acid.

14 The graph shows the results of three experiments involving the reaction of excess powdered magnesium carbonate with dilute acid.

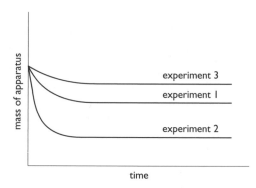

100 cm^3 of 0.5 mol l^{-1} sulphuric acid was added in experiment 1.

A	50 cm^3 of 0.5 mol l^{-1} sulphuric acid
B	100 cm^3 of 0.5 mol l^{-1} hydrochloric acid
C	50 cm^3 of 2.0 mol l^{-1} sulphuric acid
D	100 cm^3 of 1.0 mol l^{-1} hydrochloric acid
E	50 cm^3 of 2.0 mol l^{-1} hydrochloric acid

   a) Identify the solution used in experiment 2.
   b) Identify the solution used in experiment 3.

15* Three experiments were carried out in a study of the rate of reaction between magnesium (in excess) and dilute hydrochloric acid. A balance was used to record the mass of the reaction flask and its contents. The results of experiment 1, using 0.4 mol 1^{-1} acid, are shown in the graph.

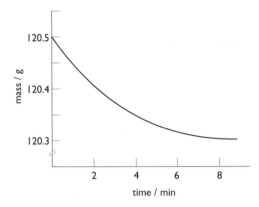

a) Why did the balance record a decrease in mass during the reaction?

b) The **only** difference between experiment 2 and experiment 1 was the use of a catalyst. On a copy of the graph, sketch a curve that could be expected for experiment 2.

c) The **only** difference between experiment 3 and experiment 1 was the use of 0.2 mol 1^{-1} acid. On your graph, sketch a curve that could be expected for experiment 3.

16* Marble chips, calcium carbonate, reacted with excess dilute hydrochloric acid. The rate of reaction was followed by recording the mass of the container and the reaction mixture over a period of time. The results of an experiment are shown in the following graph.

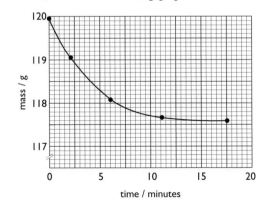

a) Write a balanced equation for the reaction.

b) Calculate the average rate of reaction over the first five minutes.

c) Why does the average rate of reaction decrease as the reaction proceeds?

d) The half-life of the reaction is the time taken for half of the calcium carbonate to be used up. Calculate the half-life for this reaction.

e) Sketch a curve showing how the volume of gas produced changes over the same period of time.

17 A group of S5 pupils were asked to carry out experiments using the following chemicals:

A 0.5 mol l^{-1} silver(I) nitrate solution

B 1.0 mol l^{-1} hydrochloric acid

C Copper powder.

a) One pupil mixed 20 cm³ of solution **A** with 15 cm³ of solution **B** and filtered off the precipitate of silver chloride. The equation for the reaction is:

$$AgNO_3(aq) + HCl(aq) \rightarrow AgCl(s) + HNO_3(aq)$$

i) Show by calculation which reactant is in excess.

ii) Calculate the mass of precipitate which was produced.

b) Another pupil added 0.25 g of substance **C** to 20 cm³ of solution **A**. The equation for this reaction is:

$$Cu(s) + 2AgNO_3(aq) \rightarrow 2Ag(s) + Cu(NO_3)_2(aq)$$

i) Show by calculation which reactant is in excess.

ii) Calculate the mass of silver displaced in this experiment.

② Enthalpy

Potential Energy

Exothermic and endothermic reactions

○ Most common reactions involve a release of energy to the surroundings, usually in the form of heat, and are said to be **exothermic**.

Examples include: combustion of fuels, neutralisation of acids by alkalis and reactive metals, displacement of metals.

○ Energy may also be released in the form of light or sound.

○ Reactions in which heat is absorbed from the surroundings are said to be **endothermic**.

Examples include: dissolving certain salts in water (e.g. ammonium nitrate), neutralising ethanoic acid with sodium hydrogencarbonate.

○ During an exothermic reaction energy possessed by the reactants, i.e. potential energy, is released to the surroundings. The products have less potential energy than the reactants.

A potential energy diagram (Figure 1) shows the energy pathway as the reaction proceeds from reactants to products.

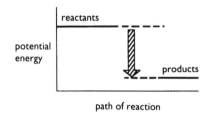

Figure 1 Exothermic reaction

○ In an endothermic reaction the reactants absorb energy from the surroundings so that the products possess more energy than the reactants. See Figure 2.

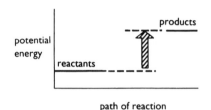

Figure 2 Endothermic reaction

Enthalpy change

○ The difference in potential energy between reactants and products is called the **enthalpy change**, symbol: ΔH.

○ Enthalpy changes are usually quoted in $kJ\ mol^{-1}$.

○ Since the reactants lose energy in an exothermic reaction, ΔH is negative (Figure 3).

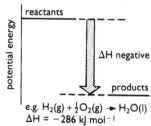

e.g. $H_2(g) + \frac{1}{2}O_2(g) \rightarrow H_2O(l)$
$\Delta H = -286\ kJ\ mol^{-1}$

Figure 3 ΔH for an exothermic reaction

○ In an endothermic reaction the products possess more energy than the reactants. An endothermic change has a positive ΔH value (Figure 4).

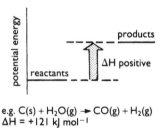

e.g. $C(s) + H_2O(g) \rightarrow CO(g) + H_2(g)$
$\Delta H = +121\ kJ\ mol^{-1}$

Figure 4 ΔH for an endothermic reaction

○ The minus sign must appear in front of the numerical value for the enthalpy change if the reaction is exothermic. The absence of a sign from the ΔH value indicates that the reaction is endothermic.

Activation energy and activated complex

○ In Chapter 1, **activation energy** was defined as the minimum kinetic energy required by colliding molecules for a reaction to occur.

○ In the potential energy diagrams (Figures 5 and 6) the activation energy appears as an 'energy barrier' which has to be overcome as the reaction proceeds from reactants to products.

○ The rate of a reaction will depend on the height of this barrier. The higher the barrier, the slower the reaction. The rate of reaction does *not* depend on the enthalpy change.

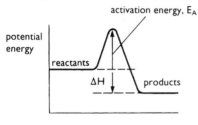

Figure 5 The activation energy for an exothermic reaction

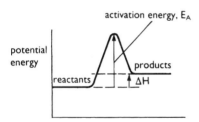

Figure 6 The activation energy for an endothermic reaction

○ As the reaction proceeds from reactants to products an intermediate stage is reached at the top of the activation energy barrier at which a highly unstable species called an **activated complex** is formed. See Figure 7, which also shows that the activation energy can be redefined as the energy needed by colliding particles to form the activated complex.

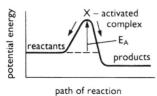

Figure 7

○ Potential energy diagrams when drawn to scale can be used to calculate the enthalpy change and/or the activation energy of a reaction.

Catalysts

● In general, catalysts provide alternative reaction pathways involving less energy, i.e. **a catalyst lowers the activation energy of a reaction**. See Figure 8.

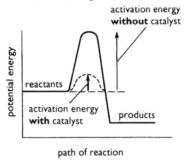

Figure 8 The lowering of the activation energy by a catalyst

Note the contrasting ways in which the use of a catalyst and the use of heat affect the rate of a reaction. Heating speeds up a reaction by increasing the number of molecules which have energy greater than the activation energy. A catalyst speeds up a reaction by lowering the activation energy. Catalysts save energy in many industrial processes.

Experimental measurement of enthalpy changes

Enthalpy of combustion

○ The **enthalpy of combustion** of a substance is the enthalpy change when one mole of the substance is burned completely in oxygen.

The equation for the complete combustion of ethane is given below along with its enthalpy of combustion.

$$C_2H_6(g) + \tfrac{7}{2}O_2(g) \rightarrow 2CO_2(g) + 3H_2O(l)$$
$$\Delta H = -1560 \text{ kJ mol}^{-1}$$

Note

1 the negative sign in the ΔH value since combustion is exothermic,
2 the equation is written showing one mole of the substance that is burning.

The equation shows that 3.5 moles of oxygen are needed per mole of ethane. If the equation is doubled, the ΔH value is doubled and is shown in kJ only.

Prescribed Practical Activity

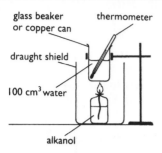

glass beaker or copper can
thermometer
draught shield
100 cm³ water
alkanol

Figure 9

The enthalpy of combustion of a simple alkanol can be determined by experiment, using an apparatus like that shown in Figure 9. The burner containing the alkanol is weighed before and after burning. The alkanol is allowed to burn until the temperature of the water in the beaker has been raised by, say, 10°C before extinguishing the flame.

The heat energy (E_h) gained by the water in the beaker can be calculated from the formula:

$$E_h = cm \, \Delta T$$

where   **c** is the specific heat capacity of water, 4.18 kJ kg^{-1} °C^{-1}

m is the mass of water heated, in kg

ΔT is the change in temperature of the water.

This is the heat released by the burning alkanol and from this the enthalpy of combustion of the alkanol can be calculated. The method of calculation is shown in Worked Example 2.1 using specimen data for the burning of ethanol. The result obtained using the above apparatus will usually be considerably less than the accepted figure given in the SQA Data Book, mainly because of heat losses.

● **Worked Example 2.1** ●

Enthalpy of combustion of ethanol, C_2H_5OH

Data:

Mass of burner + ethanol before burning	= 53.85 g
Mass of burner + ethanol after burning	= 53.49 g
Mass of water heated, m	= 100 g = 0.1 kg

Temperature rise of water, $\Delta T = 10$°C

Calculation:

Heat energy released, $E_h = cm\Delta T$
$$= 4.18 \times 0.1 \times 10$$
$$= 4.18 \text{ kJ}$$

Gram formula mass of ethanol, C_2H_5OH = 46 g

Mass of ethanol burned
$$= 0.36 \text{ g}$$

Number of moles of ethanol burned, n
$$= \frac{0.36}{46}$$

Heat energy released per mole,
$$\frac{E_h}{n} = \frac{4.18}{n} = \frac{4.18 \times 46}{0.36}$$
$$= 534 \text{ kJ}$$

Enthalpy of combustion of ethanol,
$$\Delta H = -534 \text{ kJ mol}^{-1}$$

Note that, since the reaction is exothermic, a negative sign is inserted in the final result.

Enthalpy of solution

○ The **enthalpy of solution** of a substance is the enthalpy change when one mole of the substance dissolves in water.

The enthalpy of solution can be determined experimentally as illustrated in Figure 10. The temperature of the water before adding a weighed amount of solute is measured and so is the temperature of the final solution. The method of calculating the enthalpy change is shown in Worked Example 2.2.

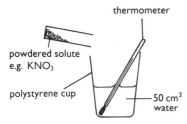

Figure 10

Enthalpy of neutralisation

○ The **enthalpy of neutralisation** of an acid is the enthalpy change when the acid is neutralised to form one mole of water.

○ When an acid such as hydrochloric acid is neutralised by an alkali such as sodium hydroxide, a salt (in this case sodium chloride) and water are formed.

$$HCl(aq) + NaOH(aq) \rightarrow NaCl(aq) + H_2O(l)$$

○ When any acid is neutralised by any alkali the reaction can be expressed by the following equation (with spectator ions omitted).

$$H^+(aq) + OH^-(aq) \rightarrow H_2O(l)$$

The enthalpy of neutralisation of an acid by an alkali can be found by experiment as shown in Figure 11. The temperature of each reactant is measured before mixing so that the average initial temperature can be calculated. The solutions are then mixed and the highest temperature of the neutral solution is noted. The method of calculating the enthalpy change is shown in Worked Example 2.3.

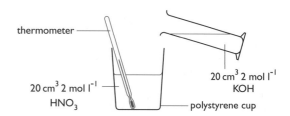

Figure 11

Worked Example 2.2

Enthalpy of solution of KNO_3

Data:

Mass of solute (potassium nitrate)
$$= 1.00 \text{ g}$$

Mass of water used, m $= 50$ g
$$= 0.05 \text{ kg}$$

Temperature of water initially
$$= 20.4°C$$

Temperature of solution $= 18.7°C$

Calculation:

Temperature fall, ΔT $= 1.7°C$

Heat energy absorbed,
$$E_h = cm\Delta T = 4.18 \times 0.05 \times 1.7 \text{ kJ}$$

Gram formula mass of potassium nitrate
$$= 101.1 \text{ g}$$

Number of moles of solute used, n
$$= \frac{1.00}{101.1} = 0.0099$$

Heat energy absorbed per mole,
$$\frac{E_h}{n} = \frac{4.18 \times 0.05 \times 1.7}{0.0099}$$
$$= 35.9 \text{ kJ}$$

Enthalpy of solution of potassium nitrate, $\Delta H = 35.9$ kJ mol^{-1}

As the reaction is endothermic, a plus sign is not needed before the numerical value.

Worked Example 2.3

Enthalpy of neutralisation of $HNO_3(aq)$ by $KOH(aq)$

Data:

Solutions used: 20 cm³ of 2 mol l⁻¹ HNO_3
20 cm³ of 2 mol l⁻¹ KOH

Temperature of acid before mixing
= 19.5°C

Temperature of alkali before mixing
= 18.5°C

Temperature of solution after mixing
= 32.0°C

Calculation:

Average initial temperature $= \dfrac{19.5 + 18.5}{2}$
$= 19.0°C$

Temperature rise, $\Delta T = 32.0 - 19.0$
$= 13.0°C$

Total volume of solution
= 40 cm³

Mass of solution heated
= 40 g = 0.04 kg

Heat energy released,
$E_h = cm\Delta T = 4.18 \times 0.04 \times 13.0$ kJ

Number of moles of H^+ ions
= number of moles of water produced.

$n = C \times V$ $= 2 \times 0.02$
$= 0.04$

Heat energy released per mole
$\dfrac{E_h}{n} = \dfrac{4.18 \times 0.04 \times 13.0}{0.04}$

$= 54.34$ kJ mol⁻¹

Enthalpy of neutralisation,
$\Delta H = -54.34$ kJ mol⁻¹

In the calculation above 0.04 moles of HNO_3 are neutralised by 0.04 moles of KOH producing 0.04 moles of water. Hence in the calculation, $cm\Delta T$ is divided by n = 0.04 so that the ΔH value obtained refers to one mole of acid being neutralised to form one mole of water.

Note that in Worked Examples 2.2 and 2.3 two approximations are being made:

1) the density of a dilute aqueous solution is the same as that of water, i.e. 1 g cm⁻³ at room temperature, and

2) the specific heat capacity of a dilute aqueous solution is the same as that of water, i.e. 4.18 kJ kg⁻¹ K⁻¹.

If sulphuric acid, a dibasic acid, is used the enthalpy of neutralisation is about the same as for hydrochloric acid, since one mole of sulphuric acid produces two moles of water when completely neutralised by sodium hydroxide as shown by the following equation.

$$H_2SO_4(aq) + 2NaOH(aq) \rightarrow Na_2SO_4(aq) + 2H_2O(l)$$

Questions

1*

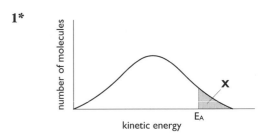

In area **X**

A   molecules always form an activated complex

B   no molecules have the energy to form an activated complex

C   collisions between molecules are always successful in forming products

D   all molecules have the energy to form an activated complex.

Questions 2 and **3** refer to the following potential energy diagram for a chemical reaction.

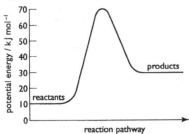

2 The activation energy, in kJ mol⁻¹, for this reaction is

   A 30   **B** 40   **C** 60   **D** 70.

3 The enthalpy change, in kJ mol⁻¹, for this reaction is

   A −20   **B** + 60   **C** − 60   **D** + 20.

4

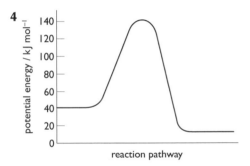

Which set of data applies to this reaction?

	Enthalpy change	E_a / kJ mol⁻¹
A	Exothermic	100
B	Endothermic	100
C	Exothermic	140
D	Endothermic	140

5* Which of the following is not a correct statement about the effect of a catalyst?

   The catalyst

   A provides an alternative route to the products
   B lowers the energy which molecules need for successful collisions
   C provides energy so that more molecules have successful collisions
   D forms bonds with reacting molecules.

6 Which of the following statements describes the effect of a catalyst in a reaction?

   A ΔH decreases and E_a increases
   B ΔH does not change and E_a decreases
   C ΔH decreases and E_a does not change
   D ΔH increases and E_a decreases

7 The potential energy diagram below refers to a reversible reaction.

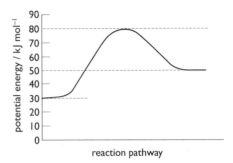

The enthalpy change, in kJ mol⁻¹, for the **reverse** reaction is

   A −20   **B** −30   **C** + 30   **D** + 20.

8 The boiling point of pentane is 36°C. Which equation illustrates the enthalpy of combustion of pentane?

   A $C_5H_{12}(l) + 8O_2(g) \rightarrow 5CO_2(g) + 6H_2O(l)$
   B $C_5H_{12}(l) + \frac{11}{2}O_2(g) \rightarrow 5CO(g) + 6H_2O(l)$
   C $C_5H_{12}(g) + 8O_2(g) \rightarrow 5CO_2(g) + 6H_2O(g)$
   D $C_5H_{12}(l) + 5O_2(g) \rightarrow 5CO_2(g) + 6H_2(g)$

9 A pupil added 0.06 mol of sodium nitrate to 100 cm³ of water at 20°C.
   The enthalpy of solution of sodium nitrate is + 20.5 kJ mol⁻¹.
   After dissolving the solute, the temperature of the solution will be

   A 17°C   **B** 20°C   **C** 23°C   **D** 26°C.

10 When 3.6 g of glucose, $C_6H_{12}O_6$, was burned, 56 kJ of energy was released.
   From this data, what is the enthalpy of combustion of glucose, in kJ mol⁻¹?

   A −15.6   **B** + 15.6   **C** −2800   **D** +2800

11* Consider the energy diagram:

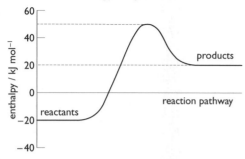

a) From the diagram, find values for
  i) the enthalpy change and the activation energy of the forward reaction;
  ii) the enthalpy change and the activation energy of the reverse reaction.
b) Which, if any, of the above values would be altered by the use of a catalyst?

12 $2N_2O(g) \rightarrow 2N_2(g) + O_2(g)$
       $\Delta H = -80 \text{ kJ mol}^{-1}$

The equation for the decomposition of dinitrogen monoxide (nitrous oxide) is shown above. The activation energy for this reaction when catalysed by platinum is 140 kJ mol^{-1}.
a) Is the catalyst heterogeneous or homogeneous?
b) Draw a potential energy diagram for the catalysed decomposition of $N_2O(g)$, with both energy values clearly indicated.
c) Elements in their natural state, such as the products of the above reaction, are assigned a value of 0 kJ mol^{-1} on a potential energy diagram.
  What would be the energy value of the activated complex for the decomposition of $N_2O(g)$ when catalysed by platinum?
d) If this reaction is carried out without a catalyst, what effect (if any) would this have on the
  i) enthalpy change
  ii) activation energy?

13 In 1780, Lavoisier and Laplace published details of their '*ice calorimeter*' which they had used to measure the heat produced when carbon is burned. The method involved burning carbon in a crucible surrounded by ice in a larger container. The heat of reaction melted some of the ice, forming water that flowed out of the bottom of the container into a pre-weighed beaker. The beaker was reweighed to find the mass of water obtained.

They found that for every gram of carbon burned, 98 g of water were collected.
a) Calculate the mass of water that would be collected when one mole of carbon was burned in the ice calorimeter.
b) One kilogram of ice at 0 °C requires 334 kJ to convert it into water. Calculate the enthalpy of combustion of carbon using the ice calorimeter.

14 Sodium hydrogencarbonate is soluble in water and it also neutralises acids, including ethanoic acid, CH_3COOH.
The equation for this reaction is:

$$NaHCO_3(s) + CH_3COOH(aq) \rightarrow$$
$$CH_3COO^-(aq) + Na^+(aq) + CO_2(g) + H_2O(l)$$

a) Calculate the enthalpy of solution of $NaHCO_3$ from the following data.

   4.2 g of solute were added to 50 cm^3 of water in a polystyrene cup.
   The temperature of the water (before mixing) was 20.0 °C and the temperature of the solution (after mixing) was 16.2 °C.
b) Calculate the enthalpy of neutralisation of ethanoic acid by solid $NaHCO_3$ from the following data.
   2.1 g of $NaHCO_3$ were added to 25 cm^3 of 1.0 mol l^{-1} ethanoic acid in a polystyrene cup.
   Temperature of acid (before mixing)
      = 19.8 °C
   Temperature of solution (after mixing)
      = 13.5 °C

15 An experiment was carried out using a methanol burner and an apparatus like that shown in Figure 9 page 14.
a) Write the equation for the complete combustion of methanol, $CH_3OH(l)$, and write down its enthalpy of combustion from your Data Book.
b) If the apparatus used is 50% efficient, calculate the mass of methanol burned when 80 cm^3 of water (in the copper can) rises in temperature from 20.5 °C to 31.0 °C.

'6* The progress of reactions can be followed by energy diagrams.

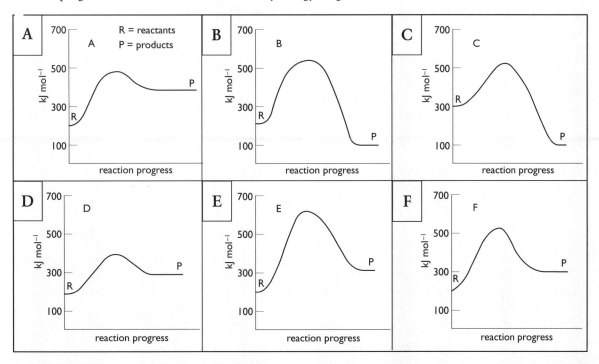

a) Identify the diagram which could represent the catalysed version of the reaction in diagram **F**.
b) Identify the diagram which represents the reaction with the highest energy of activation.
c) Identify the diagram which represents the reaction with an enthalpy change of −200 kJ mol^{-1}.

③ Patterns in the Periodic Table

The greatest step in the progress towards a Periodic Law was taken by Mendeleev in 1869. His main points were:

❍ The elements fall into a repeating pattern of similar properties if arranged in order of increasing **atomic mass**.

❍ The list was arranged into vertical and horizontal sequences, called groups and periods. The groups contained elements which were chemically similar.

❍ Blanks were left to prevent dissimilar elements coming together. Mendeleev predicted the properties for the missing elements and, after their later discovery, the predictions were found to be accurate.

❍ In the modern Periodic Table, the elements are arranged by increasing **atomic number**, each new horizontal row, or period, commences when a new layer of electrons in the atom starts to fill. Each main vertical column contains elements with the same number of electrons in the outermost layer.

Trends in physical properties

❍ Melting and boiling points and densities of the elements vary across a period and down a group.

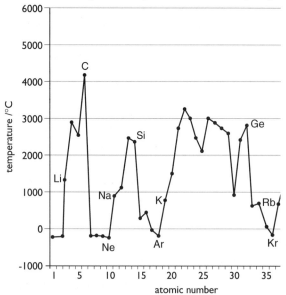

Figure 1 Variation of boiling point with atomic number

In Figures 1, 2 and 3, a repeating pattern of high and low values can be seen.

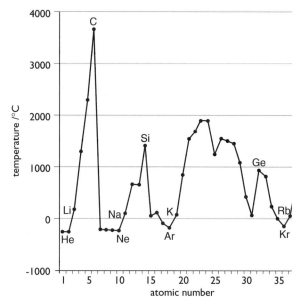

Figure 2 Variation of melting point with atomic number

Atomic Size

Covalent radius is a useful indication of atomic size.

Li	Be	B	C	N	O	F	Ne	
123	89	80	77	74	74	72	–	
Na	Mg	Al	Si	P	S	Cl	Ar	increase
157	136	125	117	110	104	99	–	in value
K	Ca	Ga	Ge	As	Se	Br	Kr	in each
203	174	125	122	121	117	114	–	column
Rb	Sr	In	Sn	Sb	Te	I	Xe	
216	191	150	140	141	137	133	–	

decrease in value in each row →

Table 1 Covalent atomic radii (10^{-12} m)

❍ In a **horizontal row** (period) of the Periodic Table, atomic size **decreases from left to right** because the atoms being considered all have

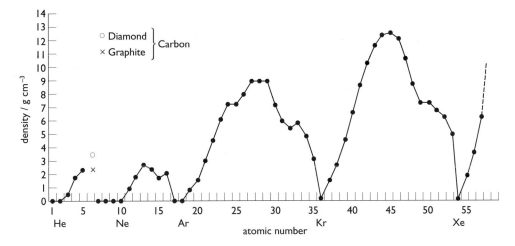

Figure 3 Variation of density (g cm⁻³) with atomic number

the same number of occupied energy levels whilst there is an increase in nuclear charge from one element to the next. This exerts an increasing attraction on the electrons resulting in the atom decreasing in size.

○ In any **vertical column** (group) all the elements have the same number of outer electrons, but one more energy level is occupied by electrons in each succeeding element, hence atomic size **increases down a group**.

First ionisation energy (or enthalpy)

○ The energy change involved in creating one mole of singly-charged positive ions from one mole of atoms in the gaseous state is called the first ionisation energy.

e.g $K(g) \rightarrow K^+(g) + e^-$

$\Delta H = (+) 425 \text{ kJ mol}^{-1}$

○ Down groups of elements, there is a decrease of first ionisation energy. The electron is being removed from the outermost layer of electrons which is increasingly distant from the nuclear attraction and so less energy is required to remove the electron.

○ In each period there is an overall increase of first ionisation energy from left to right. The electron being removed is in the same layer for any element in the same period. The nuclear charge is increasing along each period therefore the outermost electrons are more strongly held and so the energy required to remove them increases along each period.

Li	Be	B	C	N	O	F	Ne	
526	905	807	1090	1410	1320	1690	2090	
Na	Mg	Al	Si	P	S	Cl	Ar	decrease
502	744	584	792	1020	1010	1260	1530	down group
K	Ca	Ga	Ge	As	Se	Br	Kr	
425	596	577	762	953	941	1150	1350	
Rb	Sr	In	Sn	Sb	Te	I	Xe	
409	556	556	715	816	870	1020	1170	

—— overall increase along period ⟶

Table 2 First ionisation energies (kJ mol⁻¹)

○ The screening effect of electrons in inner orbitals reduces the attraction of the nucleus for outermost electrons, reducing the ionisation energy from the value expected.

e.g. Gallium's additional 11 protons should increase its ionisation energy compared with calcium's but the additional 11 electrons are in internal orbitals and screen the outer electrons from the nucleus, in fact lowering the ionisation energy.

○ The second ionisation energy is the enthalpy change associated with the loss of a second electron.

e.g $K^+(g) \rightarrow K^{2+}(g) + e$

$\Delta H = (+) 3060 \text{ kJ mol}^{-1}$

Third and successive ionisation energies can be defined in a similar way.

21

Electronegativities

◯ In a covalent bond the relative powers of the atoms in the bond to attract bonding electrons to themselves are different and are defined as their **electronegativities**.

H 2.1							
Li 1.0	Be 1.5	B 2.0	C 2.5	N 3.0	O 3.5	F 4.0	
Na 0.9	Mg 1.2	Al 1.5	Si 1.8	P 2.1	S 2.5	Cl 3.0	decrease down group
K 0.8	Ca 1.0	Ga 1.6	Ge 1.8	As 2.0	Se 2.4	Br 2.8	
Rb 0.8	Sr 1.0	In 1.7	Sn 1.8	Sb 1.9	Te 2.1	I 2.5	
Cs 0.7	Ba 0.9						

——— increase across period ⟶

Table 3 Electronegativity values

◯ The electronegativity increases from left to right along a period since nuclear charge increases in the same direction.

◯ The electronegativity decreases down a group of the periodic table since the atomic size increases down the group.

◯ The difference in electronegativity values for the atoms joined gives an indication of the relative degrees of polarity in covalent bonds.

Questions

1 Which equation represents the first ionisation enthalpy of fluorine?

A $F(g) + e^- \rightarrow F^-(g)$

B $F(g) \rightarrow F^+(g) + e^-$

C $F^-(g) \rightarrow F(g) + e^-$

D $F^+(g) + e^- \rightarrow F(g)$

2 Which equation represents the second ionisation enthalpy of copper?

A $Cu^+(g) \rightarrow Cu^{2+}(g) + e^-$

B $Cu(g) \rightarrow Cu^{2+}(g) + 2e^-$

C $Cu^+(s) \rightarrow Cu^{2+}(s) + e^-$

D $Cu(s) \rightarrow Cu^{2+}(g) + 2e^-$

3* Potassium has a larger covalent radius than sodium because potassium has

A a larger nuclear charge
B a larger nucleus
C more occupied energy levels
D a smaller ionisation enthalpy.

4 $Al(g) \rightarrow Al^{3+}(g) + 3e^-$

The energy, in kJ mol⁻¹, required to bring about the above change is

A 1752   **B** 2414   **C** 2760   **D** 5174.

5 Between 98°C and 883°C sodium exists as a liquid. Which of the following elements exists as a liquid over the greatest temperature range?

A Magnesium   **B** Aluminium
C Silicon   **D** Phosphorus

6 The bar graph shows how the first ionisation energies of 14 consecutive elements in the Periodic Table vary with atomic number. The element at which the bar graph starts is not specified.

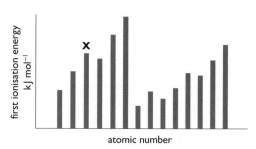

In which group of the Periodic Table is element **X**?

A 3   **B** 4   **C** 5   **D** 6

7* The difference between the covalent radius of sodium and silicon is mainly due to the difference in the

A   number of electrons
B   number of protons
C   number of neutrons
D   mass of each atom.

8 Going down Group 7 of the Periodic Table the

A   density decreases
B   covalent radius increases
C   nuclear charge decreases
D   electronegativity increases.

9* Identify the statement(s) which would describe a trend in the Periodic Table.

A	The metallic bond strengths decrease down Group 1.
B	The first ionisation energies decrease from sodium to argon.
C	The numbers of electrons in the outer energy levels increase from lithium to neon.
D	The covalent radii increase from lithium to fluorine.
E	The strengths of the Van der Waal's forces decrease down Group 0.

10* Identify the trend(s) which would occur as the relative atomic mass of the halogens increases.

A	The covalent radius decreases.
B	The density decreases.
C	The ionisation energy decreases.
D	The boiling point decreases.
E	The van der Waals' forces become stronger.

11 a) Write the equation, including state symbols, which represents the first ionisation energy of potassium.
   b) Explain why the first ionisation energy of potassium is less than
   i)   the first ionisation energy of calcium
   ii) the first ionisation energy of sodium
   iii) the **second** ionisation energy of potassium.

12* The diagram shows the first ionisation energies of successive elements (A–T), plotted against their atomic numbers.

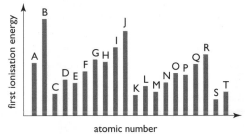

   a) Which Group of elements is represented by the letters B, J and R?
   b) Why is the first ionisation energy of element L greater than that of element K?
   c) Why is the **second** ionisation energy of element L considerably less than that of element K?

13* The table gives the ionisation energies of some of the alkali metals and some of the halogens.

Element	Ionisation Energies/kJ mol^{-1}		
	First	Second	Third
lithium	526	7310	11800
fluorine	1690	3380	6060
sodium	502	4560	6920
chlorine	1260	2310	3840
potassium	425	3060	4440
bromine	1150	2100	3480

   a) Why is the first ionisation energy of each alkali metal much less than that of the halogen **in the same period**?
   b) Why is the second ionisation energy of each alkali metal much greater than that of the halogen **in the same period**?
   c) Calculate the energy per mole required to bring about the change

$$K^+(g) \rightarrow K^{3+}(g)$$

14 The covalent radius of technetium, atomic number 43, is not known.
   a) How would you expect the covalent radius of technetium to compare with that of
   i)   manganese
   ii) cadmium (atomic number 48)?
   b) Explain your answer to **a) i)**.

15 Explain why the covalent radius
   a) increases from magnesium to barium
   b) decreases from magnesium to sulphur.

4 Bonding, Structure and Properties of Elements

Bonding is a term describing the mechanism by which atoms join together. **Structure** describes the way in which the atoms, or particles derived from them, are arranged. The resulting characteristics, whether physical or chemical, of the substances are their **properties.**

Types of bonding in elements

Metallic bonding

The mechanism of metallic bonding is described under the heading 'Groups 1, 2, and 3' below.

Covalent bonding

○ Covalent bonding is **electrostatic**, the atoms being held together by the attraction between their positive nuclei and negatively charged shared pairs of electrons. Each shared pair of electrons constitutes a covalent bond.

○ In an element all the atoms are alike in terms of protons and electrons so the bonding electrons are shared equally.

○ When more than one covalent bond is formed by an atom, the bonds are orientated in specific directions to each other.

Van der Waals' bonding

○ Van der Waals' bonding is very weak bonding between molecules. Its mechanism is explained under the heading 'Noble Gases'.

Bonding in the first 20 elements

The Noble Gases – monatomic

○ These elements, with the exception of helium, have an outer layer of eight electrons which is an especially stable arrangement.

○ The Noble Gases are monatomic, i.e. their molecules consist of only one atom.

○ The uneven distribution of the constantly moving electrons around the nuclei of the atoms causes the formation of **temporary dipoles** on the atoms (Figure 1). The atoms then attract each other.

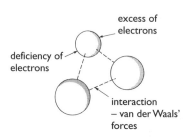

Figure 1

○ These forces are van der Waals' forces and are the weakest type of bond but are strong enough to allow the Noble Gases to liquify and solidify if they are cooled.

○ Helium, with only two electrons per atom, has the weakest van der Waals' forces between its atoms and is the element with the lowest melting point and boiling point. The other Noble Gases have increasing numbers of electrons so the van der Waals' forces, and hence melting and boiling points, increase.

Groups 7, 6 and 5 – discrete covalent molecules

○ In these groups, covalent bond formation results in eight outer electrons. These elements form small, discrete molecules.

Group 7 elements

○ Halogen atoms have one unpaired outer electron and can form one covalent bond, forming diatomic molecules F_2, Cl_2, Br_2 and I_2.

○ These molecules interact only weakly by van der Waals' forces so that all the elements are volatile, and fluorine and chlorine are gaseous.

Figure 2 Bonding in halogens

Group 6 elements

Oxygen

○ Each oxygen atom uses its two unpaired electrons to form two covalent bonds with one other oxygen atom.

○ The molecules interact by van der Waals' bonding but since the interaction is weak, O_2 is gaseous.

Sulphur

○ The atoms bond to two other atoms. Closed eight membered puckered rings are found in the crystalline forms, and zig-zag chains are found in plastic sulphur.

○ Van der Waals' forces between the molecules are strong enough to make sulphur solid at room temperature.

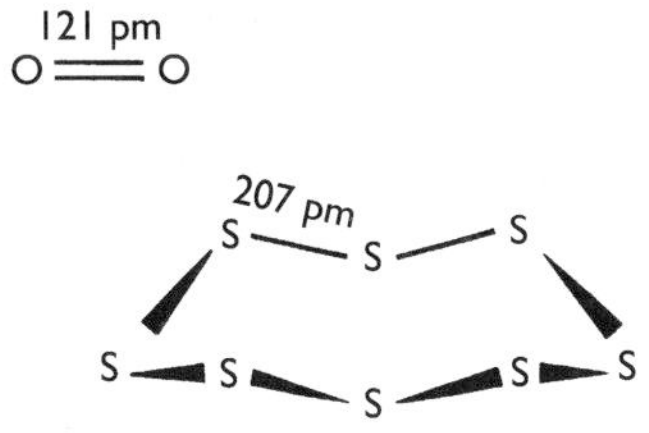

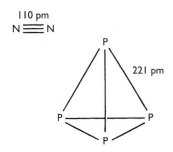

Figure 3 Bonding in oxygen and sulphur

Group 5 elements

Nitrogen

○ Nitrogen atoms form diatomic molecules with a triple bond, and weak van der Waals' interaction.

Phosphorus

○ Phosphorus makes use of single bonds to three other atoms to form tetrahedral P_4 molecules.

Figure 4 Bonding in nitrogen and phosphorus

○ In the elements of Groups 7, 6 and 5, the **intramolecular** forces, i.e. the bonds **within** the molecule are **covalent**.

○ The **intermolecular** forces, those **between** the molecules are the very weak van der Waals' forces.

Group 4 elements – usually covalent networks

Diamond

○ The standard structure is an infinite three dimensional network or lattice as in diamond and silicon, where each atom bonds covalently to four other atoms. The resultant structure is exceptionally hard and rigid. There are no discrete molecules.

○ There are no free electrons to allow conduction but in diamonds, for example, 'tunnels' between the atoms allow light to pass through, thus making them transparent.

○ These properties make diamond suitable as an abrasive and a gemstone.

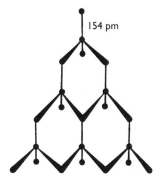

Figure 5 Diamond

Graphite

○ This other well-known variety of carbon has three covalent bonds from each atom in one plane, forming layers of hexagonal rings. The fourth unpaired electron from each carbon atom is delocalised. The result is strong bonding within the layers but only weak interaction between the layers.

○ Since the delocalised electrons are held quite weakly, they can flow across the layers. Graphite therefore conducts, like a metal. The layers separate easily so graphite is flaky. The layers are offset with respect to each other, light cannot pass through, so graphite is opaque.

○ These properties result in the use of graphite as a lubricant in electric motors and in pencils.

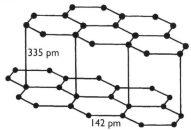

Figure 6 Graphite

Fullerenes

○ Discovered in 1985, fullerenes are discrete covalently bonded molecules. The smallest is spherical, C_{60}. Other molecules have elongated shapes e.g. C_{70}, and there are also much longer 'nanotubes'. All contain 5 and 6 membered carbon atom rings.

○ The properties of these molecules are under intensive investigation to discover uses.

Figure 7 Fullerene

Groups 1, 2 and 3 – usually metallic bonding

○ Elements in these groups have insufficient electrons to allow the achievement of an octet of electrons in their outer layer by covalent bonding.

○ Their outer electrons are delocalised, and act as a binding medium for the resultant positive ions. This is **metallic bonding.**

○ The bonding is less directional than covalent bonding, and the elements are therefore malleable and ductile.

○ The outer electrons move easily and hence the elements are electrical conductors.

○ Elements of Groups 1, 2 and 3 are typical metals, except boron which forms a structure

made up of B_{12} groups, which are interbonded with other groups. The result is an element almost as hard as diamond.

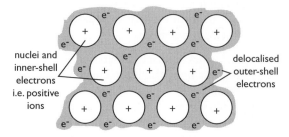

Figure 8 Metallic bonding

Summary of structures of the first 20 elements

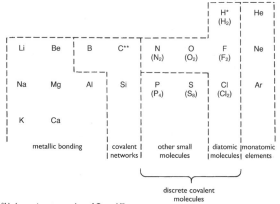

*Hydrogen is *not* a member of Group VII
**Although unusually large, the fullerene forms of carbon are discrete covalent molecules

Figure 9

Specific physical properties of elements related to bonding

Melting and boiling points

○ Where the elements consist of discrete molecules (the monatomic and diatomic gases and P_4 and S_8) the melting and boiling points are low because only the weak intermolecular van der Waals' forces have to be overcome in melting and boiling the element. The strong, covalent intramolecular forces are unaffected.

○ In the covalent network solids, such as carbon and silicon, strong covalent bonds must be broken when melting or boiling takes place. Melting and boiling points are therefore much higher.

○ For Group 1, 2 and 3 elements, strong metallic bonds have to be overcome so they have high melting and boiling points compared with covalent molecular elements.

Hardness

○ Hardness is related to bonding.

○ Giant covalent molecules have all their atoms interlinked by directional bonds so substances such as diamond are very hard, but the bonds will break on impact so that the substances are brittle.

○ Small covalent molecules like S_8 and P_4 are only attracted to each other by van der Waals' forces so the substances are soft.

○ Metallic bonds are strong but they are not directional like covalent bonds. Metals can be distorted by impact or pressure i.e. they are malleable and ductile.

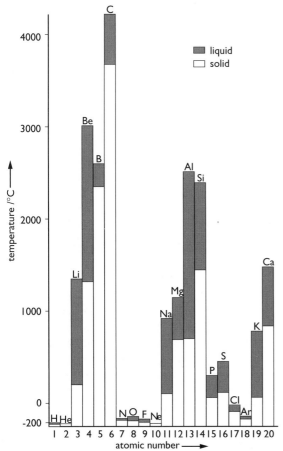

Figure 10 Melting and boiling points of elements 1–20

Questions

1 Which equation represents the first ionisation energy of bromine?

  A $Br(l) + e^- \rightarrow Br^-(g)$

  B $Br(g) \rightarrow Br^+(g) + e^-$

  C $\frac{1}{2} Br_2(l) \rightarrow Br^+(g) + e^-$

  D $\frac{1}{2} Br_2(g) + e^- \rightarrow Br^-(g)$

Questions 2 and **3** relate to the following table of data about certain elements.

Element	Melting point/°C	Boiling point/°C	Conduction when solid?
A	44	280	no
B	1083	2567	yes
C	1410	2355	no
D	114	184	no

2 Which of these elements is most likely to have a covalent network structure?

3 Which of these elements is most likely to have delocalised electrons?

4 Which element is a solid at room temperature and consists of discrete molecules?

  A Carbon **B** Silicon **C** Sulphur **D** Boron

5* The diagram shows the melting points of successive elements across a period in the Periodic Table.

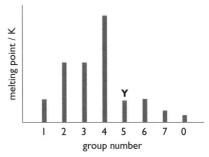

Which of the following is a correct reason for the low melting point of element **Y**?

  A It has weak ionic bonds.

  B It has weak covalent bonds.

  C It has weakly-held outer electrons.

  D It has weak forces between molecules.

6

A	$I_2(s) \rightarrow I_2(g)$
B	$I(g) \rightarrow I^+(g) + e^-$
C	$I^-(g) \rightarrow I(g) + e^-$
D	$I_2(g) \rightarrow 2I(g)$
E	$I^-(aq) \rightarrow \frac{1}{2} I_2(aq) + e^-$

Identify the equation which represents
a) the first ionisation energy of iodine
b) a change in which covalent bonds are broken
c) a change in which van der Waals' forces are broken.

7 There are various types of structure found among elements.

A	Discrete covalent molecular solid.
B	Covalent network.
C	Monatomic gas.
D	Positive ions surrounded by delocalised electrons.
E	Diatomic covalent gas.

Identify the type of structure present in
a) neon
b) nitrogen
c) phosphorus
d) potassium.

8 This question refers to elements in the third period of the Periodic Table, i.e. elements with atomic numbers 11 to 18 inclusive.
a) Which of these elements is
  i) diatomic
  ii) monatomic?
b) Why does sulphur have a much lower melting point than silicon?
c) Suggest a reason for magnesium having a higher melting point than sodium.

9 For each of the following changes, name the type of bonding being broken.
a) $C(s) \rightarrow C(g)$
b) $Ne(l) \rightarrow Ne(g)$
c) $Na(l) \rightarrow Na(g)$
d) $F_2(g) \rightarrow 2F(g)$
e) $P_4(l) \rightarrow P_4(g)$

Bonding, Structure and Properties of Compounds

Types of bonding in compounds

Ionic bonding

Ionic bonding is an electrostatic attraction between the positive ions of one element and the negative ions of another element.

Polar covalent bonding

Polar covalent bonding results from electron sharing but if the atoms being joined are not of the same element, electrons are not always shared equally, so producing a polar bond.

Intermolecular bonds

Van der Waals' forces mentioned in the last chapter are one type of intermolecular bond. Other types of these bonds include **permanent dipole-permanent dipole** interactions and **hydrogen bonds**.

Ionic bonding and structure

○ Different elements have different attractions for bonding electrons i.e. different electronegativities.

○ The greater their difference in electronegativity, the more likely are two elements to form ionic bonds. The element with the greater electronegativity is more likely to gain electrons to form a negative ion and the element with the smaller to lose electrons to form a positive ion.

○ Elements far apart in the Periodic Table are more likely to form ionic bonds i.e. ionic compounds result from metals combining with non metals (e.g. sodium fluoride and magnesium oxide). Caesium fluoride has the greatest degree of ionic bonding.

○ Electrostatic attraction holds the oppositely charged ions together in appropriate numbers so that the total charge is zero. For example in sodium chloride, there are equal numbers of Na^+ and Cl^- ions, in calcium fluoride there are twice as many F^- ions as Ca^{2+}.

○ Ionic compounds do **not** form molecules. Instead the positive and negative ions aggregate into various three dimensional structures called **lattices**.

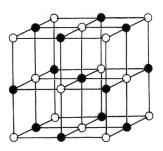

Figure 1 Sodium chloride lattice

Covalent compounds and structure

○ Most covalent compounds are formed by combinations of non-metallic elements.

○ Most are **molecular** compounds such as methane and carbon dioxide.

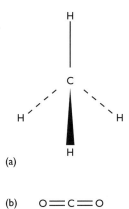

Figure 2 Bonding in methane (a) and carbon dioxide (b)

○ Molecular compounds such as CH_4, CO_2 and SiH_4 (silane) are gaseous at room temperature since there are only weak **intermolecular** forces. Melting and boiling of these compounds require only the overcoming of these weak intermolecular forces, whilst the covalent **intramolecular** forces remain intact.

29

○ A number of covalent compounds occur as **network** structures, e.g. silicon carbide and silicon dioxide.

○ Silicon carbide, SiC, has a structure similar to that of diamond and is also an abrasive.

○ Silicon dioxide, SiO_2, is formed by bonding silicon atoms to four oxygen atoms to give SiO_4 tetrahedra which are linked by sharing of each of their oxygen atoms between two silicon atoms.

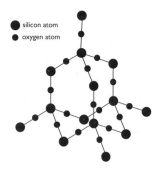

● silicon atom
● oxygen atom

Figure 3 Structure of silicon dioxide

○ Network solids have very high melting points since melting requires the breaking of strong covalent bonds. They are very hard, although brittle, because of these same strong directional bonds.

Polar covalent bonding

○ Most compounds which are covalent are formed by elements with different electronegativities, although not so different as those forming ionic bonds.

○ In these compounds, the bonding electrons are not shared equally. The atom with the greater share of electrons has a slight negative charge by comparison with the other atom.

For example chlorine, oxygen and nitrogen are all more electronegative than hydrogen.

Hydrogen chloride, water and ammonia can be represented as in Figures 4 (a), (b) and (c). The symbols δ^+ and δ^- mean 'slightly positive' and 'slightly negative'.

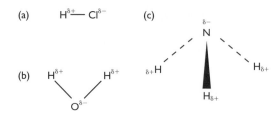

Figure 4 Bonding in hydrogen chloride (a), water (b) and ammonia (c)

○ Covalent bonds with unequal electron sharing are called **polar covalent bonds**.

○ Some molecules containing such polar bonds have an overall polarity because the bonds are not arranged symmetrically, e.g. HCl, H_2O and NH_3. Such molecules are said to have a **permanent dipole** and are described as **polar**.

○ Other molecules have a symmetrical arrangement of polar bonds and the polarity cancels out on the molecules as a whole, as in carbon dioxide and tetrachloromethane (Figure 5).

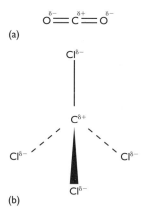

Figure 5 Bonding in carbon dioxide (a) and tetrachloromethane (b)

○ Heptane has almost **non-polar** bonds and the molecule is non-polar as a whole. Ethanol has one very polar O–H bond giving the molecule an overall polarity. Chloroform, unlike CCl_4 is polar overall because of the unsymmetrical arrangement of the C–Cl bonds (Figure 6).

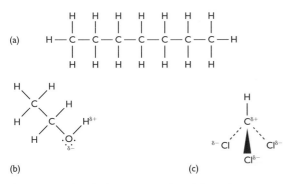

(a)

(b)   (c)

Figure 6 Bonding in heptane (a), ethanol (b) and trichloromethane (chloroform) (c)

Melting and boiling points

○ Polar molecules have melting and boiling points higher than those of non-polar molecules of a similar molecular mass. The intermolecular forces are increased by the mutual attraction of the permanent dipoles on neighbouring molecules. Propanone and butane (Figure 7) are good examples of this behaviour.

(a) Propanone: Formula mass 58
                   Boiling point 56°C

(b) Butane: Formula mass 58
             Boiling point 0°C

Figure 7

○ **All** covalent molecular compounds interact by van der Waals' bonding.

○ Permanent dipole-permanent dipole attractions are stronger than van der Waals' bonds for molecules of equivalent size.

Solvent action

○ Because it is polar, water can dissolve other polar and ionic substances.

○ Polar and ionic substances are more likely to be soluble in polar solvents and insoluble in non-polar solvents e.g. salt dissolves in water but not in heptane

○ Non-polar substances are more likely to be soluble in non-polar solvents and insoluble in polar solvents e.g. wax dissolves in heptane but not in water.

Anomalous physical properties of some hydrides

Boiling points

○ Group IV hydrides have, as expected, an increase in melting and boiling points with molecular mass.

○ In the Groups V, VI and VII, the values of melting and boiling points for NH_3, H_2O and HF (and HCl to some extent) are higher than would be expected for their molecular mass.

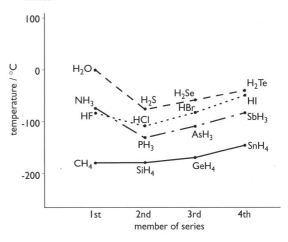

Figure 8 Melting points of hydrides of groups IV, V, VI and VII

○ These anomalous properties indicate stronger bonding between the molecules than the expected van der Waals' bonding and simple permanent dipole-permanent dipole attraction.

○ The compounds showing these anomalous properties all contain bonds which are very polar i.e. O–H, N–H, F–H (and Cl–H) as shown by the electronegativity differences in Table 1 on the next page and can therefore interact in the fashion shown in Figure 10.

31

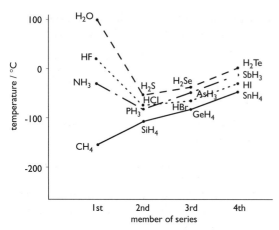

Figure 9 Boiling points of hydrides of groups IV, V, VI and VII

H–C	H–N	H–O	H–F
0.4	0.9	1.4	1.9
	H–P	H–S	H–Cl
	0.0	0.4	0.9
		H–Se	H–Br
		0.3	0.7
		H–Te	H–I
		0.0	0.4

Table 1 Electronegativity differences

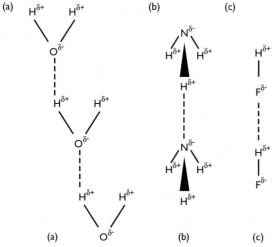

Figure 10 Hydrogen bonding in water (a), ammonia (b) and hydrogen fluoride (c)

○ This interaction is called **hydrogen bonding** since it occurs only for compounds containing a strongly electronegative element linked to hydrogen. The pull of electrons away from the hydrogen results in a positive charge located on a small atom, and hence a high positive charge density capable of interacting with the negative end of other molecules.

○ Hydrogen bonding is stronger than van der Waals' bonding, and stronger than ordinary permanent dipole-permanent dipole attractions but weaker than covalent bonds.

Viscosity

Viscosity normally increases with molecular mass but molecules with, for example, OH groups show higher viscosity than expected, i.e. hydrogen bonding occurs between molecules and increases viscosity.

Miscibility

○ Miscible liquids mix thoroughly without any visible boundary between them, e.g. ethanol and water, but water and hexane are immiscible, with the hexane forming a visible upper layer.

○ Hydrogen bonding owing to −OH groups in water and ethanol aids miscibility, but other polar liquids like propanone, although without −OH groups, are frequently miscible with water.

Density of water

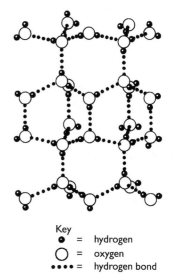

Key
● = hydrogen
○ = oxygen
••••• = hydrogen bond

Figure 11 Structure of ice

❍ As with all liquids, water contracts on cooling, but when it reaches 4°C it begins to expand again, and at its freezing point is less dense than the water which is about to freeze. The reason for this is the ordering of molecules, caused by hydrogen bonding, into an open lattice.

❍ As a result ice floats on water, seas freeze from the top downwards, allowing fish to survive in unfrozen water beneath and pipes burst when water freezes inside them.

Questions

1 Which of the following fluorides is likely to have the **most** ionic character?

   A NaF   **B** MgF_2 **C** CsF   **D** BaF_2

2* What type of bond is broken when ice is melted?

   A Ionic   **B** Polar covalent
   C Hydrogen   **D** Non-polar covalent

3 Which type of structure describes a substance which conducts electricity when solid and melts at 1500°C?

   A Covalent network   **B** Monatomic
   C Ionic lattice   **D** Metallic

4 Which of the following is an example of intramolecular bonding?

   A Polar covalent   **B** Hydrogen
   C Van der Waals'   **D** Ionic

5 Which of the following solids is most likely to dissolve in tetrachloromethane, CCl_4?

   A Calcium chloride
   B Copper(II) chloride
   C Potassium chloride
   D Phosphorus(V) chloride

6* Silicon carbide can be used as

   A a lubricant
   B a tip for cutting/grinding tools
   C a substitute for pencil 'lead'
   D an electrical conductor.

7* Which of the following shows the types of bonding in **decreasing** order of strength?

   A Covalent : hydrogen : van der Waals'
   B Covalent : van der Waals' : hydrogen
   C Hydrogen : covalent : van der Waals'
   D Van der Waals' : hydrogen : covalent

8* Carbon dioxide is a gas at room temperature while silicon dioxide is a solid because

   A van der Waals' forces are much weaker than covalent bonds
   B carbon dioxide contains double covalent bonds and silicon dioxide contains single covalent bonds
   C carbon–oxygen bonds are less polar than silicon–oxygen bonds
   D the relative formula mass of carbon dioxide is less than that of silicon dioxide.

9 Which of the following compounds has non-polar molecules?

   A HBr   **B** CO_2 **C** H_2O **D** CH_3Cl

Questions 10 and **11** relate to the following equations.

   A $H_2(g) \rightarrow 2H(g)$
   B $H_2(l) \rightarrow H_2(g)$
   C $H_2O(g) \rightarrow 2H(g) + O(g)$
   D $H_2O(l) \rightarrow H_2O(g)$

10 Which equation represents a reaction in which hydrogen bonds are broken?

11 Which equation represents a reaction in which non-polar covalent bonds are broken?

12* Identify the type(s) of bonding present in a sample of hydrogen gas.

A	van der Waals'
B	covalent (non-polar)
C	ionic
D	hydrogen
E	covalent (polar)

13* The grid shows statements which can describe different substances.

A	It conducts electricity.
B	It is soluble in water.
C	It has covalent bonding.
D	It has a network structure.
E	It has hydrogen bonding.
F	Van der Waals' forces exist.

a) Identify the **two** statements which can be applied to diamond.

b) Identify the statement(s) which can be applied to ammonia but **not** methane.

c) Identify the statement which can be applied to both argon and water.

14 Iodine monochloride, ICl, is a brown liquid produced when iodine reacts with chlorine.

a) Write a balanced equation, including state symbols, for this reaction.

b) Copy and complete the following table in which iodine monochloride is compared with bromine, which is also a brown liquid.

	Iodine monochloride	Bromine
Molecular mass		159.8
Boiling point/°C	97	
Type of bonding within molecules		Covalent (non-polar)
Type of bonding between molecules		

c) Explain why iodine monochloride has a much higher boiling point than bromine.

15 The structural formula of an amino acid called cysteine is shown below.

$$
\begin{array}{c}
\text{H} \quad \text{H} \quad \text{O} \\
| \quad\ | \quad\ || \\
\text{H—N—C—C—O—H} \\
| \\
\text{H—C—H} \\
| \\
\text{S—H}
\end{array}
$$

Refer to the SQA Data Book to help you decide which of the following bonds present in cysteine is

a) non-polar   b) the most polar.

H – N   N – C   C – S   S – H

16 The following flow diagram summarises one way of purifying silicon.

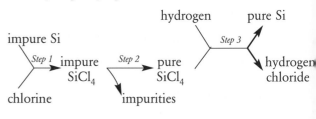

a) Write balanced equations for the reactions occurring at
   i) *step 1*   ii) *step 3*.

b) Which of the chemicals shown in the flow chart has the most polar bonds?

c) $SiCl_4$ is a liquid at room temperature while silicon is a solid with a very high melting point. Why are these substances so different?

d) Draw a diagram to show the shape of a molecule of $SiCl_4$.

e) Hydrogen chloride is very soluble in water.
   i) What are the products of electrolysis of this solution?
   ii) Why might electrolysis of this solution affect the economics of the method of purifying silicon described above?

17 The following table contains data relating to the hydrides of Group 5 elements.

Compound	Ammonia NH_3	Phosphine PH_3	Arsine AsH_3	Stibnine SbH_3
Molecular mass	17	34	77.9	124.8
Boiling point/°C	–33	–88	–55	–17

a) Why does arsine have a higher boiling point than phosphine?

b) On a graph of temperature against molecular mass, plot the boiling points of phosphine, arsine and stibnine.

c) Predict the boiling point of ammonia, **if** it followed the trend shown on the graph.

d) Why is the boiling point of ammonia much higher than this prediction?

18 The following table shows the radii, measured in picometres (pm), of ions of certain elements.

Na^+	Mg^{2+}	Al^{3+}	Si^{4-}	P^{3-}	S^{2-}	Cl^-	K^+	Ca^{2+}
95	65	50	271	212	184	181	133	99

  a) Explain why an aluminium ion is much smaller than an aluminium atom.
  b) Why is there a large increase in ionic radius between aluminium and silicon?
  c) What do all the ions from silicon to calcium have in common?
  d) Why do the ionic radii decrease from silicon to calcium?

6 The Mole

The Avogadro Constant

○ A **mole** of a substance is its **gram formula mass**, gfm.

○ One mole of any substance contains Avogadro's constant, **L**, i.e. 6.02×10^{23}, formula units. The term 'formula unit' relates to the type of particle present in the substance.

Metals and monatomic species e.g Noble Gases.

○ Here the formula unit is an **atom**.

Thus, 20.2 g of neon and 23.0 g of sodium each contain **L** (6.02×10^{23}) atoms.

Covalent substances

○ Here the formula unit is a **molecule**.

○ The total number of atoms in a mole of molecules can be found by multiplying **L** by the number of atoms in each molecule.

For example, 32 g oxygen, O_2, has L molecules. The number of atoms present is 2L.

44 g propane, C_3H_8, has L molecules. The number of atoms present is 11L (3L of C & 8L of H).

Ionic compounds

○ Here the formula unit consists of the ratio of **ions** expressed by the ionic formula of the compound. The total number of ions depends on the number of each kind of ion in the formula.

For example, 4.6 g K^+Cl^- contains L formula units comprising L K^+ & L Cl^-, i.e. 2L ions.

400 g $(Fe^{3+})_2(SO_4^{2-})_3$ contains L formula units comprising 2L Fe^{3+} & 3L SO_4^{2-} i.e. 5 L ions.

○ Equimolar quantities of different substances contain equal numbers of formula units. Each of the following quantities represents 0.2 moles of the substance and as a result contains 0.2L formula units.

4.6 g of sodium, Na, contain 0.2L **atoms**.

5.6 g of nitrogen gas, N_2, contain 0.2L **molecules**.

22.2 g of calcium chloride, $CaCl_2$, contain 0.2L **formula units**.

● Worked Example 6.1 ●

$1 \text{ g } H_2$ $0.2 \text{ mol } C_2H_6$ $6 \text{ g } H_2O$

Which of the quantities given above contains

a) the most molecules

b) the most hydrogen atoms?

$1 \text{ g } H_2 = 0.5$ mol, so it contains 0.5L molecules or L H atoms.

$0.2 \text{ mol } C_2H_6$ contains 0.2L molecules, 1.2L H atoms (6×0.2).

$6 \text{ g } H_2O = 0.33$ mol, so it contains 0.33L molecules, 0.66L H atoms.

Answers: **a)** $1 \text{ g } H_2$ **b)** $0.2 \text{ mol } C_2H_6$

● Worked Example 6.2 ●

a) What mass of $Ca_3(PO_4)_2$ contains 6.02×10^{23} positive ions?

b) What volume of 0.5 mol l^{-1} $Cu(NO_3)_2$ contains 3.01×10^{23} negative ions?

Answers:

a) 1 mole of $Ca_3(PO_4)_2 = 310$ g and contains 3L Ca^{2+} ions, so 103.3g of the compound contains 6.02×10^{23} positive ions.

b) 1 mole of $Cu(NO_3)_2$ contains 2L nitrate ions, so 0.25 mol $Cu(NO_3)_2$ contains $\frac{L}{2}$, 3.01×10^{23} nitrate ions.

$$V = \frac{n}{c} = \frac{0.25}{0.5} = 0.5$$

Hence 0.5 litres of this solution contains 3.01×10^{23} nitrate ions.

Molar volume

○ With gases it is usually more appropriate to measure volume rather than mass. The molar volume of any gas at 0°C and one atmosphere pressure can be calculated by dividing its molar mass by its density at that temperature and pressure.

For example, fluorine, F_2, gfm = 38 g and density at 0°C and 1 atmosphere pressure = 1.7 g litre^{-1}.

Hence, molar volume $= \frac{38}{1.7} = 22.4$ litres.

○ The densities of gases increase in proportion to their gram formula masses. Consequently the molar volumes of different gases are approximately the same for all gases at the same temperature and pressure.

○ Since the volume of a gas changes if the temperature and/or the pressure changes, it is important to specify the temperature and pressure at which a volume is being measured. At room temperature and pressure, i.e. 20°C and 1 atmosphere pressure, the molar volume of any gas is approximately 24 litres mol^{-1}.

○ The relationship between volume of a gas, number of moles and molar volume can be expressed as follows.

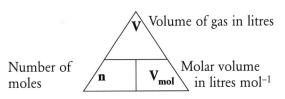

Hence, volume of gas, $V = n \times V_{mol}$ and number of moles, $n = \dfrac{V}{V_{mol}}$

Worked Example 6.3

Calculate the molar volume of oxygen from the following data obtained at 20°C and 1 atmosphere pressure.

Mass of empty flask	= 205.42 g
Mass of flask + oxygen	= 206.70 g
Volume of flask	= 960 cm^3

Calculation:

Mass of oxygen = 1.28 g
(206.70 – 205.42)
1.28 g of oxygen occupies a volume of 960 cm^3.
Gram formula mass of O_2 = 32 g

32 g of O_2 occupies a volume of

$$\frac{960 \times 32}{1.28} \text{ cm}^3 = 24\,000 \text{ cm}^3$$

Hence, the molar volume of O_2 is 24.0 litres at 20°C & 1 atmosphere pressure.

Worked Example 6.4

The molar volume at 0°C and 1 atmosphere pressure is 22.4 litres mol^{-1}.

Calculate:

a) the volume of 0.125 mol of hydrogen

b) the number of moles of oxygen in 560 cm^3 under these conditions.

Answers:

a) Volume of hydrogen,
$$V = n \times V_{mol}$$
$$= 0.125 \times 22.4$$
$$= 2.8 \text{ litres}$$

b) 560 cm^3 = 0.560 litres.

Number of moles of oxygen,
$$n = \frac{V}{V_{mol}} = \frac{0.560}{22.4} = 0.025$$

Reacting volumes

There are two main types of calculation involving molar volumes.

1 Calculations involving mass and volume

● Worked Example 6.5 ●

Calculate the volume of carbon dioxide released when 0.4 g of calcium carbonate is dissolved in excess hydrochloric acid. The gas is collected at room temperature and pressure. The molar volume is 24 litres.

The equation for the reaction is:

$CaCO_3(s) + 2HCl(aq) \rightarrow$
1 mol $\qquad CaCl_2(aq) + CO_2(g) + H_2O(l)$
100 g $\qquad\qquad\qquad$ 1 mol
$\qquad\qquad\qquad\qquad$ 24 litres

Hence, 0.4 g of $CaCO_3$ gives

$\dfrac{0.4}{100} \times 24$ litres

$= 0.096$ litres (or 96 cm^3) of CO_2.

○ In many reactions which involve gases one or more of the reactants or products may be a liquid or a solid. The volume of liquid or solid is so small compared with that of the gas or gases that it can be regarded as negligible.

If the reaction in Worked Example 6.6 is carried out when all the volumes are measured at room temperature and pressure the products include water. Since water is a liquid its volume can be ignored.

Gas volume calculations involving excess reactant

Worked Example 6.7 illustrates the application of excess reactant to the previous type of calculation. It is necessary to find out which reactant is in excess before calculating the volume of gaseous product.

2 Comparing volumes of gases

● Worked Example 6.6 ●

Calculate **a)** the volume of oxygen required for the complete combustion of 200 cm^3 of butane
b) the volume of each product.

(All volumes are measured at 150°C and 1 atmosphere pressure.)

$$2C_4H_{10}(g) + 13O_2(g) \rightarrow 8CO_2(g) + 10H_2O(g)$$

Mole ratio of reactants and products:	2	13	8	10
Volume ratio of reactants and products (at same T and P)	2	13	8	10
Simplified volume ratio:	1	6.5	4	5

Hence 200 cm^3 of butane **a)** requires 1300 cm^3 of oxygen for complete combustion
b) produces 800 cm^3 of $CO_2(g)$ and 1000 cm^3 of $H_2O(g)$.

● Worked Example 6.7 ●

A mixture of 20 cm³ of methane and 50 cm³ of oxygen was ignited and allowed to cool. Calculate the volume and composition of the resulting gaseous mixture. All volumes are measured under the same conditions of room temperature and pressure.

$$CH_4(g) \quad + \quad 2O_2(g) \quad \rightarrow \quad CO_2(g) \quad + \quad 2H_2O(l)$$

Mole ratio:	1	2	1	2
Volume ratio:	1	2	1	negligible

According to the equation,

20 cm³ of methane requires 2×20 cm³ of oxygen, i.e. 40 cm³.

Hence, oxygen is present in excess since its initial volume is 50 cm³.

Volume of excess oxygen $= (50 - 40) = 10$ cm³

Volume of carbon dioxide formed $= (1 \times 20) = 20$ cm³

Therefore the resulting gas mixture consists of 10 cm³ of O_2 and 20 cm³ of CO_2.

Questions

SECTION A:

The Avogadro Constant (L = 6.02×10^{23})

1 The Avogadro constant is the same as the number of

  A molecules in 1 mol of iodine crystals
  B atoms in 1 mol of chlorine gas
  C ions in 1 mol of KBr crystals
  D protons in 1 mol of helium gas.

2 60 g of carbon contain as many atoms as

  A 190 g of fluorine
  B 100 g of calcium
  C 60 g of cobalt
  D 20 g of helium.

3 The number of moles of ions in 1 mol of aluminium nitrate is

  A 1   **B** 2   **C** 3   **D** 4

4 The Avogadro constant is the same as the number of

  A molecules in 14 g of nitrogen gas
  B ions in 500 cm³ of 1 mol l⁻¹ KI(aq)
  C atoms in 2 g of hydrogen gas
  D molecules in 200 g of C_7H_{16}(l).

Questions **5, 6** and **7** relate to the following quantities

  A 12 g of CH_4 **B** 6 g of H_2O
  C 5 g of C_2H_6 **D** 17 g of NH_3

5 Which of the above quantities contains 6.02×10^{23} molecules?

6 Which of the above quantities contains L atoms?

7 Which of the above quantities contains one mole of hydrogen atoms?

8 200 cm³ of 3 mol l⁻¹ $ZnCl_2$ solution contains the same number of chloride ions as

  A 100 cm³ of 2 mol l⁻¹ $FeCl_3$
  B 200 cm³ of 3 mol l⁻¹ NaCl
  C 800 cm³ of 1.5 mol l⁻¹ HCl
  D 400 cm³ of 2 mol l⁻¹ $MgCl_2$

9 The number of sodium ions in 212 g of sodium carbonate is approximately

  A 6.0×10^{23} **B** 1.2×10^{24}
  C 2.4×10^{24} **D** 3.6×10^{24}

10 A mixture of sodium chloride and sodium carbonate contains 2 mol of chloride ions and 1 mol of carbonate ions. How many moles of sodium ions are present?

  A 1   **B** 2   **C** 3   **D** 4

11* A mixture of magnesium bromide and magnesium sulphate is known to contain 3 mol of magnesium and 4 mol of bromide ions. How many moles of sulphate ions are present?

A 1   **B** 2   **C** 3   **D** 4

12 How many hydrogen atoms are there in 0.25 mol of methane? ($L = 6.02 \times 10^{23}$)

A 0.25 L   **B** 0.5 L   **C** 1.0 L   **D** 2.0 L

13 The following grid contains various quantities of different substances.

A	4 g H_2
B	12 g C
C	20 g HF
D	8 g O_2
E	16 g CH_4
F	24 g Mg

a) Identify the quantity which contains the most molecules.
b) Identify the quantity which contains the most atoms.

14* 0.2 mol of $CuSO_4$ and 0.1 mol of Na_2SO_4 were dissolved in water and the solution made up to 500 cm³.
Identify the **true** statement(s).

A	The solution contained 0.1 mol of sodium ions.
B	The solution contained equal numbers of copper(II) and sodium ions.
C	The solution contained equal numbers of positive and negative ions.
D	The concentration of copper(II) ions in the solution is 0.4 mol 1^{-1}.
E	The concentration of sulphate ions in the solution is 0.8 mol 1^{-1}.

15* The value for the Avogadro Constant is 6.02×10^{23} mol^{-1}.
Identify the **true** statement(s).

A	24 g of carbon contains 6.02×10^{23} atoms.
B	1 g of hydrogen contains 6.02×10^{23} molecules.
C	500 cm³ of 2 mol 1^{-1} sodium hydroxide solution contains 6.02×10^{23} sodium ions.
D	6 g of water contains 6.02×10^{23} atoms.
E	44 g of carbon dioxide contains 6.02×10^{23} oxygen atoms.

16* The value for the Avogadro constant is 6.02×10^{23} mol^{-1}.
Identify the **true** statement(s).

A	There are 6.02×10^{23} atoms in 0.5 mol of neon gas.
B	There are 6.02×10^{23} electrons in 0.5 mol of hydrogen gas.
C	There are 6.02×10^{23} molecules in 0.5 mol of oxygen gas.
D	There are 6.02×10^{23} hydrogen atoms in 0.5 mol of water.
E	There are 6.02×10^{23} oxide ions in 0.5 mol of potassium oxide.
F	There are 6.02×10^{23} sodium ions in 0.5 mol of sodium chloride.

17 Hydrazine, N_2H_4
Hydrogen sulphide, H_2S Benzene, C_6H_6

For each of the above compounds calculate the mass that contains
a) 6.02×10^{23} molecules
b) 6.02×10^{23} atoms of hydrogen.

18 a) Using L to represent the Avogadro constant, calculate the number of
 i) positive ions in 82 g of sodium phosphate, Na_3PO_4
 ii) negative ions in 328 g of calcium nitrate, $Ca(NO_3)_2$
 iii) ions in total in 42 g of ammonium dichromate, $(NH_4)_2Cr_2O_7$
b) What volume of 2 mol 1^{-1} sulphuric acid contains
 i) L positive ions
 ii) L negative ions?

SECTION B: Gas volumes

1 The density of oxygen gas at 50°C and 1 atmosphere pressure was found to be 1.2 g l^{-1}.
Under these conditions, the molar volume in litres is

   A 13.3   **B** 24.0   **C** 26.7   **D** 32.0

2 $2NO(g) + O_2(g) \rightarrow 2NO_2(g)$

How many litres of nitrogen dioxide could be obtained by mixing 1.5 litres of nitrogen monoxide and 0.5 litres of oxygen? (All volumes are measured under the same conditions of temperature and pressure.)

   A 0.5   **B** 1.0   **C** 1.5   **D** 2.0

3 Which of the following has the same volume as 16 g of oxygen gas? (All volumes are measured under the same conditions of temperature and pressure.)

   A 4 g of helium gas
   B 16 g of methane gas
   C 2 g of hydrogen gas
   D 14 g of carbon monoxide gas

4 Using the density given in the SQA Data Book how many moles of chlorine molecules are there in a 2 litre container?

   A 0.09   **B** 0.18   **C** 0.29   **D** 0.38

Questions 5 and **6** relate to the decomposition of sodium hydrogencarbonate when heated, as shown in the following equation.

$$2NaHCO_3(s) \rightarrow Na_2CO_3(s) + CO_2(g) + H_2O(l)$$

In an experiment 0.1 mol of sodium hydrogencarbonate was heated until no further change took place.

5 The volume of gas obtained after cooling to room temperature was ($V_{mol} = 24$ litres mol^{-1})

   A 0.6 litres   **B** 1.2 litres
   C 1.8 litres   **D** 2.4 litres

6 The mass of remaining solid was

   A 5.3 g   **B** 8.4 g   **C** 10.6 g   **D** 13.7 g

7 In which reaction is the volume of the products equal to the volume of the reactants?

   A $2H_2(g) + O_2(g) \rightarrow 2H_2O(g)$
   B $3H_2(g) + N_2(g) \rightarrow 2NH_3(g)$
   C $N_2(g) + O_2(g) \rightarrow 2NO(g)$
   D $2SO_2(g) + O_2(g) \rightarrow 2SO_3(g)$

8 The equation for the complete combustion of ethene is

$$C_2H_4(g) + 3O_2(g) \rightarrow 2CO_2(g) + 2H_2O(l)$$

50 cm^3 of ethene is mixed with 200 cm^3 of oxygen and the mixture is ignited. What is the volume of the resulting gas mixture? (All volumes are measured under the same conditions of temperature and pressure.)

   A 100 cm^3 **B** 150 cm^3
   C 200 cm^3 **D** 250 cm^3

Questions 9 and **10** refers to the reaction between hydrogen gas and iodine vapour as shown in the following equation.

$$H_2(g) + I_2(g) \rightarrow 2HI(g)$$

1.2 mol of hydrogen gas and 1.0 mol of iodine vapour were mixed and allowed to react. After 5 minutes, 0.6 mol of iodine remained.

9 The number of mol of hydrogen which remain at this time was

   A 1.0   **B** 0.8   **C** 0.6   **D** 0.4

10 The number of mol of hydrogen iodide produced after 5 minutes was

   A 1.6   **B** 1.2   **C** 0.8   **D** 0.4

11 A mixture of 20 cm^3 of methane and 30 cm^3 of oxygen at 130°C was ignited.

$$CH_4 + 2O_2 \rightarrow CO_2 + 2H_2O$$

Identify the **true** statement(s) about this experiment, assuming that all volumes were measured at the same temperature and pressure.

A	Oxygen was in excess by 10 cm^3.
B	Methane was in excess by 5 cm^3.
C	15 cm^3 of carbon dioxide was produced.
D	40 cm^3 of water vapour was produced.
E	The total volume after reaction was 45 cm^3.

12 A mixture containing 0.2 mol magnesium and 0.1 mol magnesium carbonate was added to 200 cm^3 of 5 mol l^{-1} hydrochloric acid. Gas volumes were measured at room temperature and pressure (V_{mol} = 24 litres mol^{-1}). Identify the **true** statement(s) about this experiment.

A	There was 0.4 mol of excess acid.
B	1.2 litres of hydrogen gas were produced.
C	0.6 mol of magnesium chloride were produced.
D	There was 0.7 mol of excess acid.
E	2.4 litres of carbon dioxide were produced.
F	0.3 mol of water were produced.

13 Hydrogen sulphide gas reacts with zinc(II) nitrate solution, forming a precipitate of zinc(II) sulphide and a solution of nitric acid. The equation for the reaction is:

$$Zn(NO_3)_2(aq) + H_2S(g) \rightarrow$$
$$ZnS(s) + 2HNO_3(aq)$$

Hydrogen sulphide gas was passed through 200 cm^3 of 0.5 mol l^{-1} zinc(II) nitrate solution until no further reaction occurred. The precipitate was removed by filtration, washed, dried and weighed.
a) Hydrogen sulphide is a highly poisonous gas. What safety precaution should be taken during this experiment?
b) Calculate the volume of hydrogen sulphide required for complete reaction. (V_{mol} = 24 litres mol^{-1})
c) Calculate the mass of precipitate obtained.
d) Assuming that there is no loss of water during the experiment, what will be the concentration of the filtrate?

14 Silver(I) carbonate decomposes when heated according to the following equation.

$$2Ag_2CO_3 \rightarrow 4Ag + 2CO_2 + O_2$$

In an experiment, 2.758 g of silver(I) carbonate was heated as shown in the diagram until decomposition was complete.

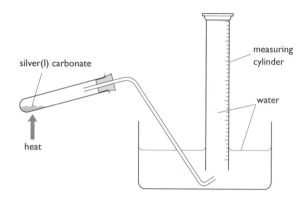

silver(I) carbonate

measuring cylinder

water

heat

a) Calculate the mass of silver obtained.
b) Calculate the volume of gas collected. (V_{mol} = 24 litres mol^{-1})
c) If sodium hydroxide solution was then added to the water, how would the volume of gas be affected? Explain why this happens.

15 Methoxymethane, CH_3OCH_3, is a gas at room temperature. The equation for the complete combustion of methoxymethane is shown below.

$$CH_3OCH_3 + 3O_2 \rightarrow 2CO_2 + 3H_2O$$

a) A mixture of 25 cm^3 of methoxymethane and 100 cm^3 of oxygen was ignited. Assume that all volumes are measured at room temperature and pressure.
   i) Show by calculation which reactant is in excess and by how much.
   ii) Calculate the volume of the gaseous product of this reaction.
b) Methoxymethane and ethanol (boiling point 78°C) are isomers.
   i) Explain the meaning of '*isomers*'
   ii) Suggest why methoxymethane has a much lower boiling point than ethanol.

16 Lime water (calcium hydroxide solution) turns cloudy at first when carbon dioxide is passed into it. When more carbon dioxide is added, the mixture turns clear again due to the production of calcium hydrogencarbonate which is soluble in water. The equation for the overall reaction is as follows.

$$Ca(OH)_2(aq) + 2CO_2(g) \rightarrow Ca(HCO_3)_2(aq)$$

Carbon dioxide was passed into a solution of calcium hydroxide containing 1.48 g l^{-1}.

a) Calculate the concentration of calcium hydroxide in moles per litre.

b) Calculate the volume of carbon dioxide which can react with 250 cm³ of this solution according to the equation shown above (V_{mol} = 24 litres mol^{-1}).

17 Ammonia burns in air which is enriched with extra oxygen. The balanced equation for this reaction is:

$$4NH_3 + 3O_2 \rightarrow 2N_2 + 6H_2O$$

a) Assuming that all volumes are measured at room temperature and pressure, calculate
   i) the volume of oxygen needed to burn 600 cm³ of ammonia, and
   ii) the volume of gas produced.

b) Write the balanced equation for the catalytic oxidation of ammonia in which nitrogen monoxide is formed instead of nitrogen.

18 Using the apparatus shown in the diagram, 0.12 mol of copper(II) oxide was completely reduced by ammonia according to the following equation.

$$3CuO(s) + 2NH_3(g) \rightarrow 3Cu(s) + N_2(g) + 3H_2O(l)$$

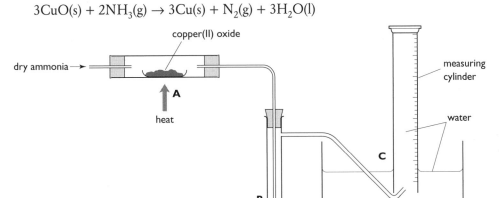

a) Calculate the mass of copper obtained at **A**.

b) What volume of water, to the nearest cm³, will be collected in tube **B**? (density of water = 1.0 g cm^{-3})

c) Calculate the volume of nitrogen collected over water at **C**. (V_{mol} = 24 litres mol^{-1})

d) To ensure complete reduction of the copper oxide, excess ammonia is used. What effect, if any, will this have on
   i) the pH of the water at **C**
   ii) the volume of gas collected?

THE WORLD OF CARBON

(7) Fuels

Fuels are substances which release energy on burning.

For Higher Chemistry, detailed additional knowledge of only one crude-oil derived fuel, petrol, is required.

Petrol

○ In addition to production from the gasoline fraction of the distillation of crude oil, petrol can also be made by **reforming** the naphtha fraction.

Figure 1 Fractions from crude oil

○ Reforming alters the arrangement of atoms in molecules. It *may* also alter the number of carbon and/or hydrogen atoms per molecule.

$$C_7H_{16} \rightarrow C_7H_8 + 4H_2$$
heptane   **methylbenzene**

$$CH_3CH_2CH_2CH_2CH_2CH_2CH_2CH_3 \rightarrow$$
octane
$$CH_3C(CH_3)_2CH_2CH(CH_3)CH_3$$
2,2,4-trimethylpentane

○ After adding the products of reforming, petrol contains branched-chain alkanes, cycloalkanes, and aromatic hydrocarbons as well as straight-chain hydrocarbons. (Aromatic hydrocarbons are dealt with in Chapter 8.)

○ To suit prevailing temperatures, any petrol is a blend of hydrocarbons of different volatilities, i.e. for low temperatures more high-volatility components are included.

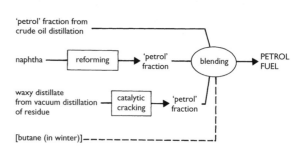

Figure 2 Making petrol

○ In a petrol engine, the petrol is mixed with air, and at the correct instant just before the end of the compression stroke of the 'four-stroke' cycle it is ignited by an electrical spark.

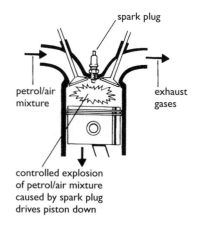

Figure 3 Petrol engine

○ 'Knocking', or 'pinking', is caused by auto-ignition, i.e. the fuel-air mixture ignites in the hot engine before the spark occurs.

○ Auto-ignition can be reduced by adding lead compounds to petrol, but leaded petrol is being phased out.

○ In unleaded petrol, more highly branched and aromatic compounds are used instead of lead compounds to reduce auto-ignition.

Alternative fuels

Ethanol

Ethanol can be mixed with petrol. The ethanol can be obtained by fermenting sucrose from surplus sugar-cane production in, for example, Brazil. The sugar cane is a **renewable** source of fuel.

$$C_2H_5OH + 3O_2 \rightarrow 2CO_2 + 3H_2O$$

Methanol

Methanol is an alternative to petrol. For its manufacture, see Chapter 11.

Advantages as a fuel
Virtually complete combustion, less carbon monoxide than from petrol.
Contains no aromatic carcinogens.
Cheaper to produce than primary fractionation gasoline.
Less volatile, and explosive, than petrol.
The car engine requires little modification.

Disadvantages as a fuel
Difficulty of mixing methanol and petrol without an extra cosolvent.
Methanol absorbs water, tending to form immiscible layers, becomes corrosive to car engine.
Methanol is toxic.
Less energy produced, volume for volume than from petrol. Bigger car fuel tanks needed.
Methanol is made from synthesis gas made from fossil methane.
Increases 'greenhouse' gases, unless 'biogas' is used to make synthesis gas.

Methane

Organic waste (e.g. animal manure, domestic refuse and human sewage) can be fermented anaerobically (in the absence of oxygen) to produce methane. Methane can be used as a domestic gaseous fuel or, from high pressure cylinders, as a motor fuel.

$$CH_4 + 2O_2 \rightarrow CO_2 + 2H_2O$$

Hydrogen

Electrolysis of water using solar energy which is a renewable resource could produce hydrogen to be used as a means of storing and distributing energy. If safety fears can be overcome, the hydrogen could be used as fuel in internal combustion engines, replacing petrol, and 'slowing' the increase of carbon dioxide in the atmosphere. The only product of hydrogen's combustion is water.

$$2H_2 + O_2 \rightarrow 2H_2O$$

Questions

Questions **1** and **2** relate to the following hydrocarbons.

A	C_2H_6	**B**	C_4H_{10}
C	C_8H_{18}	**D**	$C_{16}H_{34}$

1 Which hydrocarbon is most likely to be found in petrol?

2 Which hydrocarbon is added to petrol in winter to make it more volatile?

3* Which of the following occurs when crude oil is distilled?

 A Covalent bonds break and form again.
 B Covalent bonds break and van der Waals' bonds form.
 C Van der Waals' bonds break and covalent bonds form.
 D Van der Waals' bonds break and form again.

4 Biogas is mainly a mixture of

    A hydrogen and nitrogen
    B methane and carbon dioxide
    C hydrogen and carbon dioxide
    D methane and nitrogen.

5 Which of the following substances would **not** decrease the pre-ignition of petrol?

6 Which of the following substances is least likely to be present in petrol?

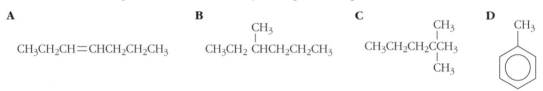

7 The following substances may be present in fuels.

A	Methanol	B	Hydrogen	C	Octane
D	Trimethylpentane	E	Ethanol	F	Methylbenzene

    a) Which substance is a renewable source of motor fuel?
    b) Which substance is aromatic?
    c) Which substance when burned would not contribute to the 'greenhouse effect'?
    d) Which substance is manufactured from 'synthesis gas'?

8 The following compounds may be present in fuels.

A	Butane	B	CH_4	C	Methanol
D	(methylbenzene structure) CH_3	E	CH_3CHOCH_3 with CH_3	F	$CH_3CCH_2CH_2CH_3$ with two CH_3

    a) Identify the main component of biogas.
    b) Identify the two compounds which can be described as oxygenates.
    c) Identify the compound(s) which could be produced by reforming heptane.

9 a) General sale of four-star petrol ceased on the 1st of January 2000. Which component of four-star justified this action?
    b) Why are levels of benzene in petrol also being reduced during 2000?
    c) Why did petrol include the substance named in your answer to **a)** as well as benzene?
    d) Name **two** types of compounds which will still be added to petrol to ensure that it continues to be satisfactory in modern car engines.

10

$$C_{18}H_{38} \xrightarrow{\text{I}} C_8H_{18} \quad + \quad C_6H_{14} \quad + \quad C_3H_6 \ + \ \textbf{X}$$

II ↓   III ↓   IV ↓

$$\underset{\displaystyle CH_3CHCH_2CHCH_2CH_3}{\overset{\displaystyle CH_3 \quad CH_3}{|\qquad\ |}} \qquad \bigcirc + \textbf{Y} \qquad -\!\!\left[CH_2\underset{|}{\overset{CH_3}{CH}}\right]_{\!n}\!-$$

Reaction **I** shows one possible outcome of cracking octadecane, $C_{18}H_{38}$.

Reactions **II**, **III** and **IV** refer to subsequent changes involving the products of cracking.

a) From the following list choose **two** terms for **each** of the reactions **II**, **III** and **IV**.

    addition   dehydrogenation   isomerisation   polymerisation   reforming

b) Which reaction produces an aromatic compound?

c) What structural feature of the product of reaction **II** makes it suitable for use in petrol?

d) Name the carbon compounds produced in **i)** reaction **III**   **ii)** reaction **IV**.

e) What substance is **X** and why is it a problem in catalytic cracking?

8 Hydrocarbons

Homologous Series

○ There are different series of hydrocarbons such as **alkanes**, **alkenes** and **cycloalkanes**.

○ Alkanes and alkenes have carbon atoms linked in chains, while cycloalkanes have a ring structure.

○ Alkanes and cycloalkanes are **saturated** as all of their carbon–carbon bonds are single bonds. Alkenes are **unsaturated** since they contain carbon–carbon double bonds.

○ The carbon–carbon double bond is an example of what is called a **functional group** since it has a major influence on the chemical behaviour of the compound.

○ Whether a hydrocarbon is saturated or unsaturated can be shown by testing it with bromine water. Alkenes rapidly decolourise the bromine water, while alkanes and cycloalkanes do not do so.

○ It is also possible to have a carbon–carbon triple bond in a molecule. The **alkynes** are a series of unsaturated hydrocarbons which possess this functional group. The first member of this series is called **ethyne** (acetylene).

Members of the three homologous series – alkanes, alkenes and alkynes – are listed below in Table 1.

○ Each of these series is an **homologous series**. Members of a given series, known as **homologues**, have the following characteristics:

1 Physical properties show a gradual change from one member to the next.

2 Chemical properties and methods of preparation are very similar.

3 Successive members differ in formula by $-CH_2-$ and in molecular mass by 14.

Alkanes	Alkenes	Alkynes
Methane CH_4 H—C—H (with H above and below)		
Ethane C_2H_6 H—C—C—H	Ethene C_2H_4 $C=C$	Ethyne C_2H_2 H—C≡C—H
Propane C_3H_8 H—C—C—C—H	Propene C_3H_6 H—C—C=C	Propyne C_3H_4 H—C—C≡C—H
Butane C_4H_{10}	Butene C_4H_8	Butyne C_4H_6
Pentane C_5H_{12}	Pentene C_5H_{10}	Pentyne C_5H_8
Hexane C_6H_{14}	Hexene C_6H_{12}	Hexyne C_6H_{10}
Heptane C_7H_{16}	Heptene C_7H_{14}	Heptyne C_7H_{12}
Octane C_8H_{18}	Octene C_8H_{16}	Octyne C_8H_{14}
General formula: C_nH_{2n+2}	General formula: C_nH_{2n}	General formula: C_nH_{2n-2}

4 They can be represented by a **general formula**.

5 Members of a series possess the same **functional group**, i.e. a certain group of atoms or type of bond which is mainly responsible for the characteristic chemical properties of that homologous series.

Naming isomers of alkanes

○ Isomers have the same molecular formula but different structural formulae.

○ The first three members of the alkane series – methane, ethane and propane – do not have isomers.

○ Butane, C_4H_{10}, has two isomers. Their full and shortened structural formulae are shown below.

$CH_3CH_2CH_2CH_3$

Á

CH_3CHCH_3

B̄

Compound A is called butane and is an example of a **straight-chain hydrocarbon.** Compound B is a **branched** hydrocarbon and its name is 2-methylpropane.

The method of naming isomers operates as follows:

1 Select and name the longest chain of carbon atoms in the molecule.

2 Find out which atom the branch is attached to by giving each carbon in the longest chain a number. Begin numbering from the end which is nearer the branch.

3 Identify the branch, e.g. as a methyl group (CH_3–), an ethyl group (C_2H_5–) etc. Figure 1 illustrates how this system applies to the above example.

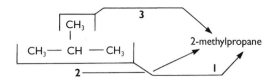

Figure 1

○ Pentane, C_5H_{12}, has three isomers as follows.

pentane

$CH_3CH_2CH_2CH_2CH_3$

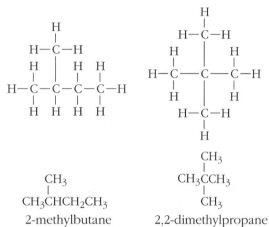

$CH_3CHCH_2CH_3$
$\quad\quad CH_3$
2-methylbutane

CH_3CCH_3
$\quad\quad CH_3$
2,2-dimethylpropane

Some of the problems which arise when dealing with structural formulae are shown below. Four other ways of representing 2-methylbutane, different from the structural formula given above, are shown.

$CH_3CHCH_2CH_3$
$\quad CH_3$

$CH_3CH_2CHCH_3$
$\quad\quad\quad\quad CH_3$

CH_3CHCH_2
$\quad CH_3 \quad CH_3$

$CHCH_2CH_3$
$CH_3 \quad CH_3$

The system of naming can be applied to more complicated molecules as shown by the following two examples.

$$\begin{array}{ccc}
CH_3 & CH_3 \\
| & | \\
CH_3CCH_2CHCH_3 \\
| \\
CH_3
\end{array}$$

2,2,4-trimethylpentane

$$\begin{array}{c}
C_2H_5 \\
| \\
CH_3C\,HCHCHCH_2CH_3 \\
| \quad | \\
CH_3 \; CH_3
\end{array}$$

3-ethyl-2,4-
dimethylhexane
(an isomer of decane,
$C_{10}H_{22}$)

Naming isomers of alkenes and alkynes

○ Ethene has no isomers. Propene has no isomers which are alkenes but it is isomeric with cyclopropane.

○ Isomers of alkenes can arise for two reasons, since
  1 the position of the double bond in the chain can vary and
  2 the chain can be straight or branched.

This is illustrated by the isomers of butene, C_4H_8.

$$\begin{array}{c}
H \;\; H \;\; H \quad\; H \\
| \quad | \quad | \quad / \\
H-C-C-C=C \\
| \quad | \qquad \backslash \\
H \;\; H \qquad\; H
\end{array}$$

$CH_3CH_2CH{=}CH_2$
but-1-ene

$$\begin{array}{c}
H \;\; H \;\; H \;\; H \\
| \quad | \quad | \quad | \\
H-C-C=C-C-H \\
| \qquad\qquad | \\
H \qquad\qquad H
\end{array}$$

$CH_3CH{=}CHCH_3$
but-2-ene

$$\begin{array}{c}
H \\
| \\
H-C-H \\
H \quad | \qquad H \\
| \quad | \quad\; / \\
H-C-C=C \\
| \qquad\quad \backslash \\
H \qquad\quad H
\end{array}$$

$$\begin{array}{c}
CH_3 \\
| \\
CH_3C{=}CH_2
\end{array}$$

2-methylpropene

○ Where necessary, the name shows the position of the double bond. Thus but-2-ene has the double bond between the second and third carbon atoms in the chain.

○ When naming a branched alkene the position of the double bond is more important than the position of the branch. The name of the alkene whose structure is shown here is 3-methylbut-1-ene (and **not** 2-methylbut-3-ene).

$$\begin{array}{c}
H \\
| \\
H-C-H \\
H \; | \qquad\qquad CH_3 \\
| \; | \qquad H \qquad | \\
H-C-C-C=C \quad\;\; CH_3CHCH{=}CH_2 \\
| \; | \; | \quad\; \backslash \\
H \; H \; H \quad\; H \qquad\; 3 \; methylbut\text{-}1\text{-}ene
\end{array}$$

○ Isomers of alkynes (from butyne) are named in a similar way to alkenes.

Addition reactions of alkenes

○ Alkenes can undergo addition reactions because they contain C=C bonds. Alkanes are unable to react by addition since they contain only single bonds.

Addition of hydrogen (H_2) – hydrogenation

An ALKENE reacts with HYDROGEN to form an ALKANE.

e.g.

$$CH_3CH_2CH{=}CH_2 + H_2 \xrightarrow[\text{Ni catalyst}]{200°C} CH_3CH_2CH_2CH_3$$

but-1-ene $\qquad\qquad\qquad\qquad$ **butane**

Addition of halogens (Br_2, Cl_2)

An ALKENE reacts with BROMINE to form a DIBROMOALKANE.

$$\text{e.g. } \begin{array}{c}
H \;\; H \quad\; H \\
| \quad | \quad / \\
H-C-C=C \quad + \; Br{-}Br \longrightarrow \\
| \qquad\quad \backslash \\
H \qquad\quad H
\end{array}$$

propene

$$\begin{array}{c}
H \;\; H \;\; H \\
| \quad | \quad | \\
H-C-C-C-H \\
| \quad | \quad | \\
H \; Br \; Br
\end{array}$$

1,2-dibromopropane

Similarly, an ALKENE reacts with CHLORINE to form a DICHLOROALKANE.

e.g.

$$CH_3CH_2CH{=}CH_2 + Cl_2 \rightarrow CH_3CH_2CHClCH_2Cl$$

but-1-ene $\qquad\qquad\qquad$ **1,2-dichlorobutane**

Addition of hydrogen halides (HX, where X = F, Cl, Br or I)

An ALKENE reacts with a HYDROGEN HALIDE to form a HALOGENOALKANE.

e.g. $CH_2{=}CH_2 + HBr \rightarrow CH_3CH_2Br$
$\quad$ **ethene** $\qquad\qquad\qquad$ **bromoethane**

Addition of water (H_2O) – Hydration

An ALKENE reacts with WATER (steam) to form an ALKANOL.

$$CH_2{=}CH_2 + H_2O \xrightarrow[\substack{\text{phosphoric} \\ \text{acid catalyst}}]{300°C} CH_3CH_2OH$$
ethene   ethanol

This method can be applied to the production of other alkanols from alkenes with more carbon atoms, e.g. the catalytic hydration of propene produces propanol.

Note: In each of the addition reactions described above the product is **saturated**. The atoms of the substance being added form bonds with the carbon atoms which were originally held together by the double bond.

Alkenes from dehydration of alkanols

○ The reverse process of the addition of water (hydration) is **dehydration** of an alkanol.

This can be easily demonstrated in the laboratory using the apparatus illustrated in Figure 2.

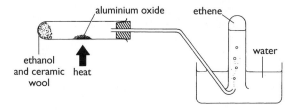

Figure 2 Dehydration of ethanol

○ When ethanol vapour is passed over heated aluminium oxide, which acts as a catalyst, dehydration occurs forming ethene.

$$C_2H_5OH \rightarrow CH_2{=}CH_2 + H_2O$$

○ Concentrated sulphuric acid has a strong attraction for water and can also be used to dehydrate alkanols.

○ Other alkenes can be produced by dehydration of alkanols, e.g. dehydration of propanol produces propene.

○ When an alkanol is dehydrated the –OH group is removed along with a hydrogen atom from an adjacent carbon atom.

○ Sometimes this produces two different alkenes, e.g. dehydration of butan-2-ol can produce either but-1-ene or but-2-ene as shown below.

$$\begin{array}{ccccccc} & H & H & H & H \\ & | & | & | & | \\ H{-}C & {-}C & {-}C & {-}C{-}H \\ & | & | & | & | \\ & H & H & OH & H \end{array}$$

$$\downarrow$$

$$CH_3CH_2CH{=}CH_2 + H_2O$$
or
$$CH_3CH{=}CHCH_3 + H_2O$$

Uses of halogenoalkanes

○ Halogenoalkanes have properties which make them suitable for a wide range of consumer products.

○ 2-bromo-2-chloro-1,1,1-trifluoroethane is the anaesthetic, 'halothane'.

$CF_3CHClBr$ halothane

CF_2Cl_2 dichlorodifluoromethane

CF_3CH_2F 1,1,1,2-tetrafluoroethane

○ Chlorofluorocarbons, or CFCs, were developed for a number of uses where a non-flammable, volatile liquid was required. Dichlorodifluoromethane was important as a refrigerant and as an aerosol propellent. Other CFCs were used as degreasing solvents and 'blowing agents' for making plastic foam, e.g. expanded polystyrene.

○ It is believed that CFCs are chiefly responsible for the depletion of the ozone layer in the upper atmosphere which absorbs ultra-violet (UV) radiation from the sun.

○ HFAs, i.e. hydrofluoroalkanes, are being developed as alternatives to CFCs, e.g. 1,1,1,2-tetrafluoroethane is a refrigerant. HFAs are more reactive than CFCs and are less likely to persist in the atmosphere sufficiently to affect the ozone layer.

Addition reactions of ethyne

○ Ethyne decolourises bromine water which shows that ethyne is unsaturated. It burns with a very sooty flame due to its high carbon content.

○ Ethyne undergoes similar addition reactions to ethene when it reacts with hydrogen, hydrogen halides, bromine and chlorine but the addition is a two-stage process. In the first stage one molecule of ethyne combines with one molecule of the addition reagent to form a compound with a C=C bond. In the second stage another molecule of the reagent is needed to form a saturated product.

Figure 3 summarises the reactions of ethyne with hydrogen, hydrogen chloride and bromine.

Aromatic hydrocarbons

○ **Aromatic** compounds contain a distinctive ring structure of six carbon atoms.

○ The simplest aromatic compound is the hydrocarbon called **benzene**, molecular formula: C_6H_6.

○ Aromatic compounds often behave in a markedly different way due to their characteristic chemical structure.

Structure of benzene

○ From its formula, C_6H_6, we might expect benzene to be unsaturated but the bromine water test shows that C=C bonds are not present in benzene.

○ Benzene has a planar molecule and all its carbon–carbon bonds are the same length, longer than the C=C bond but shorter than the C–C bond.

○ Each carbon atom has four outer electrons and in benzene three of these are used in forming bonds with a hydrogen atom and the two adjacent carbon atoms. The six remaining electrons, one from each carbon atom, occupy electron clouds which are **delocalised**.

Figure 4 illustrates the structure of benzene.

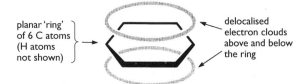

planar 'ring' of 6 C atoms (H atoms not shown)

delocalised electron clouds above and below the ring

Figure 4

○ The structure of benzene is usually represented as a regular hexagon suggesting a single bond framework (Figure 5). The circle inside the hexagon indicates the additional bonding due to the delocalised electrons. Each corner of the hexagon represents a carbon atom with one hydrogen atom attached.

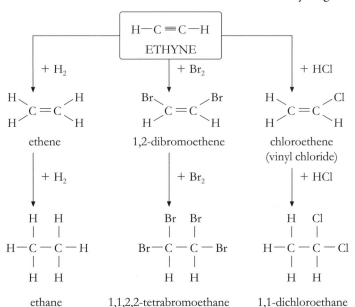

Figure 5

○ All of the above explains why benzene is reluctant to react by addition.

Aromatic compounds

○ Aromatic compounds have at least one of the hydrogen atoms on the benzene ring replaced by another atom or group of atoms.

For example, if one hydrogen atom is replaced, or substituted, by a methyl group, methylbenzene (toluene), $C_6H_5CH_3$, is produced.

CH$_3$ ◄— methyl group

phenyl group (i.e. C_6H_5)

methylbenzene

CH=CH$_2$

phenylethene

○ The **phenyl group** consists of a benzene ring minus one hydrogen atom, i.e. C_6H_5- and does not exist on its own but must be attached to another atom or group of atoms.

○ The prefix 'phenyl' is sometimes used in naming aromatic compounds.

For example, phenylethene is the systematic name for styrene which is the monomer for producing poly(phenylethene) or polystyrene as shown in Figure 6.

○ It is possible to have more than one of the hydrogen atoms in benzene replaced by methyl groups, e.g. 1,4 dimethylbenzene (para-xylene), $C_6H_4(CH_3)_2$.

CH$_3$ —◯— CH$_3$

$CH_3C_6H_4CH_3$

1,4-dimethylbenzene

Some examples of important monosubstituted aromatic compounds are given below.

◯—OH

phenol

◯—COOH

benzoic acid

◯—NH$_2$

phenylamine (aniline)

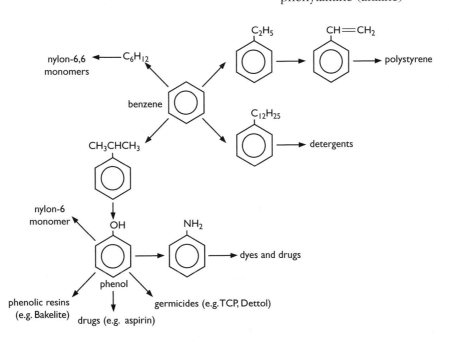

Figure 6

○ Many aromatic compounds, including benzene itself, are important as feedstocks for the production of everyday materials.

Some of these feedstocks and their products are illustrated in Figure 6 as a summary of synthetic routes emanating from benzene.

Questions

1 What kind of reaction occurs when propanol vapour is passed over hot aluminium oxide?

A Dehydration   B Hydrolysis
C Dehydrogenation D Hydration

2 One mole of a hydrocarbon combines with two moles of hydrogen gas to form a saturated hydrocarbon. The hydrocarbon could be

A benzene   B butene
C cyclopentane D propyne.

3
$$CH_3$$
$$|$$
$$CH_3CH_2CH$$
$$|$$
$$CHCH_2CH_3$$
$$|$$
$$CH_3$$

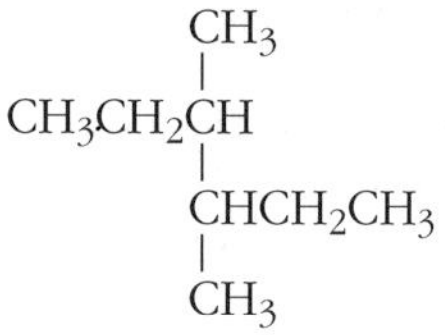

The name of this compound is

A 2,3-diethylbutane
B 2-ethyl-3-methylpentane
C 3,4-dimethylhexane
D 3-ethyl-2-methylpentane

4 When but-2-ene reacts with bromine the formula of the product is

A $CH_3CHBrCHBrCH_3$

B $CH_3CHBrCH_2CH_2Br$

C $CH_3CBr_2CH_2CH_3$

D $CH_2BrCHBrCH_2CH_3$

5 A bottle is labelled with the formula C_5H_{10}. The liquid in the bottle is **not**

A pent-1-ene   B pent-2-yne
C cyclopentane D 2-methylbut-2-ene.

6 Draw the full structural formula of each of the following compounds.
a) 3-ethyl-2-methylpentane
b) 1,3-dimethylcyclobutane
c) pent-2-ene
d) 2-methylbut-1-ene
e) hex-3-yne
f) 3-methylbut-1-yne
g) ethylbenzene
h) 1,3,5-trimethylbenzene

7 Draw the shortened structural formula of each of the following compounds.
a) 3,3-diethylpentane
b) 2,2,6-trimethylheptane
c) 3-methylhex-3-ene
d) 3-ethylpent-1-ene
e) 4,4-dimethylhex-2-yne
f) 1,3-dichloropropane

8 Name the following compounds
a)
$$CH_3 \quad CH_3$$
$$| \qquad |$$
$$CH_3CH_2CHCH_2CCH_3$$
$$|$$
$$CH_3$$

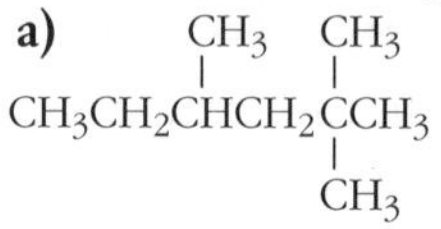

b)
$$CH_3CH=CHCHCH_2CH_3$$
$$|$$
$$C_2H_5$$

c)
$$CH_3 \diagdown \quad \overset{CH_3}{\underset{\text{CH}}{|}}$$
$$\overset{CH}{\underset{CH_2}{|}} \qquad \overset{}{\underset{CH_2}{CH_2}}$$
$$CH_2 ——— CH_2$$

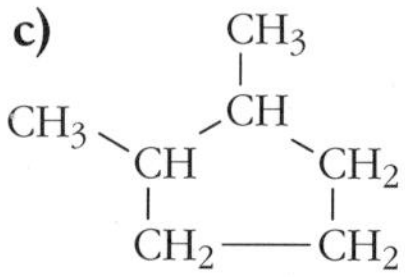

d)
$$Br$$
$$|$$
$$CH_3CH_2CCH_3$$
$$|$$
$$Br$$

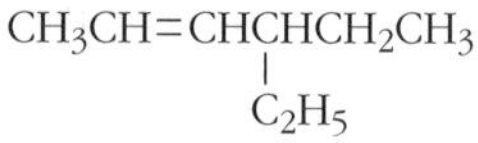

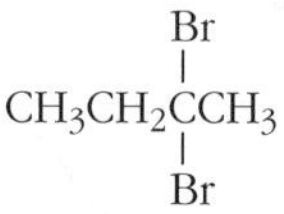

e) $CH_3C \equiv CCHCH_3$
$$|$$
$$CH_3$$

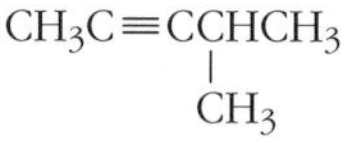

f)
$$CH_3$$

(benzene ring with two CH_3 groups)
$$CH_3$$

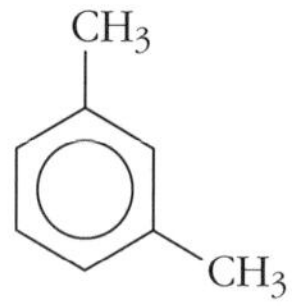

9 For each of the following reactions, draw the full structural formula and give the systematic name of the carbon compound produced.
a) But-2-ene + hydrogen chloride
b) Ethene + chlorine
c) 2-methylpropene + hydrogen
d) Ethyne + chlorine [1:2 mol ratio]
e) But-2-yne + HBr [1:1 mol ratio]
f) Propyne + hydrogen [1:1 mol ratio]

10 Iodine monochloride, ICl, reacts with alkenes in a similar manner to bromine.
a) What type of reaction occurs when an alkene reacts with iodine monochloride?
b) Draw the structural formulae of the two possible products formed when propene reacts with iodine monochloride.
c) Why is there only one product when but-2-ene reacts with iodine monochloride?

11 In the Wurtz reaction, iodoalkanes react with sodium to form alkanes. The reaction is used to make alkanes which have an even number of carbon atoms, e.g. iodomethane and sodium react to produce ethane as shown below.

$$CH_3{\vdots}I + 2Na + I{\vdots}CH_3 \rightarrow CH_3-CH_3 + 2NaI$$

a) Name the iodoalkane required to make octane.

b) Draw the structural formula of 2-iodopropane and the product when it undergoes the Wurtz reaction.

c) Alkanes such as pentane, which have odd numbers of carbon atoms per molecule, can be produced by the Wurtz reaction.

$$C_3H_7I + 2Na + C_2H_5I \rightarrow C_5H_{12} + 2NaI$$

However, **two** other alkanes are formed in this reaction. Name these alkanes.

12 The following diagram shows some reactions involving propene and propyne.

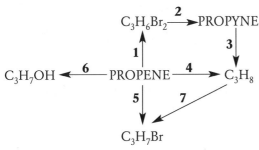

a) Which of the reactions **1** to **7** are examples of hydrogenation?

b) Which of the reactions **1** to **7** are **not** addition reactions?

c) Reaction **6** can be reversed in a laboratory experiment.
   i) What type of reaction is this reverse reaction?
   ii) Describe briefly with the aid of a diagram how it can be carried out in the laboratory.

d) Reaction **7** occurs when a mixture of propane and bromine vapour is exposed to sunlight. An acidic compound is also produced in the reaction. Work out an equation for this reaction using molecular formulae.

13 Aromatic compounds which have hydroxyl groups attached to the benzene ring are known collectively as phenols. The names and structural formulae of three examples are shown below.

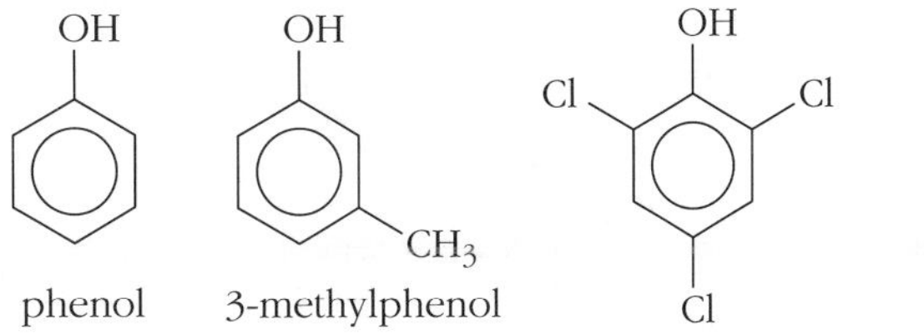

OH   OH   OH

phenol   3-methylphenol   trichlorophenol (TCP)

a) Give the molecular formula of each of these phenols.

b) Phenol is slightly soluble in water forming a weak acid known as carbolic acid. Benzene is not acidic. Write the formulae of both ions present in carbolic acid solution.

c) The name 'trichlorophenol' does not fully describe its structure. Work out the full name of this compound.

14 a) Draw the shortened structural formula of pent-2-yne.

b) Name an isomer of pent-2-yne which has
   i) a straight-chain structure
   ii) a branched-chain structure
   iii) a ring structure.

15*

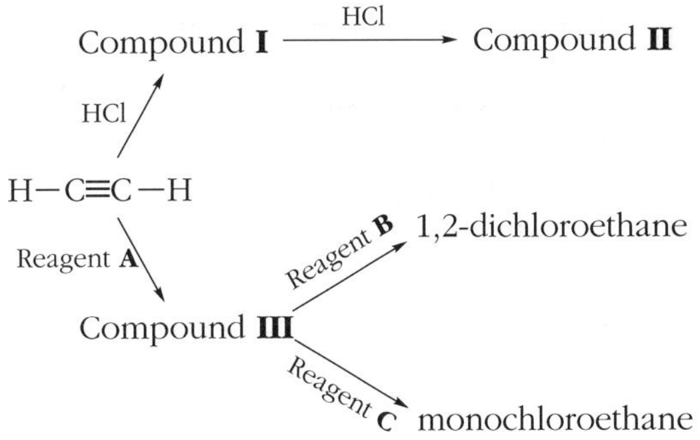

Compound **I** $\xrightarrow{\text{HCl}}$ Compound **II**

$$H-C{\equiv}C-H$$

HCl

Reagent **A**

Compound **III**

Reagent **B** → 1,2-dichloroethane

Reagent **C** → monochloroethane

All compounds in the above diagram have different structures, and the reagent and compound are in the ratio of 1 mole : 1 mole in every case.

a) Draw the full structural formulae for compounds **I, II** and **III**.

b) Name reagents **A, B** and **C**.

16*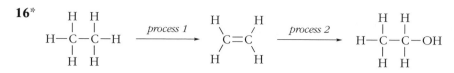

A	condensation	B	cracking	C	dehydration
D	hydration	E	hydrolysis	F	oxidation

    a) Identify process 1.
    b) Identify process 2.

17 The grid gives the names of various hydrocarbons.

A	Benzene	B	Pentyne	C	Cyclobutane
D	Butyne	E	Ethene	F	Cyclopentene

    a) Identify the compound(s) which cannot rapidly decolourise bromine water.
    b) Identify the compound which is the second member of the homologous series to which it belongs.
    c) Identify the **two** compounds which are isomers.

18 Some hydrocarbons are shown below.

A	$CH_3C{\equiv}CH$	B	$\begin{array}{c}CH_3\\|\\CH_3C{=}CH_2\end{array}$	C	$\begin{array}{c}CH_2{-}CH_2\\|\quad\quad|\\CH{=}CH\end{array}$
D	$CH_3CH_2CH_3$	E	$CH_2{=}CHCH{=}CH_2$	F	$CH_3CH{=}CHCH_3$

    a) Identify the **two** compounds which belong to the same homologous series.
    b) Identify the compound one mole of which requires 4 moles of oxygen for complete combustion.
    c) Identify the compound(s) which could combine with hydrogen bromide to form a dibromoalkane.

9 Alcohols, Aldehydes and Ketones

Alcohols

○ An alcohol is a carbon compound containing the hydroxyl functional group, –OH.

○ An alcohol name ends in -ol.

Alkanols

○ Alkanols are a homologous series of alcohols.

○ An alkanol is a substituted alkane in which one of the hydrogen atoms has been replaced by the **hydroxyl** group.

○ The name of an alkanol is obtained by replacing the final letter of the corresponding alkane by the name ending '-ol'.

Alkanes		Alkanols	
Methane	CH_4	Methanol	CH_3OH
Ethane	C_2H_6	Ethanol	C_2H_5OH
Propane	C_3H_8	Propanol	C_3H_7OH
Butane	C_4H_{10}	Butanol	C_4H_9OH
Pentane	C_5H_{12}	Pentanol	$C_5H_{11}OH$
General formula: C_nH_{2n+2}		General formula: $C_nH_{2n+1}OH$ or $C_nH_{2n+2}O$	

Table 1

Structural formulae and isomers

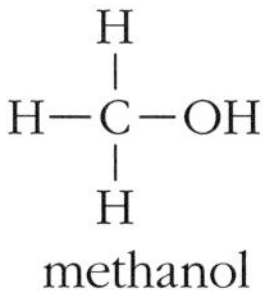

$$H-\overset{\displaystyle H}{\underset{\displaystyle H}{C}}-OH \qquad H-\overset{\displaystyle H}{\underset{\displaystyle H}{C}}-\overset{\displaystyle H}{\underset{\displaystyle H}{C}}-OH \text{ or } CH_3CH_2OH$$

methanol   ethanol

○ Methanol has no isomers. Ethanol has no isomer which is an alkanol.

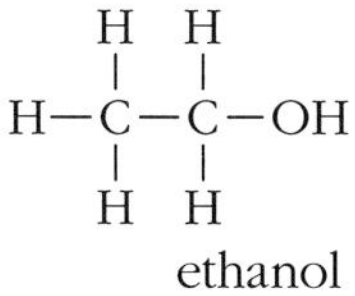

○ Propanol has two isomers since the hydroxyl group can be attached either to a carbon atom at the end of the chain or to the carbon atom in the middle of the chain.

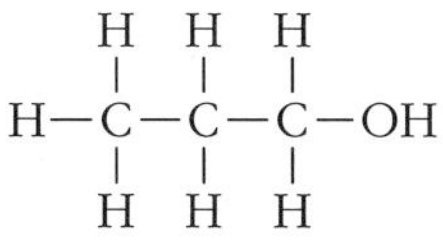

$$H-\overset{\displaystyle H}{\underset{\displaystyle H}{C}}-\overset{\displaystyle H}{\underset{\displaystyle H}{C}}-\overset{\displaystyle H}{\underset{\displaystyle H}{C}}-OH \qquad H-\overset{\displaystyle H}{\underset{\displaystyle H}{C}}-\overset{\displaystyle H}{\underset{\displaystyle OH}{C}}-\overset{\displaystyle H}{\underset{\displaystyle H}{C}}-H$$

$CH_3CH_2CH_2OH$ CH_3CHCH_3
                                              |
                                             OH

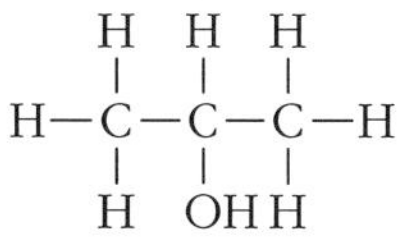

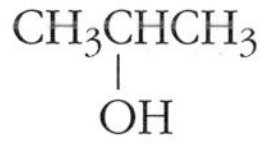

                              or $CH_3CH(OH)CH_3$

propan-1-ol   propan-2-ol

○ Butanol has more isomers since the chain may be branched. Three isomers of butanol are shown here.

$CH_3CH_2CH_2CH_2OH$ $CH_3CH_2CHCH_3$
                                                          |
butan-1-ol   OH
                                                        or
                                          $CH_3CH_2CH(OH)CH_3$
                                               butan-2-ol

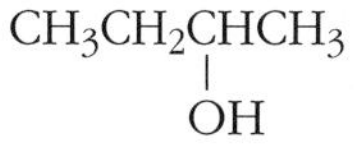

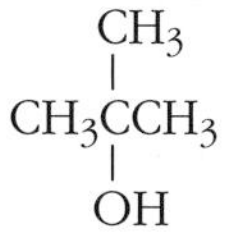

                    CH_3
                       |
            CH_3CCH_3
                       |
                     OH

        2-methylpropan-2-ol

○ When an alkanol contains three or more carbon atoms per molecule it is necessary when naming it to specify the carbon atom to which the –OH group is attached.

○ When naming alkanols which have branched chains the position of the hydroxyl group takes precedence over the position of the branch. Thus the alkanol shown below is called 3-methylbutan-2-ol, not 2-methylbutan-3-ol.

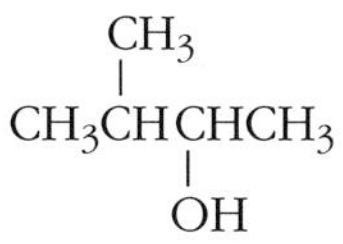

      CH_3 CH_3
         | |
$CH_3CHCHCH_3$ or $CH_3CHCH(OH)CH_3$
         |
        OH

Types of alcohol

○ Alcohols fall into three different types depending on the position of the hydroxyl group (Table 2).

○ Methanol and ethanol are examples of primary alkanols.

Type	Primary	Secondary	Tertiary
Position of –OH group.	Joined to the **end** of the carbon chain	Joined to an **intermediate** carbon atom.	Joined to an **intermediate** carbon atom which also has a **branch** attached.
	R–CH$_2$OH	**R–CH–R′** $\mid$ OH	**R″** $\mid$ **R–C–R′** $\mid$ OH
	e.g. propan-1-ol butan-1-ol	e.g. propan-2-ol butan-2-ol	e.g. 2-methylpropan-2-ol

(The symbols **R**, **R′** and **R″** stand for alkyl groups, e.g. methyl, CH$_3$–, ethyl, C$_2$H$_5$–, etc.)

Table 2

Oxidation of alcohols

○ Oxidation occurs when a substance combines with oxygen.

○ Combustion is an extreme example of oxidation. Complete combustion of an alcohol produces carbon dioxide and water. e.g.

$$C_2H_5OH(l) + 3O_2(g) \rightarrow 2CO_2(g) + 3H_2O(l)$$

○ Other oxidation reactions cause less drastic changes to the structure of the alcohol.

○ Primary and secondary alcohols can be oxidised by various oxidising agents but tertiary alcohols do not readily oxidise.

○ Acidified potassium dichromate solution is a suitable oxidising agent. The dichromate ions gain electrons from the alcohol which, therefore, has been oxidised. The equation for this reaction is:

$$\overset{\text{heat}}{Cr_2O_7{}^{2-} + 14H^+ + 6e^- \rightarrow 2Cr^{3+} + 7H_2O}$$
$$\underset{\text{ions – orange}}{\text{dichromate}} \qquad \underset{\text{ions – blue–green}}{\text{chromium(III)}}$$

○ Oxidation also results from passing the alcohol vapour over heated copper(II) oxide as shown in Figure 1.

The oxide is reduced to copper. Ethanol is oxidised to form ethanal. The equation for the reaction is:

$$CH_3CH_2OH + CuO \rightarrow$$
$$CH_3CHO + Cu + H_2O$$

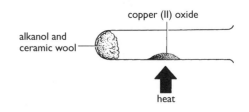

Figure 1 Oxidation of an alkanol

○ **Primary alcohols** are oxidised to produce **aldehydes**,

e.g. propan-1-ol $\rightarrow$ PROPANAL

$$CH_3CH_2CH_2OH \rightarrow CH_3CH_2CHO$$

○ **Secondary alcohols** are oxidised to produce **ketones**.

e.g propan-2-ol $\rightarrow$ PROPANONE

$$CH_3CH(OH)CH_3 \rightarrow CH_3COCH_3$$

○ Either of the oxidising agents, $Cr_2O_7^{2-}/H^+$ (aq) or CuO(s) can be used for these reactions.

○ When primary alcohols are oxidised to aldehydes and secondary alcohols are oxidised to ketones, two hydrogen atoms are removed, namely the hydrogen atom of the –OH group and a hydrogen on the adjacent carbon atom. A tertiary alcohol cannot be similarly oxidised since it does not have a hydrogen atom attached to the carbon atom adjacent to the hydroxyl group.

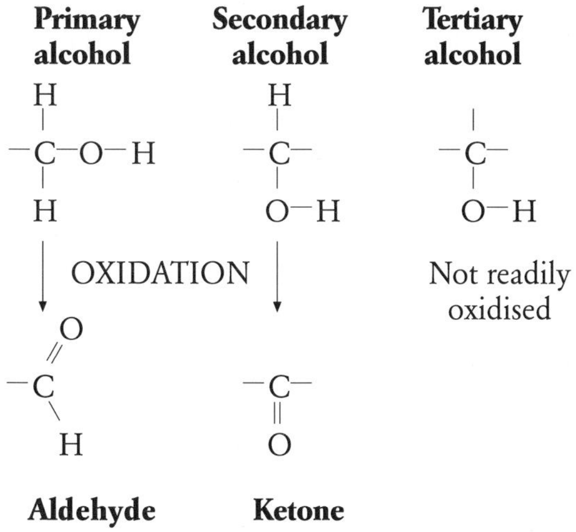

Primary alcohol   Secondary alcohol   Tertiary alcohol

OXIDATION

Not readily oxidised

Aldehyde   Ketone

Figure 2

Aldehydes and Ketones

○ Aldehydes and ketones contain a carbon–oxygen double bond, C=O, called a **carbonyl** group. In an **aldehyde** the carbonyl group is at the **end** of the carbon chain and has a hydrogen atom attached to it. In a **ketone** the carbonyl group is **joined** to two other carbon atoms.

○ There is a homologous series of aldehydes called **alkanals**, and a homologous series of ketones called **alkanones**. These are shown in Table 3.

○ Note that in the shortened structural formula of an alkanal the functional group is written as –CHO and not –COH.

○ Branched alkanals and alkanones do exist. When naming these the position of the functional group takes precedence over the position of the branch, as shown in the following examples. There is no need to indicate a number for the functional group when naming an alkanal as it must always be at the end of the chain but when naming an alkanone it is usually necessary to specify the number of the carbonyl group.

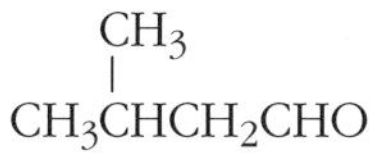

$$CH_3$$
$$CH_3CHCH_2CHO$$
3-methylbutanal

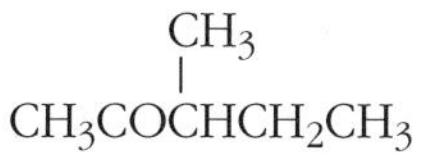

$$CH_3$$
$$CH_3COCHCH_2CH_3$$
3-methylpentan-2-one

Alkanals		Alkanones	
Methanal	HCHO		
Ethanal	CH_3CHO		
Propanal	CH_3CH_2CHO	Propanone	CH_3COCH_3
Butanal	$CH_3CH_2CH_2CHO$	Butanone	$CH_3CH_2COCH_3$
General formula:	$C_nH_{2n}O$ [n ≥ 1]		$C_nH_{2n}O$ [n ≥ 3]
Functional group:	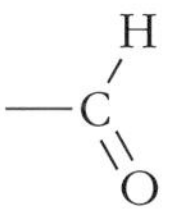 $-C\overset{H}{\underset{O}{}}$ or –CHO		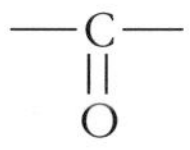 $-\overset{}{\underset{O}{C}}-$ or –CO–

Table 3

Oxidation of aldehydes

○ Aldehydes and ketones are similar in that both types of compound contain the carbonyl group and are obtained by oxidation of alcohols.

○ Aldehydes are readily oxidised while ketones are not.

Prescribed Practical Activity

Several oxidising agents can be used to distingush aldehydes from ketones:

1   Acidified potassium dichromate solution, $Cr_2O_7^{2-}(aq) + H^+(aq)$

2   Benedict's solution or Fehling's solution, $Cu^{2+}(aq)$ in alkaline solution

3   Tollen's reagent, i.e. ammoniacal silver(I) nitrate solution, $Ag^+(aq) + NH_3(aq)$.

In the experiment two samples of each oxidising agent are poured into separate test tubes. A few drops of an aldehyde are added to one set of each oxidising agent and a few drops of a ketone are added to the other set. The test tubes are placed in a hot water bath for several minutes (Figure 3).

hot water ———————— aldehyde (or ketone) + oxidising agent

Figure 3

○ Acidified potassium dichromate solution oxidises an aldehyde to form a **carboxylic acid**. If the aldehyde is an alkanal, it is oxidised to form an **alkanoic acid**, e.g.

$$CH_3CH_2CH_2CHO \rightarrow CH_3CH_2CH_2COOH$$
$$\text{butanal} \qquad\qquad \text{butanoic acid}$$

○ The other two oxidising agents are alkaline and as a result oxidise an alkanal to give the appropriate alkanoate ion, e.g.

$$CH_3CH_2CHO \rightarrow CH_3CH_2COO^-$$
$$\text{propanal} \qquad \text{propanoate ion}$$

○ The change that occurs to the functional group when an aldehyde is oxidised is shown below.

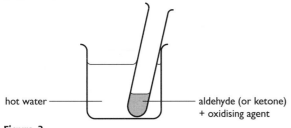

○ This shows that during the oxidation of an aldehyde the C–H bond next to the carbonyl group is broken and the hydrogen atom is replaced by a hydroxyl group. This cannot happen with a ketone since it does not have a hydrogen atom attached to its carbonyl group.

Table 4 summarises the results for the reactions of an aldehyde, ketones do **not** react

Oxidising Agent	Observations	Explanation
Acidified potassium dichromate solution	Orange solution → blue-green solution	$Cr_2O_7^{2-}(aq)$ reduced to $Cr^{3+}(aq)$
Benedict's solution or Fehling's solution	Blue precipitate → orange-red	$Cu^{2+}(aq)$ reduced to $Cu_2O(s)$ [copper(I) oxide] i.e. $Cu^{2+} + e^- \rightarrow Cu^+$
Tollen's reagent	Colourless solution → silver mirror	$Ag^+(aq)$ reduced to $Ag(s)$, i.e. $Ag^+ + e^- \rightarrow Ag$

Summary of the oxidation of alcohols

	PRIMARY ALCOHOL	$\rightarrow$	ALDEHYDE	$\rightarrow$	CARBOXYLIC ACID
	Primary Alkanol	$\rightarrow$	**Alkanal**	$\rightarrow$	**Alkanoic Acid**
e.g.	CH_3CH_2OH	$\rightarrow$	CH_3CHO	$\rightarrow$	CH_3COOH
	ethanol		ethanal		ethanoic acid
	SECONDARY ALCOHOL	$\rightarrow$	KETONE		not readily oxidised further
	Secondary Alkanol	$\rightarrow$	**Alkanone**		
e.g.	$CH_3CH(OH)CH_3$	$\rightarrow$	CH_3COCH_3		
	propan-2-ol		propanone		

TERTIARY ALCOHOLS are not readily oxidised.

In each of the examples above, oxidation of an alkanol or an alkanal has resulted in an increase in the oxygen to hydrogen ratio. The reverse of these reactions would be reductions and would involve a decrease in the oxygen to hydrogen ratio.

- **Oxidation** occurs when there is an **increase** in the oxygen to hydrogen ratio.

- **Reduction** occurs when there is a **decrease** in the oxygen to hydrogen ratio.

Questions

1 Which process occurs when ethanol is converted to ethanal?

   A Reduction   B Hydrogenation
   C Oxidation   D Dehydration

2* Which is true of a compound with the following formula?

$$CH_3CH(OH)CH_3$$

   A It is a primary alcohol.
   B It can be oxidised to an aldehyde.
   C It is a tertiary alcohol.
   D It can be oxidised to a ketone.

3 Which compound is formed by the oxidation of butan-2-ol?

   A $CH_3CH_2CH_2CHO$

   B $CH_3CH_2COCH_3$

   C $CH_3CH_2CH_2COOH$

   D $CH_3CH{=}CHCH_3$

4 Oxidation of butanal to butanoic acid results in the compound

   A gaining 2 g per mole
   B losing 16 g per mole
   C gaining 16 g per mole
   D losing 2 g per mole.

5* The dehydration of butan-2-ol can produce two isomeric alkenes, but-1-ene and but-2-ene. Which one of the following alkanols can similarly produce, on dehydration, a pair of isomeric alkenes?

   A propan-2-ol   B pentan-3-ol
   C hexan-3-ol   D heptan-4-ol

6 Which alkanol can be oxidised to produce an alkanone?

   A 2-methylpropan-1-ol
   B 3-methylbutan-2-ol
   C 2,2-dimethylpropan-1-ol
   D 2-methylbutan-2-ol

7 Which of the following statements is **not** true about aldehydes?

 A They are formed by oxidation of secondary alcohols.
 B They can be oxidised to produce carboxylic acids.
 C Their molecules contain a carbonyl group of atoms.
 D They will reduce acidified potassium dichromate solution.

8 Draw a structural formula and name the type of each of the following alcohols.
 a) hexan-3-ol
 b) 2-methylbutan-2-ol
 c) 3,3-dimethylbutan-1-ol
 d) 3-ethylpentan-2-ol

9 Give the systematic name and indicate the type of each of the following alcohols.
 a) $CH_3CH_2CH(OH)CH_2CH_3$
 b)
$$\overset{\displaystyle C_2H_5}{\underset{\displaystyle OH}{CH_3CH_2CCH_2CH_3}}$$
 c) $CH_3CH(CH_3)CH_2CH_2OH$
 d)
$$HOCH_2CH_2CH_2\underset{\displaystyle CH_3}{\overset{\displaystyle CH_3}{C}}CH_3$$

10 Butanone is an important solvent which can be made from butene in a two-stage process outlined below.

$$\text{BUTENE} \xrightarrow{H_2O(g)} \text{Compound } \mathbf{X} \xrightarrow{\text{oxidation}} \text{BUTANONE}$$

 a) Draw the full structural formula of butanone.
 b) Give the systematic name of compound **X**.
 c) Name the type of reaction occurring in the first stage.
 d) Name a suitable oxidising agent for the second stage.

11 The bromoalkane shown below can react with potassium hydroxide under different conditons to give two other carbon compounds, **Y** and **Z**.

$$\overset{\displaystyle H\quad H\quad H}{\underset{\displaystyle H\quad Br\quad H}{H-C-C-C-H}}$$

Reaction 1 ↙   ↘ *Reaction 2*

liquid Y   **gas Z**

In reaction **1** the bromine atom is replaced by a hydroxyl group.
In reaction **2** the bromine atom and a hydrogen atom from an adjacent carbon atom are removed.

 a) Name **Y** and **Z**.
 b) **Y** and **Z** can be distinguished by chemical tests.
  i) Describe one test (with result) which would give a positive result with **Y**.
  ii) Describe one test (with result) which would give a positive result with **Z**.

12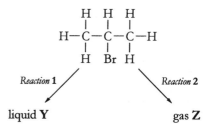

Benzoic acid can be converted into two other aromatic compounds by the reaction sequence shown above.
Work out the oxygen:hydrogen ratio for each compound and decide whether reactions **1** and **2** occur by oxidation or reduction.

13 When an alkene reacts with ozone, the molecule is split in two at the double bond to form carbonyl compounds. An example is shown below.

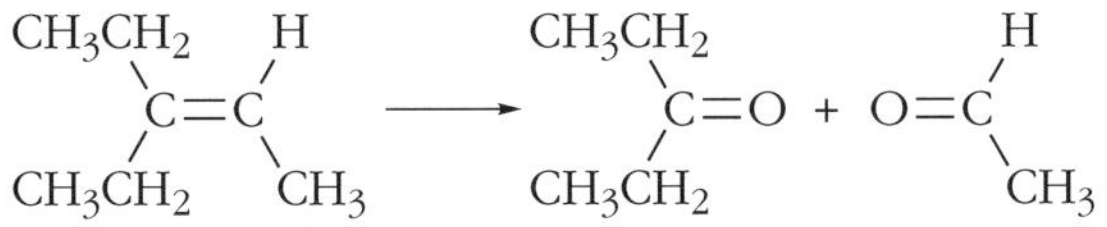

a) Name the alkene shown above.

b) Name the alkanone produced in the reaction shown above.

c) Describe a chemical test which would distinguish between the carbonyl compounds produced in the above reaction.

d) When hex-3-ene reacts with ozone there is only one compound produced. Explain why.

e) Draw a structural formula of the alkene which reacts with ozone to form only propanone.

14*

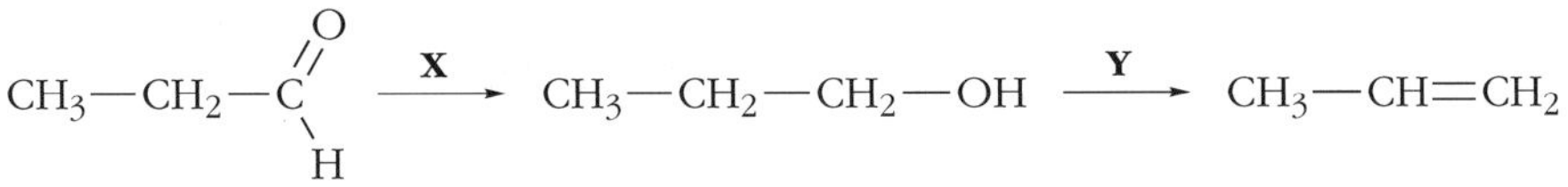

A	Oxidation	**B**	Reduction	**C**	Hydrogenation
D	Dehydrogenation	**E**	Dehydration	**F**	Condensation

a) Identify the name which could be applied to reaction **Y**.

b) Identify the name(s) which could be applied to reaction **X**.

15* Many organic compounds contain oxygen.

A	CH_3-O-CH_3	**B**	CH_3-CH_2-OH	**C** 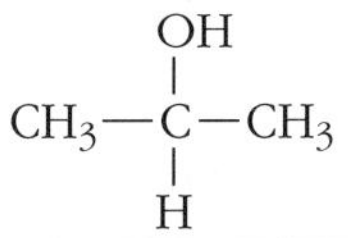	$\begin{array}{c} OH \\ \mid \\ CH_3-C-CH_3 \\ \mid \\ H \end{array}$
D	$\begin{array}{c} O \\ \parallel \\ CH_3-C-CH_3 \end{array}$	**E**	$CH_3-CH_2-C \overset{\displaystyle O}{\underset{\displaystyle H}{}}$	**F**	$\begin{array}{c} CH_3 \\ \mid \\ CH_3-C-CH_3 \\ \mid \\ OH \end{array}$

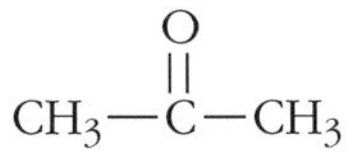

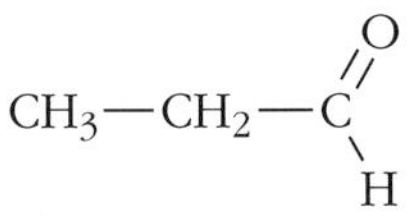

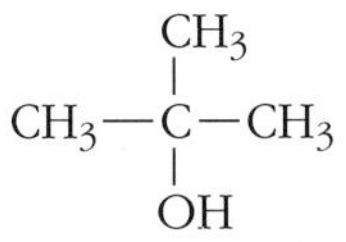

a) Identify the **two** compounds which contain the carbonyl group.

b) Identify the primary alcohol.

c) Identify the compound which can give propene on dehydration.

d) Identify the isomer of methoxyethane: $CH_3-O-CH_2-CH_3$

10 Carboxylic Acids and Esters

Carboxylic Acids

○ A carboxylic acid is characterised by the **carboxyl** functional group, and by its name ending, '-oic acid'.

The carboxyl functional group:

$$-\overset{\displaystyle O}{\underset{\displaystyle OH}{C}} \quad\text{or}\quad -COOH$$

e.g. CH_3COOH

benzoic acid COOH

ethanoic acid   benzoic acid

○ There is a homologous series of carboxylic acids called alkanoic acids which are based on the corresponding parent alkanes. This is shown in Table 1.

○ Branched-chain alkanoic acids can also be obtained and these are named with the functional group taking precedence. There is no need to give a number for the functional group as it must be at the end of the chain, i.e. the carbon atom of the –COOH group is the first carbon atom in the chain.

e.g.

$$CH_3CHCH_2COOH \overset{\displaystyle CH_3}{|}$$

3-methylbutanoic acid

Uses of carboxylic acids

○ Ethanoic acid prevents bacterial and fungal growth. Dilute solutions, vinegar, are used for pickling food.

○ Ethanoic acid is a feedstock for the production of, for example, ethenyl ethanoate (vinyl acetate), which is polymerised to give the plastic component of vinyl emulsion paints, and cellulose ethanoate, which is used to produce films and lacquers.

○ Benzene-1,4-dicarboxylic acid, is a diacid used to make polyester and hexanedioic acid is a monomer used in the production of nylon.

○ Benzoic acid, C_6H_5COOH, is the food additive, E210, acting as a preservative and antioxidant.

$CH_3COOCH=CH_2$ $HOOC-$⬡$-COOH$

ethenyl ethanoate   benzene-1,4-dicarboxylic acid

$$HOOC(CH_2)_4COOH$$
hexanedioic acid

Name of acid	Structural formulae	
Methanoic acid	HCOOH	$H-\overset{\displaystyle O}{\underset{\displaystyle OH}{C}}$
Ethanoic acid	CH_3COOH	$H-\overset{\displaystyle H}{\underset{\displaystyle H}{C}}-\overset{\displaystyle O}{\underset{\displaystyle OH}{C}}$
Propanoic acid	CH_3CH_2COOH	
Butanoic acid	$CH_3CH_2CH_2COOH$	
Pentanoic acid	$CH_3CH_2CH_2CH_2COOH$	
General formula:	$C_nH_{2n}O_2$	

Esters

○ When a carboxylic acid reacts with an alcohol a new type of carbon compound, called an **ester**, is formed.

A convenient method of preparing an ester is described below.

Prescribed Practical Activity

About 2 cm^3 of an alcohol and an equal volume of a carboxylic acid are mixed together and a few drops of concentrated sulphuric acid are added. This mixture is heated as shown in Figure 1 for several minutes.

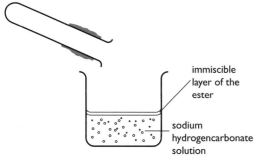

loose plug of ceramic wool

paper towel soaked in cold water and attached by an elastic band

hot water

alcohol + carboxylic acid + concentrated H$_2$SO$_4$

Figure 1

The test tube is removed from the water bath and its contents added to about 20 cm^3 of sodium hydrogencarbonate solution as shown in Figure 2. This solution neutralises the sulphuric acid as well as any unreacted carboxylic acid releasing carbon dioxide in the process. The ester appears as an immiscible layer on the surface of the solution. The ester can also be detected by its characteristic smell.

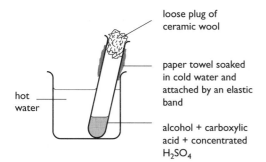

immiscible layer of the ester

sodium hydrogencarbonate solution

Figure 2

○ The functional groups present in the reactants interact to form an ester link and, at the same time, produce a water molecule, i.e. the process of making an ester is an example of a **condensation** reaction (Figure 3).

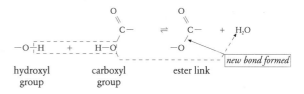

hydroxyl group

carboxyl group

ester link

new bond formed

Figure 3

e.g.

| H   H |
| H—C—C—O—H + |

ethanol

ethanoic acid

ethyl ethanoate

This equation can be rewritten using shortened structural formulae:

$$CH_3CH_2OH + HOOCCH_3 \rightleftharpoons$$
$$CH_3CH_2OOCCH_3 + H_2O$$

To show the reaction between the functional groups, in the example above the formula of the carboxylic acid has been reversed. The equation can, of course, be written with the formula of the carboxylic acid shown first and the formula of the alcohol written in reverse.

i.e.

$$CH_3COOH + HOCH_2CH_3 \rightleftharpoons$$
ethanoic acid   ethanol

$$CH_3COOCH_2CH_3 + H_2O$$
ethyl ethanoate

○ Concentrated sulphuric acid provides hydrogen ions which catalyse the reaction. It also helps to increase the yield of ester by absorbing water, the other product. (See Chapter 15.)

Naming esters

○ The name of an ester depends on which alcohol and which carboxylic acid have been used in preparing it. The first part of the name, which ends in '-yl', comes from the alcohol and the second part,which ends in '-oate', comes from the acid.

An example is illustrated in Figure 4. The formula of the ester is shown twice since there are two ways of drawing it as explained above.

○ Esters prepared from alkanols and alkanoic acids which have the same total number of carbon atoms will have the same molecular formula.

For example, ethyl ethanoate and methyl propanoate are isomers with molecular formula $C_4H_8O_2$. Butanoic acid, C_3H_7COOH, is also an isomer but it belongs to a different homologous series.

Uses of esters

○ Different esters differ widely in smell. They are used in perfumes and as artificial flavourings in food, e.g. pentyl ethanoate has a pear-like flavour. Artificial perfumes or flavourings have several natural and synthetic materials blended together.

○ The principal use of esters is as solvents, e.g. in car body paints, radiator enamels, adhesives and cosmetic preparations. Rapid evaporation of the solvent requires esters with few carbon atoms, e.g. ethyl ethanoate, as they tend to be more volatile.

○ Esters also have medicinal uses, e.g. methyl salicylate or 'oil of wintergreen' is used as a liniment.

Hydrolysis of Esters

○ The formation of an ester, **esterification**, is a reversible reaction. The reverse process in which the ester is split by reaction with water to form an alcohol and a carboxylic acid is an example of **hydrolysis**. Hydrolysis is the opposite of condensation. The C–O bond formed when an ester is made is the bond which is broken when the ester is hydrolysed.

○ Hydrolysis of an ester can be carried out by heating in the presence of a dilute acid, e.g. HCl(aq) or H_2SO_4(aq), to provide hydrogen ions to catalyse the reaction.

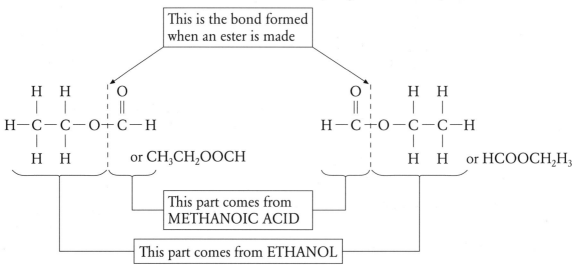

Hence, this ester is called ETHYL METHANOATE

The equation for the acid-catalysed hydrolysis of ethyl ethanoate is as follows:

$$CH_3CH_2OOCCH_3 + H_2O \rightleftharpoons$$
ethyl ethanoate

$$CH_3CH_2OH + HOOCCH_3$$
ethanol   **ethanoic acid**

◯ Acid-catalysed hydrolysis is reversible and is incomplete.

◯ Complete hydrolysis can be achieved by adding the ester to a strong alkali, e.g. NaOH(aq) or KOH(aq), and heating under reflux for about 30 minutes as shown in Figure 5.

◯ The products are the alcohol and the salt of the carboxylic acid and these can be separated by distillation. The alcohol is distilled off and the salt of the carboxylic acid is left behind in the aqueous solution. When this solution is acidified with hydrochloric acid the salt is converted to the carboxylic acid.

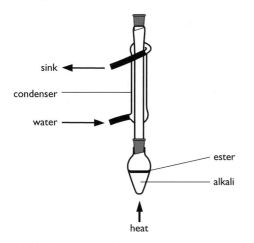

Figure 5 Heating under reflux

The equations for **a)** the hydrolysis of ethyl ethanoate by sodium hydroxide solution and **b)** subsequent acidification of the salt solution (after removal of ethanol by distillation) are as follows:

a) $CH_3COOCH_2CH_3 + Na^+ + OH^- \rightarrow$
    ethyl ethanoate
           $CH_3COO^- + Na^+ + HOCH_2CH_3$
           sodium ethanoate   **ethanol**

b) $CH_3COO^- + Na^+ + H^+ + Cl^- \rightarrow$
    sodium ethanoate
           $CH_3COOH + Na^+ + Cl^-$
           ethanoic acid

◯ Ester hydrolysis, especially by alkali, is an important process in the manufacture of soap from fats and oils. (See Chapter 12.)

Percentage yield

◯ The expected quantity of product from a known mass of reactant can be calculated from the balanced equation. This is called the **theoretical yield**.

◯ The **actual yield** is usually less than the theoretical yield, particularly so when carrying out a reaction involving carbon compounds because:

– the reaction may not go to completion, e.g. preparation of an ester,

– other reactions may also occur which 'compete' with the main reaction,

– separation of the desired product may be difficult,

– the product may be impure and some of it lost during purification.

◯ In industrial processes a high percentage yield as well as high purity of product is desirable. Unconverted reactants are frequently recycled for further reaction, e.g. making ammonia by the Haber process and making ethanol by hydration of ethene.

◯ The **percentage yield** of product can calculated by using the following relationship:

$$\text{Percentage yield} = \frac{\text{Actual yield}}{\text{Theoretical yield}} \times 100\%$$

Also: Actual yield = Percentage yield × Theoretical yield

Worked Example 10.1

A sample of methyl ethanoate weighing 6.9 g was obtained from a reaction mixture containing 9.0 g of ethanoic acid, excess methanol and a small volume of concentrated sulphuric acid. Calculate the percentage yield of ester using the following equation.

$$CH_3OH + HOOCCH_3 \rightleftharpoons CH_3OOCCH_3 + H_2O$$

$$\underset{= 60\ g}{\underset{1\ mol}{}} \qquad \underset{= 74\ g}{\underset{1\ mol}{}}$$

In theory, 60 g of ethanoic acid should yield 74 g of methyl ethanoate. Hence, 9.0 g of ethanoic acid should yield $9.0 \times \dfrac{74}{60}\ g = 11.1\ g$ of methyl methanoate.

Thus, the theoretical yield is 11.1 g, while the actual yield is 6.9 g.

Percentage yield $= \dfrac{6.9}{11.1} \times 100\ \% = 62.2\ \%$

Questions

1* Propanoic acid is reacted with ethanol. The formula for one of the products is

A $CH_3CH_2C\overset{\displaystyle O}{\underset{\displaystyle OCH_2CH_2CH_3}{}}$

B $CH_3C\overset{\displaystyle O}{\underset{\displaystyle OCH_2CH_2CH_3}{}}$

C $CH_3CH_2CH_2C\overset{\displaystyle O}{\underset{\displaystyle OCH_2CH_3}{}}$

D $CH_3CH_2C\overset{\displaystyle O}{\underset{\displaystyle OCH_2CH_3}{}}$

2 The compound with formula CH_3OOCCH_3 can be hydrolysed to give

A ethanol and methanoic acid
B methanol and ethanoic acid
C ethanol and ethanoic acid
D methanol and methanoic acid.

3* Aspirin is one of the most widely used pain relievers in the world. It has the structure:

Which two functional groups are present in an aspirin molecule?

A Hydroxyl and carboxyl
B Aldehyde and ketone
C Carboxyl and ester
D Ester and aldehyde

4* Ethyl butanoate is used in pineapple flavouring. The formulae for the molecules from which it is made are

A C_3H_7OH and CH_3COOH

B C_2H_5OH and C_2H_5COOH

C C_3H_7COOH and C_2H_5OH

D C_2H_5COOH and C_3H_7OH

5 The compound with the formula $CH_3CH_2CH_2CH_2COOH$ can be obtained when

A pentan-1-ol is oxidised
B methyl butanoate is hydrolysed
C 3-methylbutan-1-ol is oxidised
D pentanal is reduced.

6 Draw a structural formula for each of the following compounds.

a) Hexanoic acid
b) 2,3-dimethylbutanoic acid
c) 3-ethyl-4-methylpentanoic acid
d) Butyl methanoate
e) Propyl propanoate

7 Name the following compounds.

a)
$$C_2H_5$$
$$CH_3CH_2CHCH_2CH_2COOH$$

b) CH_3OOCCH_3

c)
$$CH_3$$
$$CH_3CCH_2COOH$$
$$CH_3$$

d) $HCOOCH_2CH_2CH_3$

8
$$CH_3$$
$$CH_3-C-OH \quad \text{Compound } \mathbf{Y}$$
$$CH_3$$

5.0 g of compound **Y** was mixed with a slight excess of propanoic acid and heated for several minutes.

a) What other chemical should be added to the mixture before heating?

b) Describe briefly the method of heating that should be used.

c) What type of reaction occurs between compound **Y** and propanoic acid?

d) Draw a structural formula for the carbon compound produced in this reaction.

e) How could you show that a new substance had been produced?

f) Calculate the percentage yield if the actual yield of ester (molecular formula, $C_7H_{14}O_2$) was 6.2 g.

9
$$CH_3 \qquad CH_3$$
$$CH_3CHCOOCHCHCH_3$$
$$CH_3$$

10.0 g of the compound shown above were added to 50 cm³ of dilute hydrochloric acid and heated under reflux for about 30 minutes.

a) What type of reaction occurred?

b) Draw a labelled diagram of an apparatus which could be used in this experiment showing clearly what is meant by the phrase 'heated under reflux'.

c) Draw the structural formulae and give the names of the two carbon compounds produced in this reaction.

d) Calculate the mass of alcohol obtained if the percentage yield is 65%.

10* Esters are important and useful compounds. They occur in nature and can also be made in the laboratory.

a) An ester can be made from ethanol and methanoic acid. Draw the full structural formula for this ester.

b) Name the catalyst used in the laboratory preparation of an ester.

c) How can this ester be separated from unreacted ethanol and methanoic acid?

11* Esters are a widely used class of organic compounds.

a) Draw a labelled diagram to show how to prepare an ester from an alkanol and an alkanoic acid.

b) State any safety precaution that would be taken (apart from wearing eye protection) and give a reason for it.

c) Give a use for an ester.

d) Draw a structural formula for the ester produced in the reaction between methanol and ethanoic acid.

Questions 12 to 20 relate to work covered in Chapters 8, 9 and 10.

12 Partial dehydration of ethanol produces a compound called ethoxyethane, which is commonly called ether. The equation for this reaction is shown below.

$$2C_2H_5OH \rightarrow C_2H_5OC_2H_5 + H_2O$$

High yields of ether are difficult to achieve for various reasons, such as

i) complete dehydration of some of the ethanol

ii) the high volatility of ether.

a) What is the product of complete dehydration of ethanol?

b) Draw the full structural formula of ethoxyethane and suggest why it is so volatile when compared with ethanol.

c) In an experiment, 4.5 g of ethoxyethane were obtained from 20.0 g of ethanol. Calculate the percentage yield of ether.

13 Phenol reacts with chlorine to produce the important antiseptic, trichlorophenol [TCP] according to the following equation.

$$C_6H_5OH + 3Cl_2 \longrightarrow \text{(TCP)} + 3HCl$$

a) Give the molecular formula of TCP.
b) In an experiment to make some TCP in the lab, 28 g of phenol was used. Calculate
   i)   the number of moles of phenol used
   ii) the volume of chlorine required at room temperature and pressure ($V_{mol} = 24$ litres)
   iii) the mass of TCP (1 mol = 197.5 g) obtained if the percentage yield is 83%.

14 Oil of wintergreen   Aspirin

a) What is the molecular formula of aspirin?
b) Which of the following functional groups is/are present in oil of wintergreen?

   Carbonyl   Carboxyl   Ester   Hydroxyl
c) When hydrolysed both compounds yield a compound called salicylic acid.
   i)   Suggest an alternative name for oil of wintergreen.
   ii) Work out the structural formula of salicylic acid.
d) Theoretically one mole of salicylic acid (138 g) produces one mole of aspirin (180 g). In an experiment 9.2 g of aspirin was obtained from 9.6 g of salicylic acid. Calculate the percentage yield of aspirin.

15

$$\text{ETHENE} \xrightarrow{\text{I}} C_2H_5OH$$

a) In reaction **II**, ethene undergoes addition with hydrogen cyanide (structural formula: $H-C\equiv N$). Draw the full structural formula of ethyl cyanide, the product of reaction **II**.
b) Reaction **I** is also an addition reaction. What other name can be used to describe this reaction?
c) In reaction **III**, ethyl cyanide reacts with water and HCl(aq). Ammonium chloride is also produced in this reaction. Write a balanced equation for reaction **III**.
d) In reaction **IV**, the products of reactions **I** and **III** react to form another carbon compound, **Q**.
   i)   Name compound **Q** and draw its full structural formula.
   ii) Describe how reaction **IV** can be carried out in the laboratory.

16* Many organic functional groups contain oxygen.

A 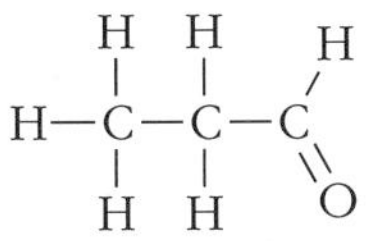	B 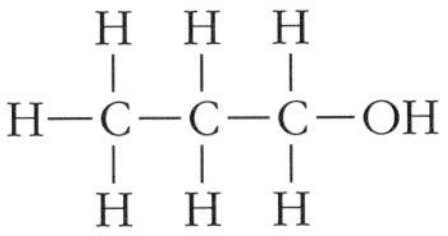	C 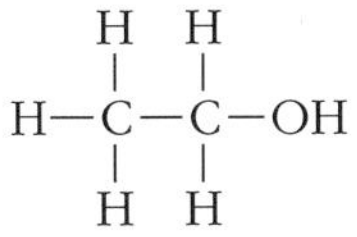

H H H
  | | |
H—C—C—C≡O
  | |
H H
	H H H
	  | | |
	H—C—C—C—OH
	  | | |
	H H H
		H H
		  | |
		H—C—C—OH
		  | |
		H H

D 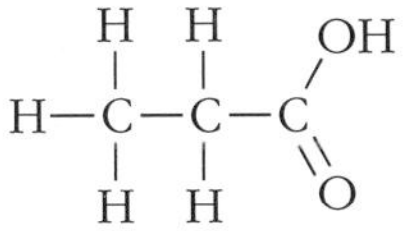	E 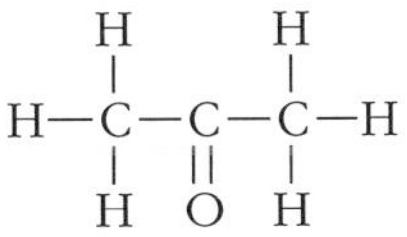	F 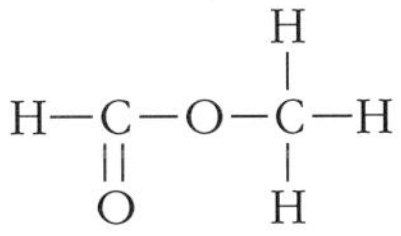

H H OH
  | |
H—C—C—C≡O
  | |
H H
	H H
	  | |
	H—C—C—C—H
	  | | |
	H O H
		H
		  |
		H—C—O—C—H
		  | |
		O H H

a) Identify the aldehyde.
b) Identify the compound which could be hydrolysed when warmed with sodium hydroxide solution.
c) Identify the **two** compounds which could be oxidised to produce the compound shown in box **D**.
d) Identify the **two** isomers.

17

A	B	C
Butan-2-ol	Ethyl butanoate	Butanone

D	E	F
Butanal	Butanoic acid	Butyl methanoate

a) Identify the compound which can be hydrolysed to give butanol .
b) Identify the compound which could be formed when the compound shown in box **E** is reduced.
c) Identify the compound which could be formed by the hydration of but-1-ene.
d) Identify the **two** isomers.

18*

A 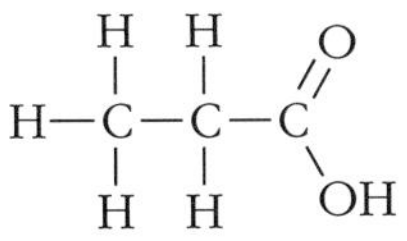	B 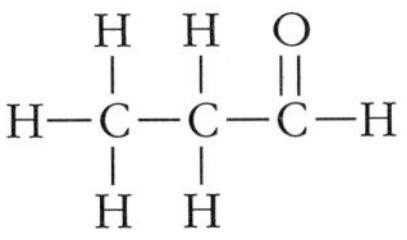	C 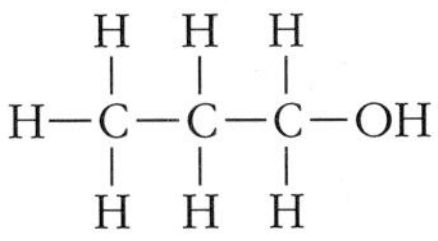

H H O
  | | //
H—C—C—C
  | | \
H H OH
	H H O
	  | | ||
	H—C—C—C—H
	  | |
	H H
		H H H
		  | | |
		H—C—C—C—OH
		  | | |
		H H H

D 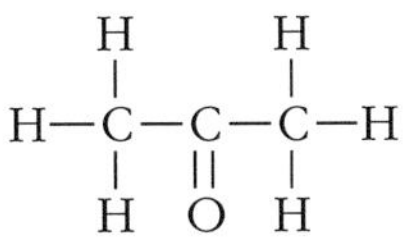	E 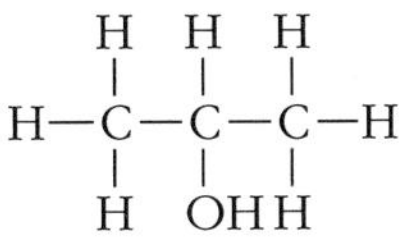	F 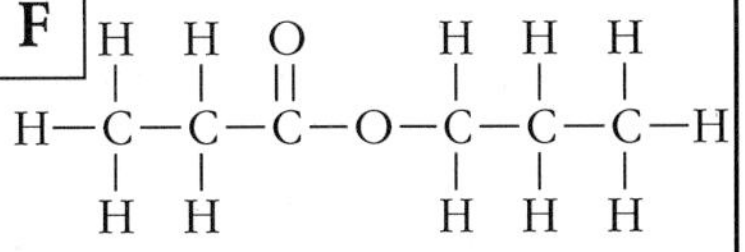

H H
  | |
H—C—C—C—H
  | | |
H O H
	H H H
	  | | |
	H—C—C—C—H
	  | | |
	H OH H
		H H O H H H
		  | | || | | |
		H—C—C—C—O—C—C—C—H
		  | | | | |
		H H H H H

a) Identify the two compounds which would react to produce the compound shown in box **F**.
b) Identify the alkanone.

19 The structural formulae of six aromatic compounds are shown below.

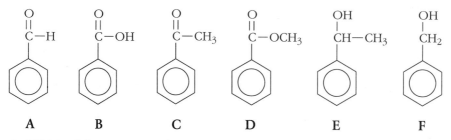

    A   **B**   **C**   **D**   **E**   **F**

a) Which of these compounds is **i)** a carboxylic acid **ii)** a secondary alcohol?
b) Classify each of the four remaining compounds.
c) Which of these compounds is formed when
    i)   A is oxidised
    ii)   A is reduced
    iii) E is oxidised
    iv) B reacts with methanol.
d) What is the molecular formula of **D**?
e) Which two compounds react with NaOH(aq)? In each case name the type of reaction occurring.
f) Describe a chemical test, with result, which would distinguish **A** and **C**.

20 In the following flow diagram, compound **X** is converted into two other compounds, one of which is then converted into various products as shown.

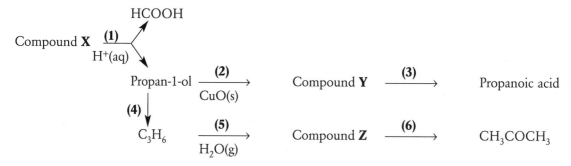

a) Draw the full structural formula of
    i)   compound **X**
    ii)   compound **Z**.
b) Name compound **Y**.
c) Which reaction in the sequence shown above is an example of
    i)   dehydration
    ii) hydrolysis?
d) Which pair of compounds shown above
    i)   are isomers belonging to the same homologous series
    ii) are isomers but belong to different homologous series?
e) Describe briefly how reaction **(4)** can be carried out in the laboratory.
f) **i)**   What happens to the copper oxide during reaction **(2)**?
    ii) Name another reagent suitable for use in carrying out reactions **(3)** and **(6)**.

Polymers

Polymers are very large molecules, macromolecules, made by joining small molecules, monomers, in long chains or networks.

Addition polymers

○ Addition polymers are made from **unsaturated monomers**. The polymers are saturated.

○ Ethene is the starting material for many products of the chemical industry, especially for addition polymers. Ethene can be made by cracking ethane from natural gas or the gas fraction of crude oil or by cracking the naphtha fraction of crude oil. It can then be polymerised:

$$n\ CH_2{=}CH_2 \rightarrow \text{+}CH_2{-}CH_2\text{+}_n$$
ethene   **poly(ethene)**

○ Propene is made by cracking propane from the gas fraction of crude oil or by cracking naphtha. It can be polymerised into poly(propene) as shown in Figure 1.

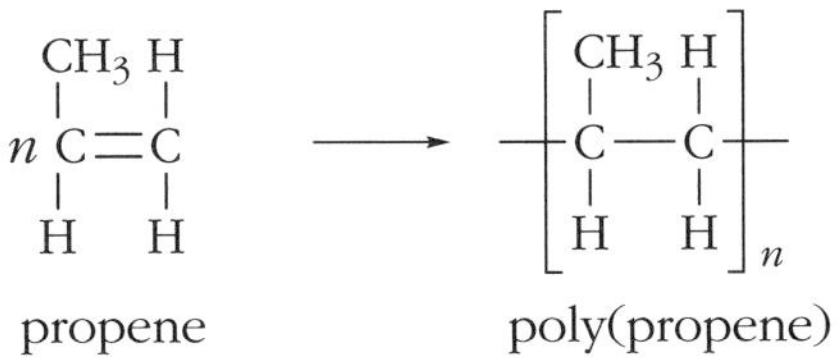

CH₃ H   ⎡ CH₃ H ⎤
 | | ⎢ | | ⎥
n C═C   ───→   ⎢─C─C─⎥
 | | ⎢ | | ⎥
 H H   ⎣ H H ⎦ₙ
propene   poly(propene)

Figure 1

Condensation polymers

○ Condensation polymers are made from monomers with two functional groups per molecule. The monomers and repeating units or structure of some condensation polymers are shown below. In each case, water is formed as a by-product.

Polyester

○ Polyesters are synthesised by condensation of two monomers. One having two hydroxyl groups is called a **diol** and the other, with two carboxyl groups, is a **diacid**. Their structures are shown in Figure 2, and the structure of polyester, obtained by condensing two diol molecules and two diacid molecules, is shown in Figure 3.

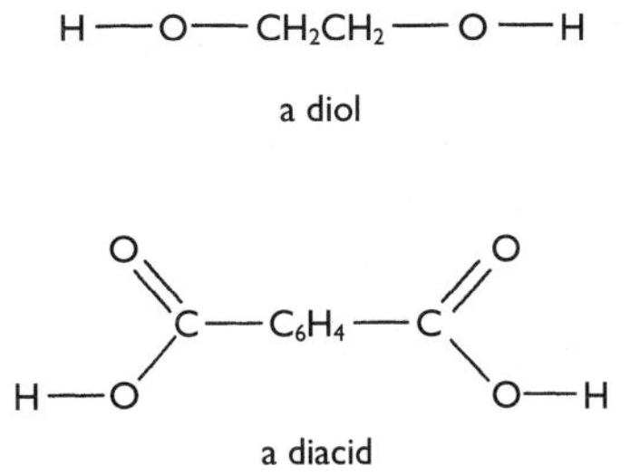

H —O— CH₂CH₂ — O —H

a diol

a diacid

Figure 2

Repeating unit

—O—CH₂CH₂—O+C—C₆H₄—C—O—CH₂CH₂—O+C—C₆H₄—C—

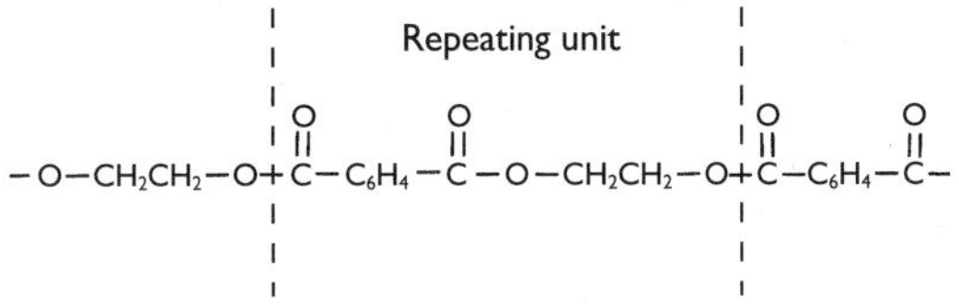

Figure 3

The dotted lines indicate the **repeating unit**.

○ Polyesters with a linear structure are used for fibres.

○ Polyesters which are cross-linked to produce a network, 3-dimensional structure are used for moulding resins.

Polyamide

○ An amide link is formed by the reaction of an amine functional group with a carboxyl group.

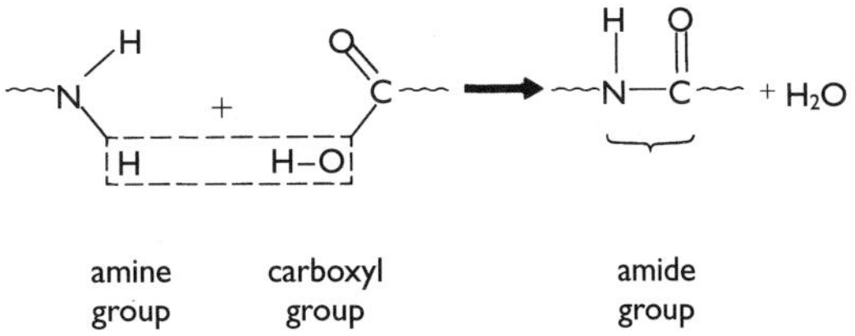

amine   carboxyl   amide
group   group   group

Figure 4

73

○ Nylon is an example of a polyamide. It is used as a fibre and as an engineering plastic.

○ The strength of nylon is related to hydrogen bonding between its chains.

Figure 5 shows the structures of typical monomers for making a polyamide, and Figure 6 shows the resulting polyamide made from two molecules of each monomer. Once again the dotted lines show the repeating unit, starting from the middle of the -NH-CO- amide linkage.

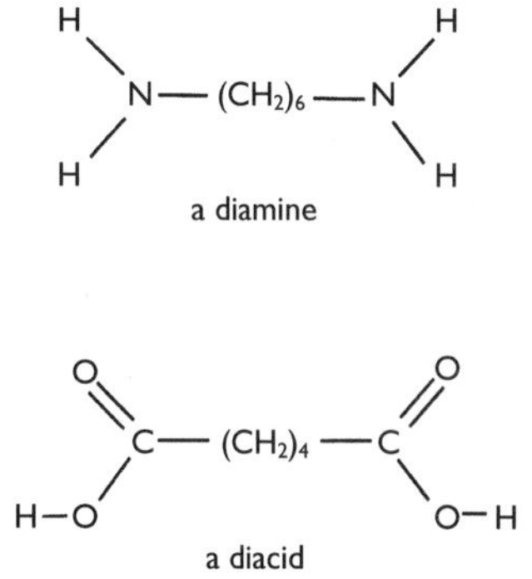

a diamine

a diacid

Figure 5

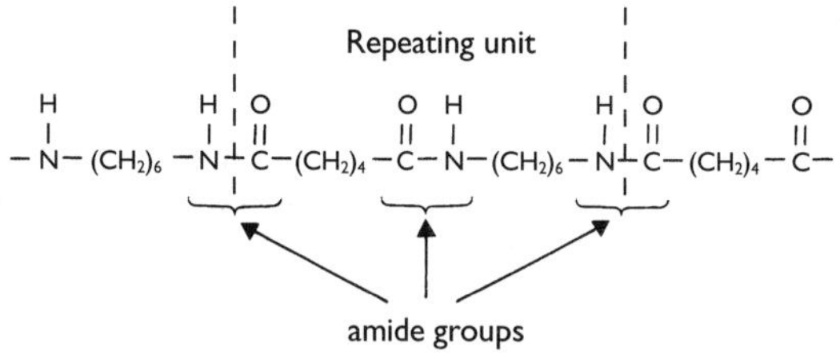

Repeating unit

amide groups

Figure 6

Methanal-based thermosetting polymers
○ Thermosetting polymers harden on heating. They cannot be softened by warming or be remoulded. (Polymers which can be remoulded after warming are thermoplastic.)

○ Examples of methanal-based polymers are urea-methanal and bakelite (Figure 7).

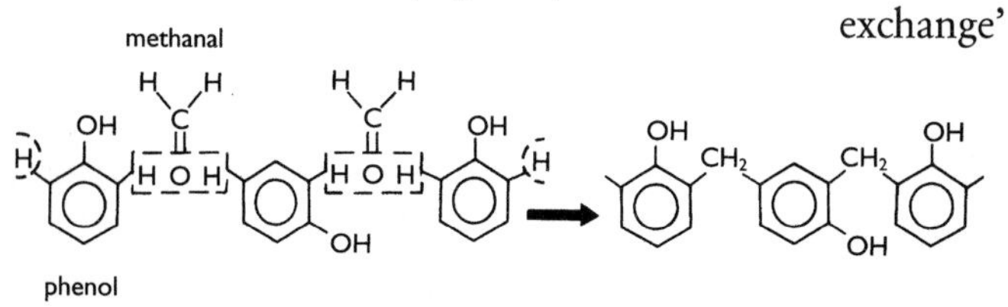

methanal

phenol

Figure 7 Bakelite

○ A major use of both polymers is for electrical fittings because of their good insulating properties.

○ Methane or coal is steam reformed to give synthesis gas, a mixture of carbon monoxide and hydrogen.

$$CH_4(g) + H_2O(g) \rightarrow CO(g) + 3H_2(g)$$
$$\text{(synthesis gas)}$$

○ The synthesis gas is the feedstock for the production of methanol, which, in turn, is the feedstock for producing methanal.

$$CO(g) + 2H_2(g) \rightarrow CH_3OH(g)$$
$$\text{(methanol)}$$

$$CH_3OH(g) + \tfrac{1}{2}O_2(g) \rightarrow HCHO(g) + H_2O(g)$$
$$\text{(methanal)}$$

Recent developments

Kevlar
○ Kevlar is an aromatic polyamide.

○ It is very strong because of the way the rigid linear molecules are packed together.

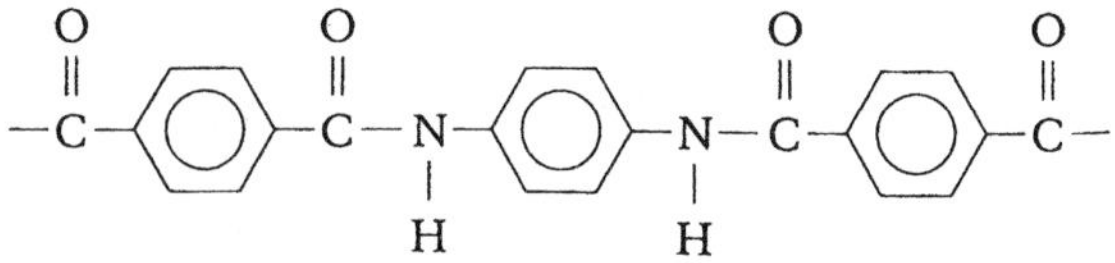

Figure 8 Kevlar

○ Kevlar is used in sail fabric, crash helmets and in body armour.

Poly(ethenol)
○ Poly(ethenol) is a water-soluble plastic.

○ It is made from another polymer by 'ester exchange'

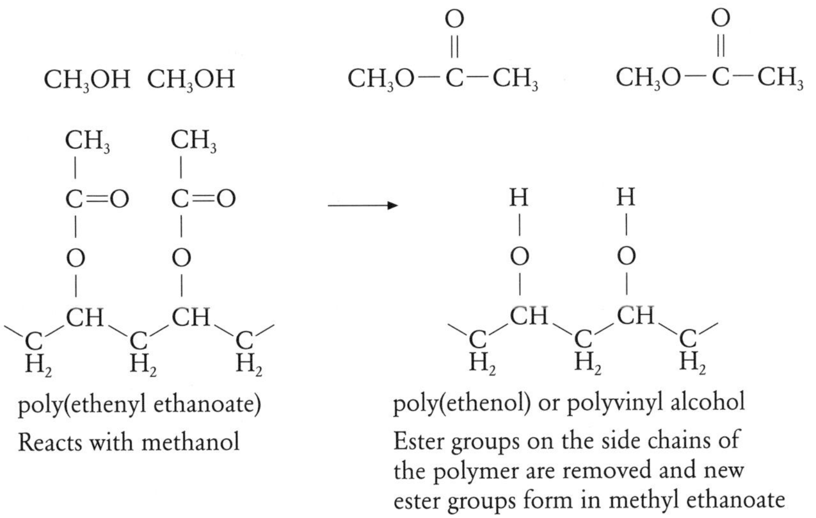

$$CH_3OH \quad CH_3OH \qquad\qquad \underset{\displaystyle CH_3O-\overset{\textstyle O}{\overset{\|}{C}}-CH_3}{} \qquad\qquad \underset{\displaystyle CH_3O-\overset{\textstyle O}{\overset{\|}{C}}-CH_3}{}$$

poly(ethenyl ethanoate)

Reacts with methanol

poly(ethenol) or polyvinyl alcohol

Ester groups on the side chains of the polymer are removed and new ester groups form in methyl ethanoate

Figure 9 Formation of poly(ethenol)

○ The proportion of acid groups removed in the production process determines the strength of the intermolecular forces upon which the solubility depends.

○ Poly(ethenol) is used to make adhesives, water-soluble protective coatings for cars in storage and soluble hospital laundry bags.

Poly(ethyne)

○ Poly(ethyne) is a polymer which can be made to conduct electricity.

$$HC\equiv CH + HC\equiv CH + HC\equiv CH$$

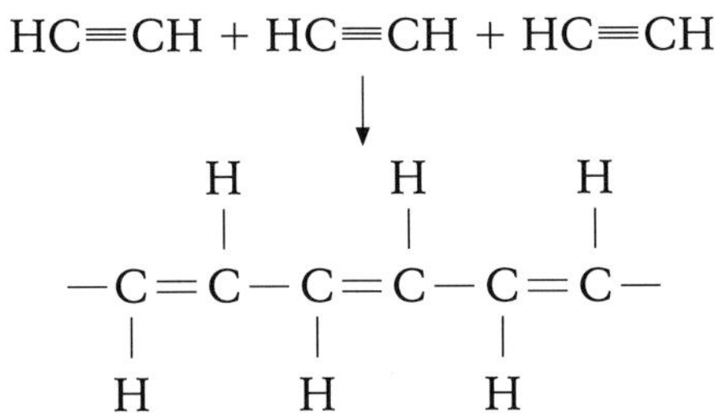

Figure 10

○ Poly(ethyne)'s conductivity depends on delocalised electrons. It is used to make loud speaker membranes.

Poly(vinylcarbazole)

○ Poly(vinylcarbazole) is able to conduct electricity when exposed to light. It is used in photocopiers.

Biopol

○ Biopol is a biodegradable polymer. It is not proving to be popular because it is not in keeping with the present move to encourage recycling.

○ Biopol included with other polymers can make the mixture unsuitable for recycling.

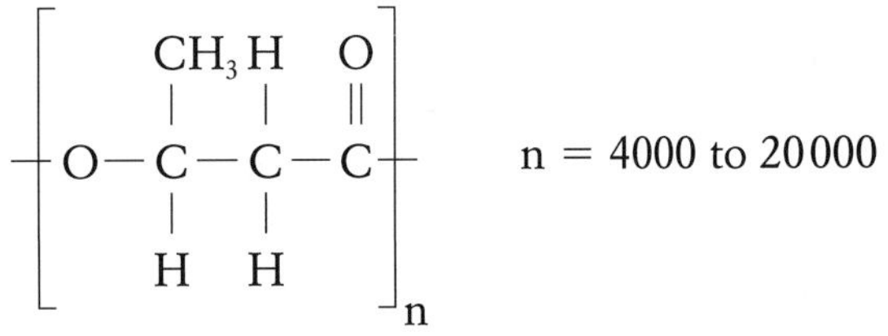

$$\left[\begin{array}{c} CH_3\ H\ \ O \\ |\ \ \ |\ \ \ \| \\ -O-C-C-C- \\ |\ \ \ | \\ H\ \ H \end{array} \right]_n \qquad n = 4000\ \text{to}\ 20\,000$$

Figure 11 The structure of Biopol

Photodegradable LDPE

○ Low density poly(ethene) can be made photodegradable i.e. to break up under the action of light.

Questions

1* Part of a polymer is shown.

Which pair of alkenes was used as monomers?

  A Ethene and propene   **B** Ethene and but-1-ene
  C Propene and but-1-ene   **D** Ethene and but-2-ene

$$-\overset{\displaystyle H}{\underset{\displaystyle H}{C}}-\overset{\displaystyle C_2H_5}{\underset{\displaystyle H}{C}}-\overset{\displaystyle H}{\underset{\displaystyle H}{C}}-\overset{\displaystyle H}{\underset{\displaystyle H}{C}}-\overset{\displaystyle H}{\underset{\displaystyle H}{C}}-\overset{\displaystyle C_2H_5}{\underset{\displaystyle H}{C}}-\overset{\displaystyle H}{\underset{\displaystyle H}{C}}-\overset{\displaystyle H}{\underset{\displaystyle H}{C}}-$$

2* Part of a polyester chain is shown below.

$$-O-\overset{O}{\overset{\|}{C}}-(CH_2)_4-\overset{O}{\overset{\|}{C}}-O-(CH_2)_6-O-\overset{O}{\overset{\|}{C}}-(CH_2)_4-\overset{O}{\overset{\|}{C}}-O-(CH_2)_6-O-$$

Which compound, when added to the reactants during polymerisation, would stop the polyester chain from getting too long?

A $HO-\overset{O}{\overset{\|}{C}}-(CH_2)_4-\overset{O}{\overset{\|}{C}}-OH$ **B** $HO-(CH_2)_6-OH$

C $HO-(CH_2)_5-\overset{O}{\overset{\|}{C}}-OH$ **D** CH_3-OH

3* Polyester fibres and cured polyester are both very strong.
What kinds of structure do their molecules have?

	Fibre	Cured resin
A	cross-linked	cross-linked
B	linear	linear
C	cross-linked	linear
D	linear	cross-linked

4* There are many different types of reactions.

A addition	**B** condensation	**C** dehydration
D hydrogenation	**E** hydrolysis	**F** polymerisation

Poly(ethenol) is a recently developed plastic which is soluble in water.
It is made by the reactions shown.

$$n\ \overset{\displaystyle H}{\underset{\displaystyle H}{C}}=\overset{\displaystyle O-\overset{O}{\overset{\|}{C}}-CH_3}{\underset{\displaystyle H}{C}} \xrightarrow{\textit{Step 1}} \left(-\overset{\displaystyle H}{\underset{\displaystyle H}{C}}-\overset{\displaystyle O-\overset{O}{\overset{\|}{C}}-CH_3}{\underset{\displaystyle H}{C}}-\right)_n \xrightarrow{\textit{Step 2}} \left(-\overset{\displaystyle H}{\underset{\displaystyle H}{C}}-\overset{\displaystyle OH}{\underset{\displaystyle H}{C}}-\right)_n$$

poly(ethenol)

a) Identify the type of reaction takaing place at *Step 2*.
b) Identify the term(s) which can be applied to the reaction taking place at *Step 1*.

5 Compounds **A** to **F** are important monomers in manufacturing plastics.

A

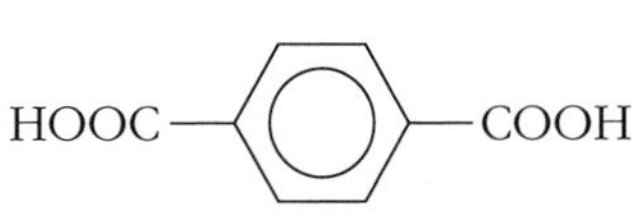

HOOC—⟨benzene ring⟩—COOH

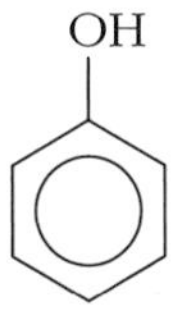

B OH
⟨phenol⟩

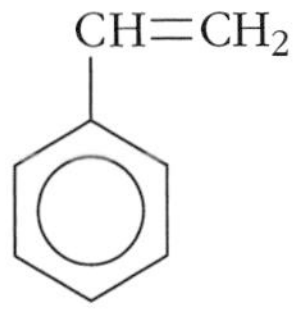

C H$_2$N—⟨benzene ring⟩—NH$_2$

D HOCH$_2$CH$_2$OH

E CH=CH$_2$
⟨phenyl⟩

F CN
CH=CH$_2$

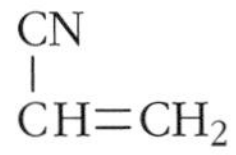

a) Kevlar is a polyamide made from two of the monomers shown above.
   i)   Which **two** monomers are used to make kevlar?
   ii) Draw a structural formula to show the repeating unit of kevlar.
   iii) Describe one use of kevlar.
b) Terylene is a polyester made from two of the monomers shown above.
   i)   Which **two** monomers can be used to make terylene?
   ii) Draw a structural formula to show the repeating unit of terylene.
c) SAN is a plastic made by co-polymerising compounds **E** and **F**. Draw a section of this polymer's structure in which two molecules of compound **E** have joined one on each side of a molecule of compound **F**.
d) Bakelite is a condensation thermosetting polymer made from compound **B** and methanal. Explain the meaning of the terms '*condensation*' and '*thermosetting*'.

6

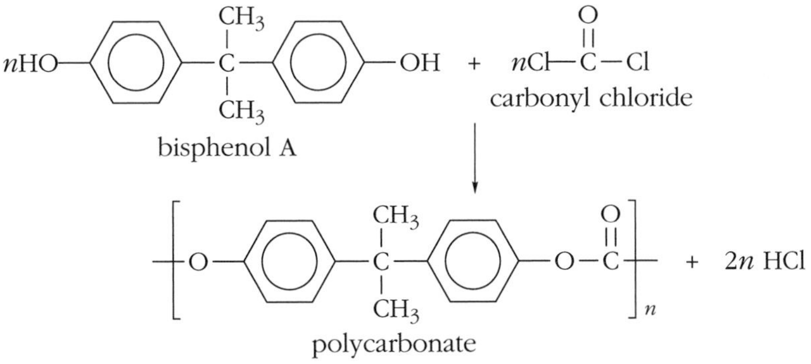

nHO—⟨benzene ring⟩—C(CH$_3$)(CH$_3$)—⟨benzene ring⟩—OH + nCl—C(=O)—Cl
bisphenol A   carbonyl chloride

↓

[—O—⟨benzene ring⟩—C(CH$_3$)(CH$_3$)—⟨benzene ring⟩—O—C(=O)—]$_n$ + $2n$ HCl
polycarbonate

The condensation reaction shown above is used to manufacture 'polycarbonates'. Polycarbonates are transparent, strong and have good resistance to heat and chemicals. They are thermoplastic and are used in making compact discs, safety glass and feeding bottles.

a) How does the above reaction differ from more familiar condensation reactions?
b) What part of the structure gives rise to the name 'polycarbonate'?
c) In the manufacturing process, bisphenol A is dissolved in NaOH(aq) and carbonyl chloride is bubbled through the solution. Sodium hydroxide solution is a better solvent for the monomer than water alone. Suggest another reason why the presence of NaOH is helpful.
d) The polymer is insoluble in NaOH(aq) and is removed by dissolving it in dichloromethane, CH$_2$Cl$_2$, which has to be stirred continuously and vigorously with the NaOH(aq).
   What property of CH$_2$Cl$_2$ and water makes this stirring necessary?
e) Suggest how the polymer is removed from the dichloromethane.
f) Explain what property of polycarbonates makes them potentially more environmentally friendly than, say, urea-methanal polymer.

7* The compound C_2H_2 can be used to make various plastics:

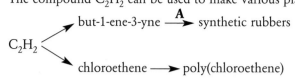

a) To which homologous series does C_2H_2 belong?
b) Draw the structure of but-1-ene-3-yne.
c) Which type of polymerisation occurs in reaction **A**?
d) Draw the structure of part of poly(chloroethene) showing at least three monomer units linked together.

8 The 'polyurethane' group of polymers are made by the following reaction.

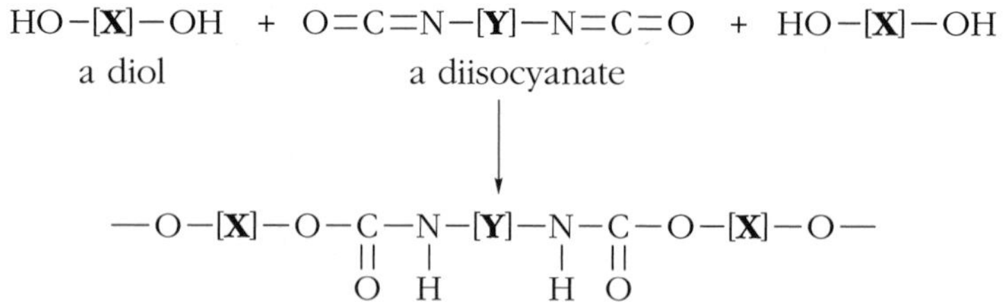

$$HO-[\mathbf{X}]-OH \quad + \quad O=C=N-[\mathbf{Y}]-N=C=O \quad + \quad HO-[\mathbf{X}]-OH$$

a diol a diisocyanate

$$-O-[\mathbf{X}]-O-\underset{\underset{O}{||}}{C}-\underset{\underset{H}{|}}{N}-[\mathbf{Y}]-\underset{\underset{H}{|}}{N}-\underset{\underset{O}{||}}{C}-O-[\mathbf{X}]-O-$$

This reaction is exothermic.

a) The 'urethane link' is similar to but not identical to the amide link.
   Copy the polymer structure and mark on it the urethane link.
b) Explain why the polymerisation shown above is neither
   i) a typical addition process, nor
   ii) a typical condensation process.
c) Name and give the structural formula of a diol containing three carbon atoms per molecule.
d) In what way would the presence of some monomer molecules with a third −OH group or a third −NCO group alter the structure of the polymer?
e) When polyurethane was made, an inert gas, CFC 11, was sometimes passed into the reaction mixture. What would the function of CFC 11 have been?
f) CFC 11 is now being replaced by HFAs similar to CH_2FCF_3. What environmental reason is there for this change?

12 Natural Products

Fats and oils

○ Natural fats and oils can be of animal, vegetable or marine origin.

○ Oils are liquid at room temperature because they contain more unsaturated molecules (i.e. carbon–carbon double bonds) than fats which are solid. The lower melting point of oils is caused by smaller van der Waals' forces of attraction between their molecules. This is in turn caused by the distorted structure of the unsaturated oils which prevent close packing.

Figure 1 Diagrammatic representation of the structure of fat molecules

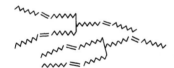

Figure 2 An exaggerated picture of oil molecules

○ Oils can be converted into solid fats by the addition of hydrogen which decreases the unsaturation.

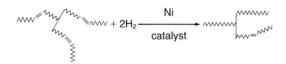

Figure 3 Partial hydrogenation of an oil molecule

○ Fats and oils in the diet are a source of energy. They supply more energy per gramme than carbohydrates, but the energy is released more slowly.

○ Fats and oils are esters. When hydrolysed, they produce three moles of 'fatty' acids to one mole of glycerol.

○ Glycerol is a trihydric alcohol i.e. it has three –OH groups per molecule. It is propan-1,2,3-triol.

Foodstuff	Energy yield kJ/100g
Sucrose ('sugar' – carbohydrate)	1672
Sunflower oil	3700
Cooking margarine	3006
'Low fat' spread	1569
Butter	3140
White bread (carbohydrate)	961

Table 1

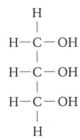

propane -1,2,3-triol or glycerol

Figure 4

○ Fatty acids are straight-chain carboxylic acids, either saturated or unsaturated, containing between 4 and 24 carbon atoms per molecule. The commonest are C_{16} and C_{18}.

e.g. Palmitic acid $CH_3(CH_2)_{14}COOH$
Stearic acid $CH_3(CH_2)_{16}COOH$
Oleic acid
$CH_3(CH_2)_7CH = CH(CH_2)_7COOH$
Linoleic acid
$CH_3(CH_2)_3(CH_2CH=CH)_2(CH_2)_7COOH$
Ricinoleic acid
$CH_3(CH_2)_5CH(OH) CH_2CH=CH(CH_2)_7COOH$

○ Fats and oils are largely mixtures of molecules in which three molecules of fatty acid are joined, with the loss of water, to one molecule of glycerol. This is called a triglyceride. The fatty acid molecules can be saturated or unsaturated and may or may not be identical.

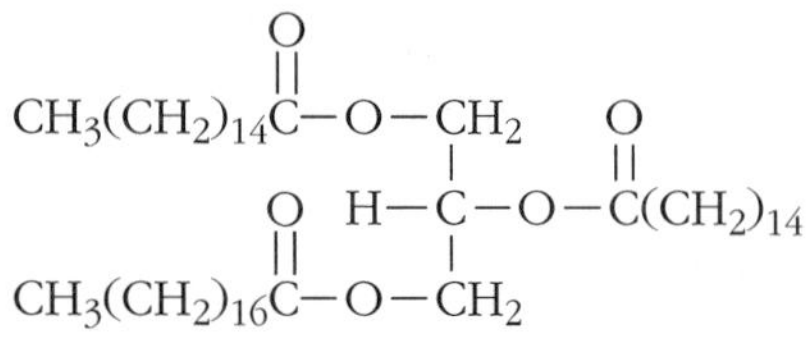

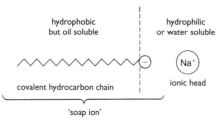

$$CH_3(CH_2)_{14}\overset{\overset{O}{\|}}{C}-O-CH_2$$

Figure 5 A triglyceride

○ Hydrolysis of fats and oils using sodium hydroxide produces soaps, the sodium salts of carboxylic acids.

| hydrophobic but oil soluble | | hydrophilic or water soluble |

covalent hydrocarbon chain   ionic head

'soap ion'

Figure 6 The structure of a 'soap ion'

Proteins

○ All proteins contain nitrogen. It is essential for their formation by plants and animals.

○ Proteins are condensation polymers made by many amino acid molecules linking together. An amine group of one molecule condenses with the carboxyl group of another molecule to form an amide or peptide link.

○ Proteins specific to the body's needs are built up within the body from the appropriate sequence of amino acids.

○ The body cannot make all the amino acids required to build proteins. It relies on dietary protein for the supply of some amino acids, these are known as essential amino acids.

○ Digestion of protein involves hydrolysis to amino acids.

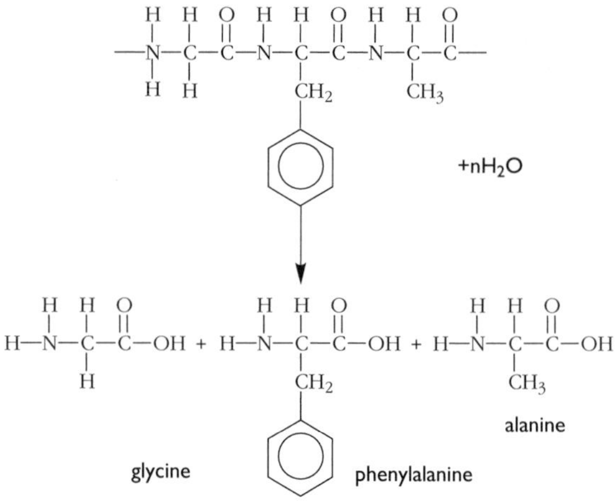

$+nH_2O$

glycine   phenylalanine   alanine

Figure 8 Hydrolysis of a protein to amino acids

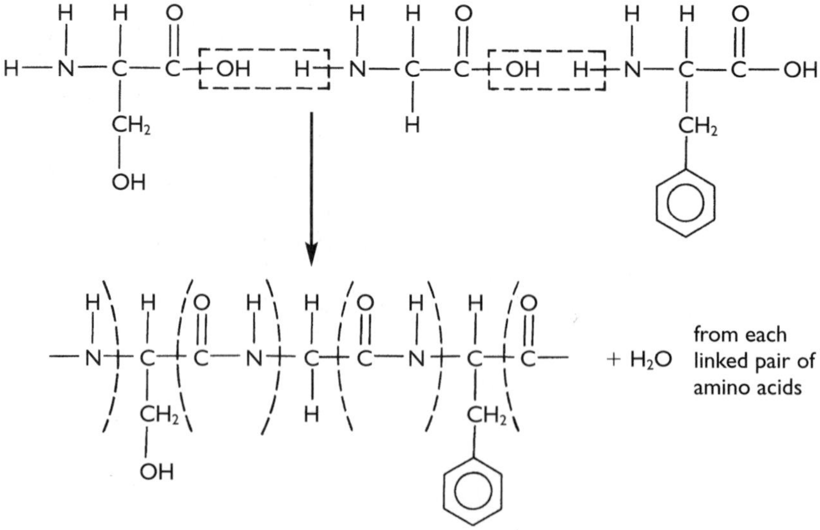

from each linked pair of amino acids

$+ H_2O$

Figure 7 Condensation of amino acids to form amide links in a protein. The amide links are shown in brackets.

Classification of proteins

○ Fibrous proteins, the major structural materials of animal tissue, are long and thin.

○ Globular proteins are the proteins involved in the regulation of life processes, e.g. haemoglobin, enzymes, hormones like insulin. Their amino acid chains form helices which are then folded into compact units.

Enzymes

○ Enzyme function is related to the molecular shapes of proteins. The enzyme and its substrate fit together on the 'lock and key' principle.

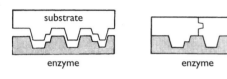

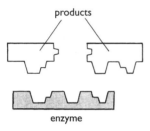

Figure 9 The 'lock and key' principle. A complex molecule being split by an enzyme

○ All proteins can be denatured by changes in temperature or pH which bring about physical changes in the molecules. Enzymes are therefore affected by changes in pH and temperature and operate best within a narrow range of each.

Prescribed Practical Activity

It is possible to investigate the factors affecting the activity of **catalase**, an enzyme which catalyses the breakdown of hydrogen peroxide into water and oxygen, with the apparatus shown.

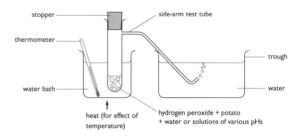

Figure 10

The basic procedure is to place three discs of potato (a source of catalase) in the side-arm tube with 5 cm³ of water. 1 cm³ of 30 volume hydrogen peroxide solution is added with a syringe and the tube is stoppered. The number of bubbles of oxygen emerging from the delivery tube in three minutes is counted.

To investigate the effect of temperature, the experiment is carried out at temperatures close to 20°C, 30°C, 40°C, 50°C and 60°C, by heating the water bath. Fresh potato, water and hydrogen peroxide are used each time. The potato and water are left for a few minutes to reach the chosen temperature before the peroxide is added.

To investigate the effect of pH, the water is replaced in turn by buffer solutions of pH 4, 7, and 10 and by 0.1 mol l⁻¹ hydrochloric acid (pH 1) and 0.1 mol l⁻¹ sodium hydroxide solution (pH 13). This time the water bath is kept at room temperature.

Questions

1* Which of the following decolourises bromine solution **least** rapidly?

    A Palm oil
    B Hex-1-ene
    C Cod liver oil
    D Mutton fat

2* When two amino acids condense together, water is eliminated and a peptide link is formed.
Which of the following represents this process?

    A

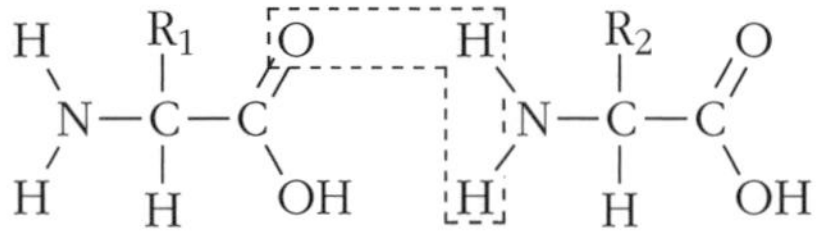

    B

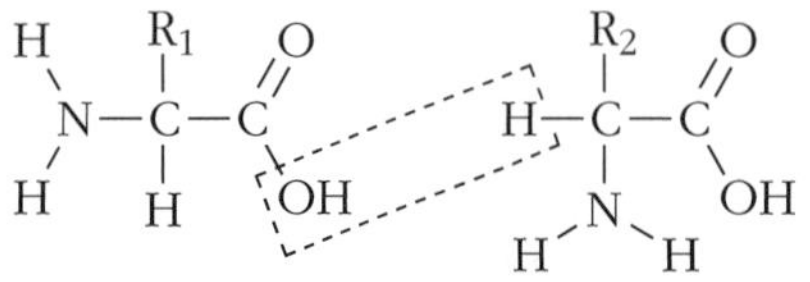

    C

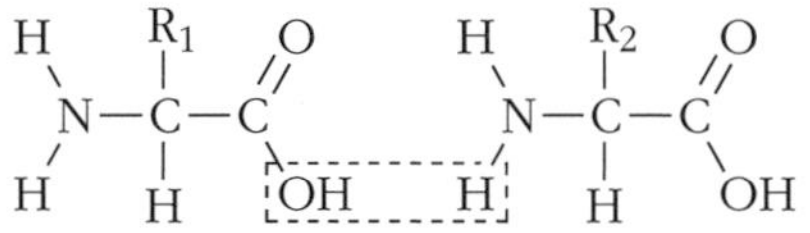

    D

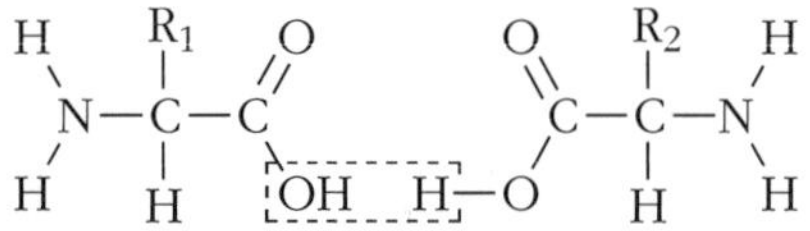

3* Proteins can be denatured under acid conditions. During this denaturing, the protein molecule

    A changes shape   **B** is dehydrated
    C is neutralised   **D** is polymerised.

4* The conversion of linoleic acid, $C_{18}H_{32}O_2$ into stearic acid, $C_{18}H_{36}O_2$, is likely to be achieved by

    A hydrogenation   **B** hydrolysis
    C hydration   **D** dehydrogenation.

5* The production of fatty acids and glycerol from fats in foods is an example of

    A hydrolysis   **B** hydrogenation
    C dehydration   **D** dehydrogenation.

6* The monomer units used to construct enzyme molecules are

    A esters   **B** amino acids
    C fatty acids   **D** monosaccharides.

7* In the formation of 'hardened' fats from vegetable oils, the hydrogen

    A causes cross-linking between chains
    B causes hydrolysis to occur
    C increases the carbon chain length
    D reduces the number of carbon–carbon double bonds.

8* Which type of reaction is involved in the conversion of vegetable oils into 'hardened' fats?

    A Condensation   **B** Hydration
    C Hydrogenation   **D** Polymerisation

9* Some amino acids are called α-amino acids because the amino group is on the carbon atom next to the acid group. Which of the following is an α-amino acid?

    A $CH_3-CH-COOH$
               $|$
              CH_2-NH_2

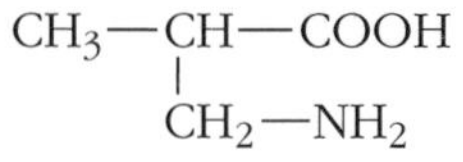

    B $CH_2-CH-COOH$
          $|$ $|$
        SH NH_2

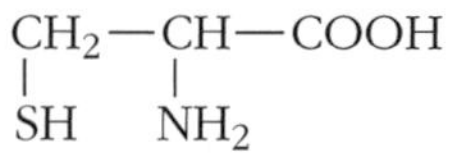

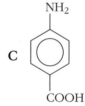

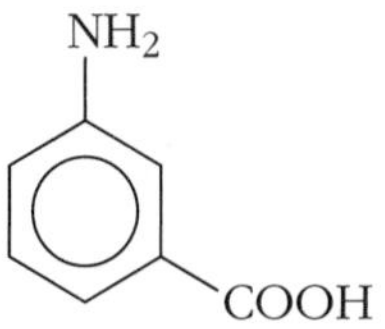

'0* The rate of hydrolysis of a protein, using an enzyme, was studied at different temperatures. Which graph could be obtained?

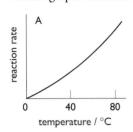
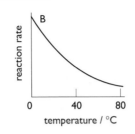
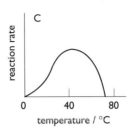
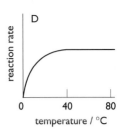

11*

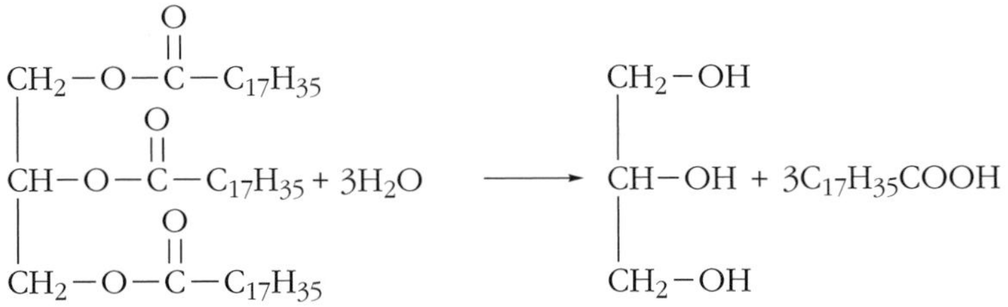

$$CH_2-O-\overset{\overset{\displaystyle O}{||}}{C}-C_{17}H_{35}$$
$$CH-O-\overset{\overset{\displaystyle O}{||}}{C}-C_{17}H_{35} + 3H_2O \longrightarrow$$
$$CH_2-O-\overset{\overset{\displaystyle O}{||}}{C}-C_{17}H_{35}$$

$$CH_2-OH$$
$$CH-OH + 3C_{17}H_{35}COOH$$
$$CH_2-OH$$

Which process is represented by the equation?

A   Condensation   B   Hydrolysis
C   Oxidation   D   Dehydration

12

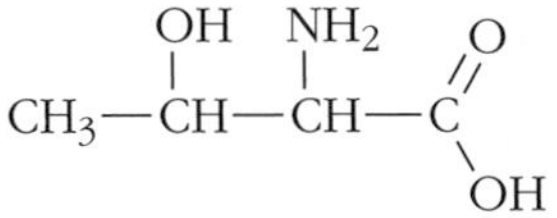

$$CH_3-\overset{\overset{\displaystyle OH}{|}}{CH}-\overset{\overset{\displaystyle NH_2}{|}}{CH}-\overset{\overset{\displaystyle O}{//}}{\underset{\underset{\displaystyle OH}{\backslash}}{C}}$$

The molecule show above can be classified as

A an enzyme   B an amino acid   C a peptide   D a protein.

13 What is the structural formula of glycerol?

A $CH_2-CH_2-CH_2$
        $|$ $|$
        OH   OH

B $CH_2-CH-CH$
        $|$ $|$ $||$
        OH   OH   O

C CH_2-C-CH_2
        $|$ $||$ $|$
        OH   O   OH

D $CH_2-CH-CH_2$
        $|$ $|$ $|$
        OH   OH   OH

14* Fats and oils are naturally occurring esters. Identify the **true** statement(s).

A	Fats and oils in the diet can supply the body with energy.
B	Fats and oils are a less concentrated source of energy than carbohydrates.
C	Fats are likely to have relatively low melting points compared to oils.
D	Fats are likely to have a higher degree of unsaturation than oils.
E	Molecules in fats are packed more closely together than molecules in oils.

15* Proteins and fats are hydrolysed during digestion.

A	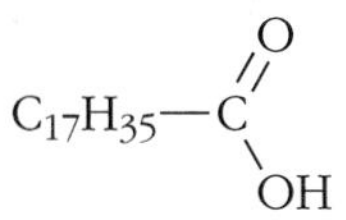 B	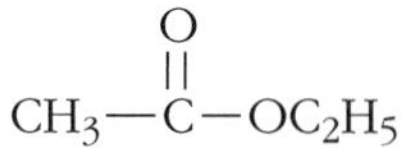 C 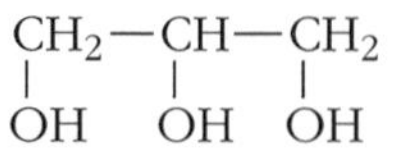
$C_{17}H_{35}-C\overset{O}{\underset{OH}{\diagdown}}$	$CH_3-\overset{\overset{O}{\|}}{C}-OC_2H_5$	$\begin{array}{ccc} CH_2-CH-CH_2 \\ \| \quad \| \quad \| \\ OH \quad OH \quad OH \end{array}$
D	**E**	**F**
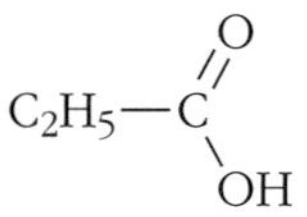 $C_2H_5-C\overset{O}{\underset{OH}{\diagdown}}$	$C_3H_7-NH_2$	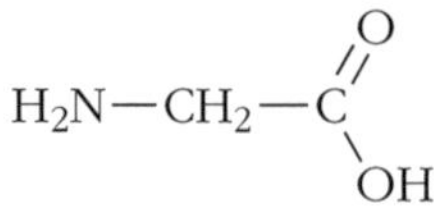 $H_2N-CH_2-C\overset{O}{\underset{OH}{\diagdown}}$

    a) Identify the compound which could be produced by the hydrolysis of a protein.
    b) Identify the compound(s) which could be produced by the hydrolysis of a fat.

16* Many different compounds are associated with foods.

A	B	C
glucose, a carbohydrate	glycerol, an alcohol	starch, a carbohydrate
D	**E**	**F**
glycine, an amino acid	oleic acid, a fatty acid	glyceryl tristearate, a fat

    a) Identify the polymer.
    b) Identify the compound which could be formed by the hydrolysis of a protein.
    c) Identify the **two** compounds which could be formed by the hydrolysis of an oil.

17 There are many different groups of atoms present in carbon compounds.

A	B	C
$-CHO$	$-COOH$	$\diagdown CHOH \diagup$
D	**E**	**F**
$-NH_2$	$-NH-CO-$	$-CH_2OH$

    a) Identify the group(s) present in a protein chain.
    b) Identify the group(s) present in glycerol.
    c) Identify the group(s) produced when a compound containing the group in box **F** is oxidised.
    d) Identify the group which gives a positive result with Tollen's reagent, i.e. ammoniacal silver nitrate solution.

18* Triglycerides are important in our diet. Three are shown below.

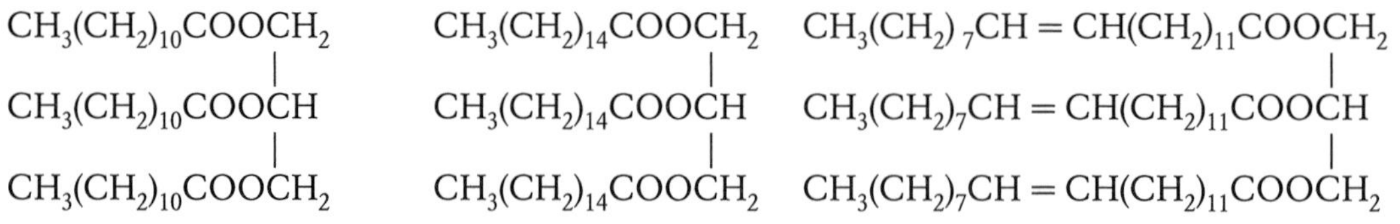

$CH_3(CH_2)_{10}COOCH_2$ $CH_3(CH_2)_{14}COOCH_2$ $CH_3(CH_2)_7CH=CH(CH_2)_{11}COOCH_2$
         $\|$ $\|$ $\|$
$CH_3(CH_2)_{10}COOCH$ $CH_3(CH_2)_{14}COOCH$ $CH_3(CH_2)_7CH=CH(CH_2)_{11}COOCH$
         $\|$ $\|$ $\|$
$CH_3(CH_2)_{10}COOCH_2$ $CH_3(CH_2)_{14}COOCH_2$ $CH_3(CH_2)_7CH=CH(CH_2)_{11}COOCH_2$
glyceryl trilaurate   glyceryl tripalmitate   glyceryl trierucate

    a) Why are triglycerides an important part of our diet?
    b) Glyceryl trilaurate is a liquid at 25°C, but glyceryl tripalmitate is a solid at the same temperature. Why does the triglyceride with the greater molecular mass have the higher melting point?
    c) Explain why glyceryl trierucate is a liquid at 25°C, whereas glyceryl tripalmitate is a solid at that temperature even though it has a smaller molecular mass.

19 There are many different enzymes in the human body.

a) Which **four** elements do all enzymes contain?

b) Salivary amylase is an enzyme which can convert starch into maltose. The pH of saliva is about 7, which is close to the optimum pH for that enzyme. Amylase stops functioning when it enters the stomach where the pH is about 2. What happens to the enzyme, on entering the stomach, that would cause it to stop functioning?

c) Many enzymes are specific and can catalyse only one reaction. For example, salivary amylase can catalyse the hydrolysis of starch to maltose, but cannot catalyse the hydrolysis of proteins to amino acids. Give a reason for this.

20 The triglyceride shown below can be present in fats and oils.

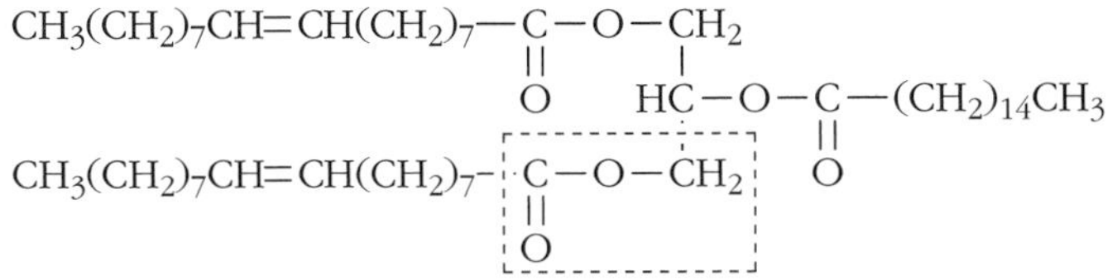

$$CH_3(CH_2)_7CH{=}CH(CH_2)_7{-}\underset{\underset{O}{\|}}{C}{-}O{-}CH_2$$

$$HC{-}O{-}\underset{\underset{O}{\|}}{C}{-}(CH_2)_{14}CH_3$$

$$CH_3(CH_2)_7CH{=}CH(CH_2)_7{-}\underset{\underset{O}{\|}}{C}{-}O{-}CH_2$$

a) Name the functional group inside the dotted lines.

b) Explain the meaning of the word '*triglyceride*'.

c) Give the molecular formula of the unsaturated acid which can be obtained from the triglyceride shown above.

21 Vegetable oils can be converted into important everyday products.

$$\text{Product } \mathbf{X} \xleftarrow[\text{H}_2/\text{Ni/heat}]{\text{I}} \text{VEGETABLE OIL} \xrightarrow[\text{NaOH(aq)/heat}]{\text{II}} \begin{array}{l} \text{SOAP} \\ + \\ \text{Compound } \mathbf{Y} \end{array}$$

a) Condensation   Hydration   Hydrolysis   Hydrogenation   Reforming

Choose one word from the list given above to describe
  i) reaction **I**
  ii) reaction **II**.

b) What is the function of nickel in reaction **I**?

c) Product **X** is used to make an important substance in the home. What is this substance?

d) Name compound **Y** and draw its structural formula.

e) Oleic acid, $CH_3(CH_2)_7CH{=}CH(CH_2)_7COOH$, is the most common acid obtained from vegetable oils. Give the formula of the soap 'molecule' produced when this acid reacts with NaOH(aq).

f) With the help of a diagram explain how soap cleans a greasy dish.

CHEMICAL REACTIONS

(13) The chemical industry

○ The UK chemical industry is a major contributor to our quality of life.

Major products include:

Plastics	Pharmaceuticals
Cosmetics & toiletries	Paints
Aerosols	Disinfectants
Detergents	Fertilisers
Explosives	Pesticides
Adhesives	Herbicides
Veterinary health products	
Inks, dyestuffs & pigments	
Chemicals used in treating water, metals, paper & fabrics	
Domestic polishes & cleaners	
Intermediates for making synthetic fibres	

○ The UK chemical industry also plays a vital role in our national economy.

○ The chemical industry is one of the UK's largest manufacturing industries. Its share of the total gross value added, i.e. the money raised in converting raw materials into end-products, achieved by all manufacturing industries in the UK was 11.5% in 1995.

○ The average growth rate of the chemical industry, 2.7% per year between 1987 and 1997, is nearly twice that of all manufacturing industries in the UK.

○ The chemical industry has maintained a positive trade balance, i.e. exports exceeding imports, for many years.

○ The UK chemical industry was sixth after USA, Japan, Germany, China and France in 1997 in terms of total sales of chemicals.

○ The chemical industry also contributes to our 'invisible' exports. In 1995, income from licensing of chemical processes developed in the UK was, at £1.3 billion; about three and a half times payments made to overseas countries for their technology.

New products

The stages needed before a new product can be manufactured are shown below.

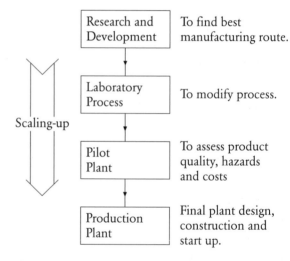

Figure 1

The manufacturing process

○ A chemical manufacturing process usually involves a sequence of steps.

For example, sulphuric acid is still a vital substance in the chemical industry. It is manufactured from sulphur by the Contact Process in a series of steps outlined below.

Step 1: Sulphur burning

$$S(l) + O_2(g) \rightarrow SO_2(g) \quad \Delta H = -297 \text{ kJ mol}^{-1}$$

Step 2: SO_2 conversion

$$SO_2(g) + \tfrac{1}{2}O_2(g) \overset{450°C}{\rightleftharpoons} SO_3(g) \quad \Delta H = -94 \text{ kJ mol}^{-1}$$

Step 3: SO₃ absorption

$$SO_3(g) + H_2O(l) \xrightarrow{V_2O_5 \text{ catalyst}} H_2SO_4(l)$$

Choosing a manufacturing route

○ Several factors may need to be taken into account when choosing a particular route to manufacture a product.

These factors include:

 – the cost, availability and suitability of the feedstock(s)
 – the yield of product(s)
 – whether or not unreacted materials can be recycled
 – how marketable are the by-products
 – energy consumption
 – environmental considerations e.g. emissions to the atmosphere, waste disposal.

Raw materials and feedstocks

○ A **feedstock** is a reactant from which other chemicals can be extracted or synthesised. Feedstocks are themselves derived from **raw materials**.

The major raw materials which are used in the chemical industry are:

Crude oil
Crude oil gives naphtha, a fraction obtained by distillation, used as an important feedstock for various chemical processes such as

1 steam cracking to produce ethene and propene for the manufacture of plastics, and

2 reforming to produce aromatic hydrocarbons for the manufacture of dyes, drugs etc.

Ores and minerals
Two examples are:

1 bauxite produces alumina, Al_2O_3, to manufacture aluminium

2 rock salt produces NaOH, Cl_2 & HCl on electrolysis of its aqueous solution.

Air
Air provides:

1 nitrogen for the production of ammonia, and

2 oxygen for the oxidation of
   a) sulphur to sulphur oxides to manufacture sulphuric acid
   b) ammonia to nitrogen oxides to manufacture nitric acid.

Water
Water is a raw material in the steam cracking of naphtha and ethane and in the hydration of ethene to produce ethanol.

Air and water have other functions in the chemical industry. Both can be used as coolants, while water is of course an important solvent.

Batch or continuous process

○ In a batch process the reactants are added to the reactor. The reaction is started and its progress carefully monitored. At the end of the reaction the reactor is emptied and the product mixture passes on to the separation and purification stages. A batch reactor is usually a large cylindrical tank.

Continuous process	Batch process
Advantages: Ideal for large quantities of product. Cheaper product if operated to full capacity. Smaller workforce. Good for fast, single-step reactions.	Better suited to small quantities. Plant cheaper to build. More versatile plant. Good for multi-step reactions. Can use reactants in any physical state.
Disadvantages: Can be difficult to use with solid reactants unless 'fluidised'. Can be difficult to control when starting-up, but easier to control when in operation.	Filling and emptying plant increases production time. Can be hard to control if reaction is exothermic.

Table 1

○ In a continuous process reactants flow into the reactor at one end and the products flow out at the other end. The design of the reactor varies from one process to another.

○ Batch and continuous processes each have their advantages and disadvantages (Table 1).

Economic aspects

○ Each industrial chemical process has its characteristic set of conditions under which it operates. These conditions are chosen so as to maximise economic efficiency.

○ The chemical industry is research-based.

○ The chemical industry can be described as capital intensive rather than labour intensive. The entire chemical industry only employs about 1.5% of the British workforce.

○ Manufacturing costs in the chemical industry can be divided into different categories:

Capital costs	Fixed costs	Variable costs
Research & development	Depreciation of plant	Raw materials
Plant construction	Labour	Energy
Buildings	Land purchase or rental	Overheads
Infrastructures	Sales expenses	Effluent treatment or disposal

Table 2

Variable costs relate to the chemical process involved. These costs will not be incurred if production is halted but **fixed costs** will still have to be paid. A company will incur fixed costs whether it manufactures one tonne of product or thousands of tonnes. The effect of the fixed cost on the selling price of the product diminishes as the scale of operation increases.

Capital costs are recovered as depreciation included under fixed costs. Depreciation occurs as chemical plants frequently operate under severe and/or corrosive conditions or become obsolete through technological progress.

The use of energy

○ Energy is a major variable cost. At times of international tension, the price of energy from oil has risen very rapidly.

○ The chemical industry has responded to the high cost of oil by

– switching where possible to processes which use less energy
– saving energy by using heat from exothermic processes elsewhere in the plant
– using 'waste' heat to generate electricity for the plant
– selling energy to supply district heating schemes for local housing.

○ Apart from its cost, wasted energy is causing needless pollution. When derived from fossil fuels it is contributing to global warming.

The location of chemical industry

Major chemical manufacturing sites have been established as a result of historical and practical considerations as illustrated by the following case study:

Grangemouth chemical works

Grangemouth Works started in 1919 as a dyeworks and has since expanded to produce pharmaceuticals, agrochemicals, pigments and speciality chemicals.

It was sited at Grangemouth for several important practical reasons.

– A large area of flat land was available.
– There was plenty of water for manufacturing processes.
– There were good transport links by railway and by Grangemouth docks to import raw materials (from coal tar) and to export products.
– There was a pool of skilled labour with experience in the chemical industry because of the nearby shale-oil works.
– Effluent could be disposed of to the sea.

Historical reasons for the siting of the Grangemouth Works included the following.

– A shortage of dyes, which had normally

been imported from Germany until the start of the First World War.

– The company's founder wanted to set up the works in his native Scotland!

Safety in the chemical industry

❍ The chemical industry has, like all industries, a duty to its employees and to the public to operate without causing accidental injury and without causing risks to health.

❍ Yet disastrous incidents in the industry have occurred.

For example, in 1974 at Flixborough in Lincolnshire a plant making cyclohexane suffered an explosion and fire. Casualties were 28 killed and 104 injured, some in neighbouring housing. Lessons learnt included building new plants away from housing and ensuring that control rooms were fire- and blast-proof.

In 1984 at Bhopal, India, a leak of toxic gas killed several thousand people in the worst chemical plant incident ever. The company had to pay huge sums in compensation, its reputation throughout the world was damaged greatly. Other companies realised the need to avoid similar accidents, not only for economic reasons.

❍ To put this matter in perspective, deaths on the roads in the UK exceed accidental deaths in the chemical industry by a factor of 1000.

❍ Chemical industry has a history of causing long-term damage to the health of its workers. Now the rules governing exposure to harmful chemicals are very strict and rigorously enforced.

❍ In the 1980's the chemical industry recognised that it needed to make a significant improvement in its safety, health and environmental performance. In the UK, the USA and Canada, a programme called Responsible Care has been adopted.

Questions

1   In Spring 2000, it was announced that crude oil prices were expected to rise considerably. Suggest different reasons why the retail price of each of the following could increase.
   a) Petrol
   b) Fertilisers
   c) Bottled mineral water

2   Draw up a table with the headings:

Capital Costs, Fixed Costs, Variable Costs.

Place each of the following costs under the appropriate heading.

Staff training
Advertising
Fuel bills
Construction of new plant
Landfill tax
Construction of rail siding,
Rental of land for expansion,
Wages
Development of new product.

3   In February 2000, millions of litres of highly toxic cyanide solution from a gold mine in Romania leaked into a tributary of the River Danube which flows through Hungary, Serbia and Bulgaria into the Black Sea.
   What could be the consequences for
   a) the aquatic environment
   b) the large human populations along the Danube
   c) international relations?

4   The technology used in the oil industry had its origins in West Lothian where a rock, oil shale, was mined and then distilled to produce crude oil products. In the nineteenth century, a batch process was used and the main products were lamp oil, candle wax and lubricants.
   If the remaining deposits of oil shale were mined today, suggest
   a) what would be the main products
   b) two reasons why a continuous process would be the preferred method of refining
   c) a major reason why a continuous process would be difficult to introduce in this case.

5

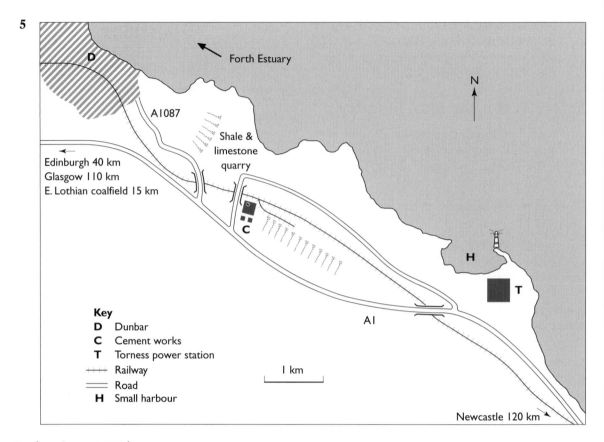

Dunbar Cement Works

Chemical reactions involved in the manufacture of cement include:

$$CaCO_3 \xrightarrow{\text{heat}} CaO + CO_2 \quad \text{and} \quad CaO + SiO_2 \xrightarrow{\text{heat}} CaSiO_3$$
$$\text{[from shale]}$$

a) Use the sketch map to answer the following:
   i) Cement manufacture requires shale as a raw material.
      What other essential materials are available nearby?
   ii) What other advantages does the specific site for the works have?
b) The cement works takes in quantities of waste paint, resins and solvents for use as fuel.
   How would this benefit
   i) the operating company
   ii) the wider community?
c) In the UK about 10 million car tyres are dumped on landfill sites each year. Rubber consists of hydrocarbon polymers. Reduction in landfill waste would benefit the wider community, but how could the use of 'chipped' tyre rubber benefit the cement company?

6 During the 1970's and the 1980's an aluminium smelter operated at Invergordon on the Cromarty Firth, the site of a former naval base. Its raw material was imported alumina (i.e. purified aluminum oxide) which was electrolysed using power from the National Grid.

Suggest **two** favourable and **two** unfavourable factors affecting the siting of the industrial plant. You may find it helpful to consult a map of the north of Scotland.

7 The following diagram summarises the manufacture of epoxyethane (which itself is used in sterilising and fumigating) and three possible processes for converting it into ethane-1,2-diol.

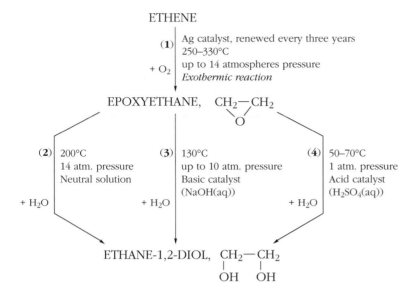

a) Name **two** feedstocks from which ethene can be obtained.
b) Write a balanced equation for reaction **(1)**.
c) In order to prevent another, more common, reaction competing with reaction **(1)** the ethene and oxygen spend less than 4 seconds in the reactor.
What would you expect the products of the competing reaction to be?
d) Give **one** advantage and **one** disadvantage for each of the processes **(2)** and **(4)**.
e) Give **one** important use of ethane-1,2-diol.
f) Explain one factor which has a significant effect on the high **capital** cost of the plant for process **(1)**.
g) Give **two variable** costs in the operating of process **(1)**.

14 Hess's Law

Hess's Law states:

'The enthalpy change of a chemical reaction depends only on the chemical nature and physical states of the reactants and products and is independent of any intermediate steps.'

i.e. the enthalpy change of a chemical reaction does not depend on the route taken during the reaction.

Hess's Law can be tested by experiment as this example shows. Solid potassium hydroxide is converted into potassium chloride solution by two different routes illustrated in Figure 1.

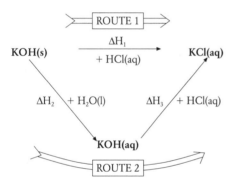

Figure 1

According to Hess's Law: $\Delta H_1 = \Delta H_2 + \Delta H_3$

Prescribed Practical Activity

Route 1: a one-step process. 25 cm³ of dilute hydrochloric acid is added to a known mass, about 1.2 g, of solid potassium hydroxide in a polystyrene cup to produce potassium chloride solution. The initial temperature of the acid, and the highest temperature of the resulting solution after stirring are measured.

Route 2: *Step 1:* The same mass of solid potassium hydroxide is added to water to form potassium hydroxide solution. The initial temperature of the water, and the highest temperature of the resulting solution after stirring are measured.

Step 2: The temperature of the potassium hydroxide solution from step 1 is remeasured, the temperature of 25 cm³ of dilute hydrochloric acid is measured and the two temperatures averaged to give a starting temperature. The two solutions are mixed, stirred and the highest temperature reached is measured.

For each of the experiments, the energy released can be calculated using: $E_h = cm\Delta T$, where c is the specific heat of water (a reasonable approximation), m is the mass of solution (assumed to be the same as for the same volume of water) and ΔT is the temperature rise.

The enthalpy change for each experiment is then obtained by dividing E_h by the number of moles of potassium hydroxide.

Then: $\Delta H_1 = \Delta H_2 + \Delta H_3$

Calculations using Hess's Law

○ Only certain enthalpy changes can be measured directly, as shown in Chapter 2.

○ Hess's Law enables the calculation of enthalpy changes which are very difficult or even impossible to measure. The calculation of the enthalpies of formation of carbon compounds from their constituent elements is an example.

● Worked Example 14.1 ●
$$2C(s) + H_2(g) \rightarrow C_2H_2(g)$$

Calculate the enthalpy of formation of ethyne gas from carbon and hydrogen using the enthalpies of combustion of carbon, hydrogen and ethyne.

$$2C(s) \quad + \quad H_2(g) \xrightarrow{\Delta H_x} C_2H_2(g)$$

$\Delta H① \Big| +2O_2(g) \quad \Delta H② \Big| +\tfrac{1}{2}O_2(g) \quad \Delta H③ \Big| -2\tfrac{1}{2}O_2(g)$

$$2CO_2(g) \quad + \quad H_2O(l)$$

In the alternative route,

Step 1 is the combustion of 2 moles of carbon,

$$2C(s) + 2O_2(g) \rightarrow 2CO_2(g)$$
$$\Delta H_1 = -(2 \times 394) \text{ kJ} = -788 \text{ kJ}$$

Step 2 is the combustion of 1 mole of hydrogen,

$$H_2(g) + \tfrac{1}{2}O_2(g) \rightarrow H_2O(l)$$
$$\Delta H_2 = -286 \text{ kJ}$$

Step 3 is the **reverse** of combustion of 1 mole of ethyne,

$$2CO_2(g) + H_2O(l) \rightarrow C_2H_2(g) + 2\tfrac{1}{2}O_2(g)$$
$$\Delta H_3 = +1300 \text{ kJ*}$$

Adding these three equations gives the required equation, namely

$$2C(s) + H_2(g) \rightarrow C_2H_2(g)$$

According to Hess's Law,

$$\Delta H_x = \Delta H_1 + \Delta H_2 + \Delta H_3$$
$$= -788 - 286 + 1300$$
$$= +226 \text{ kJ mol}^{-1}$$

(*The sign has been altered since the reaction has been reversed.)

● Worked Example 14.2 ●

The following equation shows the formation of methanol from carbon, hydrogen and oxygen.

$$C(s) + 2H_2(g) + \tfrac{1}{2}O_2(g) \rightarrow CH_3OH(l)$$

Use the enthalpies of combustion of carbon, hydrogen and methanol to calculate the enthalpy change of this reaction.

$$C(s) \quad + \quad 2H_2(g) + \quad \tfrac{1}{2}O_2(g) \xrightarrow{\Delta H_x} CH_3OH(l)$$

$$\Delta H_1 \Big| {+O_2(g)} \quad \Delta H_2 \Big| {+O_2(g)} \qquad\qquad \Delta H_3 \Big| {-2O_2(g)}$$

$$CO_2(g) \quad + \quad 2H_2O(l) \quad + \quad \tfrac{1}{2}O_2(g)$$

In the alternative route,

Step 1 is the combustion of 1 mole of carbon,

$$C(s) + O_2(g) \rightarrow CO_2(g) \quad \Delta H_1 = -394 \text{ kJ}$$

Step 2 is the combustion of 2 moles of hydrogen,

$$2H_2(g) + O_2(g) \rightarrow 2H_2O(l)$$
$$\Delta H_2 = -(2 \times 286) \text{ kJ} = -572 \text{ kJ}$$

Step 3 is the **reverse** of combustion of methanol,

$$CO_2(g) + 2H_2O(l) \rightarrow CH_3OH(l) + \tfrac{3}{2}O_2(g)$$
$$\Delta H_3 = +727 \text{ kJ}$$

Adding these three equations gives the required equation, namely

$$C(s) + 2H_2(g) + \tfrac{1}{2}O_2(g) \rightarrow CH_3OH(l)$$

According to Hess's Law,

$$\Delta H_x = \Delta H_1 + \Delta H_2 + \Delta H_3$$
$$= -394 - 572 + 727$$
$$= -239 \text{ kJ mol}^{-1}$$

Note: Oxygen is one of the elements present in methanol but it is not involved in deriving the required enthalpy change. The calculation is based on enthalpies of combustion. Oxygen gas supports combustion; it does not itself have an enthalpy of combustion. Also note that in all enthalpy calculations, the **states** of the substances involved are important, since changes of state involve enthalpy changes.

Questions

1* Consider the reaction pathway shown below.

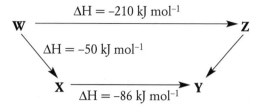

According to Hess' Law, the ΔH value, in kJ mol^{-1}, for reaction **Z** to **Y** is

A +74   B −74
C +346   D −346

2* $N_2(g) + 2O_2(g) \rightarrow 2NO_2(g)$ $\Delta H = + 88$ kJ
$N_2(g) + 2O_2(g) \rightarrow N_2O_4(g)$ $\Delta H = + 10$ kJ

The enthalpy change for the reaction $2NO_2(g) \rightarrow N_2O_4(g)$ will be

A +98 kJ   B +78 kJ
C −78 kJ   D −98 kJ

3* What is the relationship between a, b, c and d?

$S(s) + H_2(g) \rightarrow H_2S(g)$ $\Delta H = a$

$H_2(g) + \frac{1}{2}O_2(g) \rightarrow H_2O(l)$ $\Delta H = b$

$S(s) + O_2(g) \rightarrow SO_2(g)$ $\Delta H = c$

$H_2S(s) + 1\frac{1}{2}O_2(g) \rightarrow H_2O(l) + SO_2(g)$ $\Delta H = d$

A $a = b + c - d$
B $a = d - b - c$
C $a = b - c - d$
D $a = d + c - b$

4 Enthalpies of combustion of ethene, hydrogen and ethane can be found in the SQA Data Book.
What is the enthalpy of hydrogenation of ethene to form ethane, in kJ mol^{-1}?

A +137   B −137
C −149   D +149

5 The enthalpy of combustion of methane is −891 kJ mol^{-1}. The enthalpy change for the following reaction is −566 kJ.

$$2CO(g) + O_2(g) \rightarrow 2CO_2(g)$$

Using this data, what is the enthalpy of partial combustion of methane, in kJ mol^{-1}?

$$CH_4(g) + \tfrac{3}{2}O_2(g) \rightarrow CO(g) + 2H_2O(l)$$

A −325   B −608
C −1174   D −1457

6 Three reactions involving metals and metal oxides are shown below. (All metals and oxides are solids.)

$Mg + FeO \rightarrow Fe + MgO$ $\Delta H = x$ kJ mol^{-1}

$Fe + CuO \rightarrow Cu + FeO$ $\Delta H = y$ kJ mol^{-1}

$Mg + CuO \rightarrow Cu + MgO$ $\Delta H = z$ kJ mol^{-1}

Which of the following is true, according to Hess's Law?

A $y + z = -x$ B $y + z = x$
C $x + y = -z$ D $x + y = z$

7* A pupil tried to confirm Hess's Law using the reactions shown below.

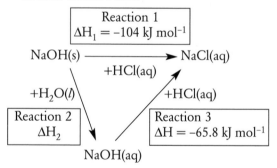

In reaction 1, the pupil measured the mass of NaOH(s) and the temperature change of the reaction mixture.

a) Which further measurement would have been taken?
b) Use the enthalpy changes in the diagram to calculate the enthalpy change for reaction 2.
c) Write, in words, a statement of Hess's Law.

8 Use appropriate enthalpies of combustion from the SQA Data Book to calculate the enthalpy changes of the following reactions.

a) $3C(s) + 4H_2(g) \rightarrow C_3H_8(g)$
(propane)

b) $2C(s) + 2H_2(g) + O_2(g) \rightarrow CH_3COOH(l)$
(ethanoic acid)

9 Methane can be converted into ethyne at very high temperatures (about 1500°C). The equation for the reaction is:

$$2CH_4(g) \rightarrow C_2H_2(g) + 3H_2(g)$$

Use enthalpies of combustion from the SQA Data Book to calculate the enthalpy change for this reaction
i) in kJ mol^{-1} of ethyne
ii) in kJ mol^{-1} of methane.

10 The simplest silicon hydride has the formula SiH_4. It is a gas at room temperature. The equation for the complete combustion of this compound is:

$$SiH_4(g) + 2O_2(g) \rightarrow SiO_2(s) + 2H_2O(l)$$

Calculate the enthalpy change for this reaction using the following data:

$Si(s) + 2H_2(g) \rightarrow SiH_4(g)$ $\Delta H = +34$ kJ mol^{-1}

$Si(s) + O_2(g) \rightarrow SiO_2(s)$ $\Delta H = -911$ kJ mol^{-1}

$H_2(g) + \frac{1}{2}O_2(g) \rightarrow H_2O(l)$ $\Delta H = -286$ kJ mol^{-1}

11 Methanal, HCHO, is made industrially by the oxidation of methanol. The boiling point of methanal is −21°C and its enthalpy of combustion is −561 kJ mol^{-1}.

a) Write the equation, including state symbols, for the complete combustion of methanal.

b) Calculate the enthalpy change for the oxidation of methanol to methanal. Refer to the SQA Data Book page 9. The equation for this reaction is:

$$CH_3OH(l) + \tfrac{1}{2}O_2(g) \rightarrow HCHO(g) + H_2O(l)$$

c) In the industrial process, a catalyst (either copper or silver) is used.
What effect, if any, will the catalyst have on
i) the enthalpy change
ii) the activation energy of the reaction?

d) In the industrial process, methanol vapour is passed over the catalyst at 500°C.
Give one reason why the enthalpy change for the industrial process will be different from your answer in part **b)**.

e) Give **one** important use of methanal.

(15) Equilibrium

○ Reversible reactions attain a state of equilibrium when the rate of the forward reaction is equal to the rate of the reverse reaction.

○ The reaction does **not** stop when equilibrium is attained. For this reason, chemical equilibrium is described as being **dynamic.**

○ When equilibrium is reached this does not imply that the equilibrium mixture consists of 50% reactants and 50% products. This will only very rarely be the case. The concentrations of reactants and products do however remain constant.

○ Equilibrium is reached when the opposing reactions occur at an equal rate. Any condition which changes the rate of one reaction more than the other should change the position of equilibrium, i.e. the relative proportions of reactants and products in the mixture.

Changing the position of equilibrium

This section deals with the influence of changing the concentration, the pressure, the temperature and the catalyst on the equilibrium position.

○ The effect of these changes can be summarised by 'Le Chatelier's Principle' which states that:

'If a system at equilibrium is subjected to any change, the system readjusts itself to try and counteract the applied change.'

Note: This statement *only* refers to reversible reactions which have reached equilibrium.

A summary of results of changes is shown in Table 1.

Example 1
Bromine water

$$Br_2(l) + H_2O(l) \rightleftharpoons$$
$$2H^+(aq) + Br^-(aq) + BrO^-(aq)$$

The addition of NaOH removes H^+ ions and the equilibrium shifts to the right. Adding HCl increases the concentration of H^+ ions moving the equilibrium back to the left.

Change applied	Effect on equilibrium position
Concentration Addition of reactant or removal of product	Equilibrium shifts to the right
Addition of product or removal of reactant	Equilibrium shifts to the left
(See example 1)	
Temperature Increase	Shifts in direction of endothermic reaction
Decrease	Shifts in direction of exothermic reaction
(See example 2)	
Pressure Increase	Shifts in direction which reduces the number of molecules in gas phase
Decrease	Shifts in direction which increases the number of molecules in the gas phase
(See example 3)	
Catalyst	No effect on equilibrium position; equilibrium more rapidly attained
(See Figure 1)	

Table 1

Example 2

$$N_2O_4(g) \rightleftharpoons 2NO_2(g)$$
$$\text{(colourless)} \quad \text{(dark brown)}$$

The forward reaction is endothermic.

Increase in temperature favours the endothermic reaction, the equilibrium moves to the right, the proportion of NO_2 increases and the gas mixture becomes darker in colour.

Decrease in temperature favours the exothermic

reaction, the equilibrium moves to the left, and the gas mixture lightens in colour.

Example 3

$$N_2O_4(g) \rightleftharpoons 2NO_2(g)$$

1 mole   2 moles

1 volume 2 volumes (at the same

temperature and pressure)

Increase in pressure causes the system to counteract this effect, i.e. to reduce the pressure within the system. The equilibrium adjusts to the left, forming more N_2O_4 molecules, reducing the number of molecules per unit volume which reduces the pressure.

Potential energy diagram:

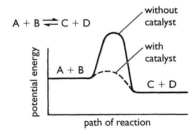

Figure 1 Potential energy: catalysed and uncatalysed reactions

Activation Energy is lowered equally for forward and backward reactions, both are speeded up and the same equilibrium is reached more quickly.

Equilibrium and the Haber process

○ The Haber process is used to synthesise ammonia from hydrogen and nitrogen.

○ If a closed reaction vessel is used, an equilibrium is set up:

$$N_2(g) + 3H_2(g) \rightleftharpoons 2NH_3(g) \quad \Delta H = -92 \text{ kJ}$$

A summary of the results of changes applied industrially to the Haber Process are shown in Table 2.

New conditions	Equilibrium change	Explanation
Increase pressure	To right, [NH$_3$] increases	Forward direction involves a decrease in number of moles of gas (4 moles → 2 moles) and hence a decrease in volume. Decrease in volume is assisted by increase in pressure.
Decrease temperature	To right, [NH$_3$] increases	Decreasing temperature removes energy from system, making reverse endothermic reaction less favourable, less NH$_3$ splits up, but reaction slows so catalyst needed.
Catalyst	No change	Both forward and reverse reactions are accelerated. The same equilibrium is reached more rapidly.

Table 2

Questions

1* Chemical reactions are in a state of dynamic equilibrium only when

A   the rate of the forward reaction equals that of the backward reaction
B   the concentrations of reactants and products are equal
C   the activation energies of the forward and backward reactions are equal
D   the reaction involves no enthalpy change.

2   When a reversible chemical reaction is at equilibrium,

A   the concentrations of reactants and products remain equal
B   the forward reaction is unable to continue
C   the concentrations of reactants and products remain constant
D   the forward and reverse reactions proceed at different rates.

Questions 3 and 4 refer to the following equilibrium which exists in bromine water.

$$Br_2(aq) + H_2O(l) \rightleftharpoons 2H^+(aq) + Br^-(aq) + BrO^-(aq)$$

3   Which of the following substances, when added, would move the equilibrium position to the right?

A   Potassium nitrate   B   Sodium bromide
C   Sulphuric acid   D   Sodium carbonate

4   Which of the following substances, when added, would increase the pH of the equilibrium mixture?

A   Potassium nitrate   B   Sodium bromide
C   Bromine   D   Sodium chloride

5* The equation refers to the preparation of methanol from synthesis gas.

$$CO(g) + 2H_2(g) \rightleftharpoons CH_3OH(g)$$
$$\Delta H = -91 \text{ kJ mol}^{-1}$$

The formation of methanol is favoured by

A   high pressure and low temperature
B   high pressure and high temperature
C   low pressure and low temperature
D   low pressure and high temperature.

6* In which of the following systems will the equilibrium be **unaffected** by a change in pressure?

A $2NO(g) + O_2(g) \rightleftharpoons 2NO_2(g)$
B $2NO_2(g) \rightleftharpoons N_2O_4(g)$
C $H_2(g) + I_2(g) \rightleftharpoons 2HI(g)$
D $N_2(g) + 3H_2(g) \rightleftharpoons 2NH_3(g)$

7   $NO_2(g) \rightleftharpoons NO(g) + \frac{1}{2}O_2(g)$
$$\Delta H = +56 \text{ kJ mol}^{-1}$$

Which two conditions favour the decomposition of NO_2?

A   Low temperature, high pressure
B   High temperature, low pressure
C   Low temperature, low pressure
D   High temperature, high pressure

8* Which entry in the table shows the effect of a catalyst on the reaction rates and position of equilibrium in a reversible reaction?

	Rate of forward reaction	Rate of reverse reaction	Position of equilibrium
A	increased	unchanged	moves right
B	increased	increased	unchanged
C	increased	decreased	moves right
D	unchanged	unchanged	unchanged

9* Which of the following is likely to apply to the use of a catalyst in a chemical reaction?

	Position of equilibrium	Effect on value of ΔH
A	Moved to right	Decreased
B	Unaffected	Increased
C	Moved to left	Unaffected
D	Unaffected	Unaffected

10* Consider the following equilibrium:

$$N_2(g) + O_2(g) \rightleftharpoons 2NO(g) \ \Delta H_{(forward)} = +180 \text{ kJ}$$

How would the equilibrium concentration of nitrogen oxide be affected by:
a)   increasing the temperature
b)   decreasing the pressure
c)   decreasing the concentration of oxygen?

11* Consider the following equilibrium:

$$N_2O_4(g) \rightleftharpoons 2NO_2(g) \qquad \Delta H_{(forward)} \text{ is + ve}$$
(pale yellow)   (dark brown)

What would be **seen** if the equilibrium mixture was
a) placed in a freezing mixture
b) compressed?

12* Changes in concentration can alter the position of an equilibrium.

$$Cl_2(aq) + H_2O(l) \rightleftharpoons 2H^+(aq) + ClO^-(aq) + Cl^-(aq)$$

A	KCl(s)
B	KOH(s)
C	$Na_2SO_4(s)$
D	$AgNO_3(s)$
E	KF(s)
F	$NaNO_3(s)$

a) Identify the compound which if added to the equilibrium mixture would move the equilibrium to the left.
b) Identify the compound(s) which if added to the equilibrium mixture would move the equilibrium to the right.

13* An industrial gas mixture is produced by the catalytic steam reforming of methane.

$$CH_4(g) + H_2O(g) \rightleftharpoons CO(g) + 3H_2(g)$$
$$\Delta H = +206 \text{ kJ mol}^{-1}$$

Identify the change(s) which would move the equilibrium to the right.

A	increasing temperature
B	increasing the concentration of hydrogen
C	increasing pressure
D	adding more catalyst
E	decreasing pressure
F	decreasing temperature

14* Iodine dissolves only slightly in water, the process being endothermic. With excess iodine present, the following equilibrium is set up.

$$I_2(s) + aq \rightleftharpoons I_2(aq) \qquad \Delta H \text{ positive}$$

The concentration of dissolved iodine was measured over a period of time. The graph below was obtained as the iodine dissolved.

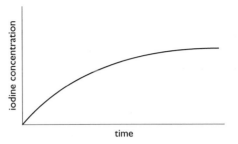

a) Copy the graph and add a curve to show how the iodine concentration would change with time if the measurements were repeated at a higher temperature.

b) The dissolved iodine reacts with water as follows.

$$I_2(aq) + H_2O(l) \rightleftharpoons 2H^+(aq) + I^-(aq) + IO^-(aq)$$

i) Copy and complete the table to show the effect on the equilibrium of adding each of the solids.

Solid	Effect on equilibrium position
potassium iodide	
potassium sulphate	

ii) Why does the position of equilibrium move to the right when solid potassium hydroxide is added?

15 Lead(II) chloride is slightly soluble in cold water. In a saturated solution of lead(II) chloride the following equilibrium is set up.

$$PbCl_2(s) \rightleftharpoons Pb^{2+}(aq) + 2Cl^-(aq)$$

a) What would be the effect on the equilibrium position of adding
i) hydrochloric acid
ii) lead(II) nitrate solution
iii) silver(I) nitrate solution?
b) Lead(II) chloride is highly soluble in very hot water. What does this indicate about the enthalpy of solution of lead(II) chloride?

16 In the Contact process, sulphur trioxide is formed from sulphur dioxide and oxygen in a reversible reaction. The equation for the reaction is:

$$2SO_2(g) + O_2(g) \rightleftharpoons 2SO_3(g)$$

The forward reaction is exothermic.

a) One litre of sulphur dioxide and one litre of oxygen were mixed under certain conditions and allowed to reach equilibrium. Analysis of the equilibrium mixture showed that 60% conversion of the sulphur dioxide had taken place. Calculate the volume of each gas present in the equilibrum mixture.

b) What effect, if any, will there be on the equilibrium position if
i) the temperature is increased
ii) a catalyst is used
iii) the pressure is increased?

17 Carbon in the form of graphite can be converted into diamond at high temperatures and high pressure. This change can be expressed in the following equation.

$$C(s) \text{ (graphite)} \rightleftharpoons C(s) \text{ (diamond)}$$

a) Calculate the enthalpy change for the forward reaction given the following data. Enthalpy of combustion of graphite is -393.5 kJ mol^{-1}. Enthalpy of combustion of diamond is -395.4 kJ mol^{-1}.

b) Is your answer to **a)** consistent with the use of high temperatures when making diamond from graphite? Explain why.

c) Refer to the densities of graphite and diamond given in the SQA Data Book to suggest why high pressures are also used.

18 Iodine monochloride, a brown liquid, reacts with chlorine to form a yellow solid called iodine trichloride according to the following equation.

$$ICl(l) + Cl_2(g) \rightleftharpoons ICl_3(s)$$

a) What effect, if any, will there be on the mass of yellow solid in an equilibrium mixture if
i) the pressure is increased
ii) some chlorine is removed?

b) Raising the temperature of the equilibrium mixture decreases the mass of yellow solid present. What can you deduce about the forward reaction from this information?

(16) Acids and bases

The pH scale

○ The concentration of hydrogen ions in solution is measured in pH units. pH stands for the negative logarithm (to base 10) of the hydrogen ion concentration, i.e. $pH = -\log_{10}[H^+(aq)]$

○ The pH scale is a continuous scale with values ranging from less than zero to more than 14. (A concentration of more than 1 mole l^{-1} of H^+ ions will give a positive $\log_{10}[H^+]$ and hence a negative pH value). Integral values of pH can be related to hydrogen ion concentrations $[H^+]$ as in Table 1.

$[H^+]$ mol l^{-1}	$\log_{10}[H^+]$	$pH(-\log_{10}[H^+])$
1	0	0
1/10 or 10^{-1}	−1	1
1/100 or 10^{-2}	−2	2
$1/10^7$ or 10^{-7}	−7	7
$1/10^{14}$ or 10^{-14}	−14	14

Table 1

○ For water and neutral solutions in water, the sole source of H^+ and OH^- ions is the very slight ionisation of some of the water molecules:

$$H_2O(l) \rightleftharpoons H^+(aq) + OH^-(aq)$$

○ An equilibrium is reached with the concentration of both H^+ and OH^- equal to 10^{-7} moles l^{-1} at 25 °C.

i.e. $[H^+] = [OH^-] = 10^{-7}$ mol l^{-1}, $pH = 7$

Then:

$$[H^+][OH^-] = 10^{-7} \text{ mol } l^{-1} \times 10^{-7} \text{ mol } l^{-1}$$
$$= 10^{-14} \text{ mol}^2 \text{ } l^{-2}$$

○ This value is called the **ionic product** of water.

○ It follows that we can calculate $[H^+]$, pH, $[OH^-]$ for acidic and alkaline solutions using the basic relationship:

$$[H^+][OH^-] = 10^{-14} \text{ mol}^2 \text{ } l^{-2}$$

From which we derive:

$$[H^+] = \frac{10^{-14}}{[OH^-]} \text{ mol } l^{-1}$$

and

$$[OH^-] = \frac{10^{-14}}{[H^+]} \text{ mol } l^{-1}$$

● Worked Example 16.1 ●

What is the concentration of OH^- ions in a solution containing 0.01 mol l^{-1} of H^+ ions?

$[H^+] = 10^{-2}$ mol l^{-1}

$[OH^-] = \dfrac{10^{-14}}{[H^+]} = \dfrac{10^{-14}}{10^{-2}} = 10^{-12}$ mol l^{-1}

● Worked Example 16.2 ●

What is **a)** the concentration of H^+ ions

b) the pH, in a solution containing 0.1 mol l^{-1} of OH^- ions?

Answer:

a) $[OH^-] = 10^{-1}$ mol l^{-1}

$[H^+] = \dfrac{10^{-14}}{[OH^-]} = \dfrac{10^{-14}}{10^{-1}} = 10^{-13}$ mol l^{-1}

b) $pH = -\log_{10}[H^+] = 13$

Strong and weak acids

○ Strong acids are acids that dissociate completely into ions in solution.

e.g. $HCl(aq) \rightarrow H^+(aq) + Cl^-(aq)$

○ Strong acids include HCl, HNO_3 and H_2SO_4.

○ Other acids dissociate only partially into ions in solution, i.e. an equilibrium exists between the ions and undissociated molecules.

For ethanoic acid:

$$CH_3COOH(aq) \rightleftharpoons CH_3COO^-(aq) + H^+(aq)$$

For carbon dioxide solution:

$$CO_2(g) + H_2O(l) \rightleftharpoons H_2CO_3(aq)$$
$$\text{carbonic acid}$$

$$\rightleftharpoons H^+(aq) + HCO_3^-(aq)$$
$$\text{hydrogencarbonate ion}$$

$$\rightleftharpoons 2H^+(aq) + CO_3^{2-}(aq)$$
$$\text{carbonate ion}$$

For sulphur dioxide solution:

$$SO_2(g) + H_2O(l) \rightleftharpoons H_2SO_3(aq)$$
$$\text{sulphurous acid}$$

$$\rightleftharpoons H^+(aq) + HSO_3^-(aq)$$
$$\text{hydrogensulphite ion}$$

$$\rightleftharpoons 2H^+(aq) + SO_3^{2-}(aq)$$
$$\text{sulphite ion}$$

○ Such incompletely dissociated acids are called weak acids. (Note that '*strong*' and '*weak*' refer to the inherent ability of acids to ionise. These words should not confused with '*concentrated*' and '*dilute*'.)

○ Solutions of strong and weak acids differ in pH, conductivity and reaction rates since their hydrogen ion concentrations are different. Solutions should be equimolar for a fair comparison.

For example, 0.1 mol l⁻¹ CH_3COOH has a lower hydrogen ion concentration, higher pH, lower conductivity and slower rate of reaction with magnesium or calcium carbonate than 0.1 mol l⁻¹ HCl.

○ The undissociated molecules of weak acids are in equilibrium with their ions. As a reaction proceeds, consuming H⁺ ions, the equilibrium shifts in favour of more dissociation until eventually all the molecules are dissociated. Thus the same number of moles of base is required to neutralise a

certain volume of either 0.1 mol l⁻¹ HCl or 0.1 mol l⁻¹ CH_3COOH. Hence the **stoichiometry** (the mole ratio of reactants) of a neutralisation reaction is the same:

$$NaOH + HCl \rightarrow NaCl + H_2O$$
$$NaOH + CH_3COOH \rightarrow CH_3COONa + H_2O$$
$$\text{1 mole acid} \equiv \text{1 mole alkali in each case.}$$

Strong and weak bases

○ A base is any substance which will neutralise the H⁺ ions of an acid to form water.

○ Bases which are soluble in water, producing OH⁻ ions, are alkalis.

○ Alkalis which are fully dissociated into ions are strong alkalis, e.g. NaOH and KOH.

$$NaOH(aq) \rightarrow Na^+(aq) + OH^-(aq)$$

○ Alkalis showing incomplete dissociation are weak alkalis, e.g. ammonia solution.

$$NH_3(aq) + H_2O(l) \rightleftharpoons NH_4^+(aq) + OH^-(aq)$$

In the example above an equilibrium, normally well to the left, is set up in the ammonia solution. This results in the lower concentration of OH⁻ ions, lower conductivity and lower pH of a weak alkali compared with an equimolar solution of sodium hydroxide.

○ The stoichiometry of neutralisations of strong and weak alkalis is the same.

$$\text{e.g. } NaOH + HCl \rightarrow NaCl + H_2O$$
$$NH_3 + HCl \rightarrow NH_4Cl + H_2O$$
$$\text{1 mole alkali} \equiv \text{1mole acid in each case}$$

The weak alkali dissociates further as its OH⁻ ions react with acids. Eventually it will dissociate fully so that a certain volume of either 0.1 mol l⁻¹ NaOH or 0.1 mol l⁻¹ NH_3 solution will neutralise the same number of moles of acid.

pH of salt solutions

○ It is normally assumed that since salts can be made by neutralisation of an acid by an alkali the pH will be neutral, i.e. 7. In fact, the measured pH of salts is often not 7.

In general terms, in solution:

○ Salts of **strong acid** and **strong alkali** have **pH 7** (e.g. NaCl and KNO$_3$)

○ Salts of **strong acid** and **weak alkali** have **pH < 7** (e.g. NH$_4$Cl)

○ Salts of **strong alkali** and **weak acid** have **pH > 7** (e.g. CH$_3$COONa)

Ammonium chloride in water

The pH of ammonium chloride in water can be explained as follows.

Ions present initially, NH$_4^+$ from the salt and OH$^-$ from the water, combine to form ammonia and water molecules:

$$NH_4^+(aq) + OH^-(aq) \rightarrow NH_3(aq) + H_2O(l)$$

Removal of OH$^-$ ions causes the water equilibrium to move to the right.

$$H_2O(l) \rightarrow H^+(aq) + OH^-(aq)$$

Excess H$^+$ ions are formed and the solution has pH less than 7.

Sodium ethanoate in water

The pH of sodium ethanoate in water can be explained as follows.

Ions present initially, CH$_3$COO$^-$ from the salt and H$^+$ from the water, combine to form ethanoic acid molecules:

$$CH_3COO^-(aq) + H^+(aq) \rightarrow CH_3COOH(aq)$$

Removal of H$^+$ ions causes the water equilibrium to be disturbed.

$$H_2O \rightarrow H^+(aq) + OH^-(aq)$$

Excess OH$^-$ ions are formed, and the solution has pH greater than 7.

Similar considerations apply to sodium and potassium salts of other carboxylic acids and of carbonic and sulphurous acids.

○ Soaps are the salts of strong alkalis like NaOH and KOH with weak long chain carboxylic acids such as stearic and oleic acids. Soaps therefore are usually alkaline in solution.

Questions

1 The concentration of OH$^-$(aq) in a solution is 0.01 mol l^{-1}. What is the pH of the solution?

   A 8   **B** 10   **C** 12   **D** 14

2* 0.5 mol of hydrogen chloride is dissolved in water, and the resulting solution is made up to a total of 5 litres. The pH of this solution is

   A 0   **B** 1   **C** 2   **D** 3.

3* A trout fishery owner added limestone to his loch to combat the effects of acid rain. He managed to raise the pH of the water from 4 to 6. This caused the concentration of the H$^+$(aq) to

   A increase by a factor of 2
   B increase by a factor of 100
   C decrease by a factor of 2
   D decrease by a factor of 100.

4 The pH of a solution of nitric acid was found to be 1.6. The concentration of H$^+$(aq) ions in the acid must be

   A more than 0.1 mol l^{-1}
   B between 0.1 and 0.01 mol l^{-1}
   C between 0.01 and 0.001 mol l^{-1}
   D less than 0.001 mol l^{-1}.

5 Butanoic acid is described as a weak acid because in water

   A its pH is about 4
   B its O–H bonds are partially dissociated
   C it is only slightly soluble
   D it gives only one hydrogen ion per molecule.

6* A fully dissociated acid is progressively diluted by the addition of water. Which of the following would increase with increasing dilution?

   A The pH value
   B The electrical conductivity
   C The rate of its reaction with chalk
   D The volume of alkali which it will neutralise

7* Which of the following is the same for equal volumes of equimolar solutions of sodium hydroxide and ammonia?

  A pH of solution
  B Mass of solute present
  C Conductivity of solution
  D Moles of acid needed for complete reaction

8* Excess marble chips (calcium carbonate) were added to 100 cm³ of 1 mol l⁻¹ hydrochloric acid. The experiment was repeated using the same mass of the marble chips and 100 cm³ of 1 mol l⁻¹ ethanoic acid. Which would have been the same for both experiments?

  A The time taken for the reaction to be completed
  B The rate at which the first 10 cm³ of gas is evolved
  C The mass of marble chips left over when reaction has stopped.
  D The average rate of the reaction

9 Which of the following correctly describes the concentration of ions in an aqueous solution which has a pH of 10?

	$[H^+]/\text{mol l}^{-1}$	$[OH^-]/\text{mol l}^{-1}$
A	10^4	10^{-10}
B	10^{-4}	10^{-10}
C	10^{-10}	10^{-4}
D	10^{-10}	10^4

10* On the structure shown, four hydrogen atoms have been replaced by the letters A, B, C and D.

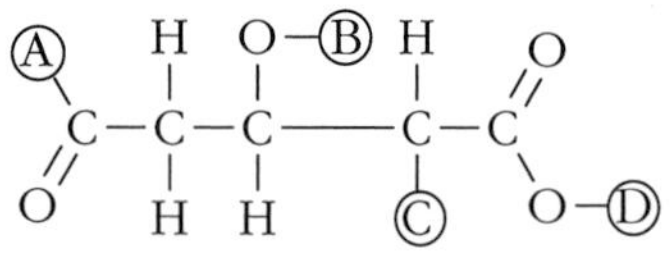

Which letter corresponds to the hydrogen atom which can ionise most easily in aqueous solution?

11 1 cm³ of a solution of KOH, which has a pH of 10, was diluted to 100 cm³. 1 cm³ of this solution was also diluted to 100 cm³. The pH of the **final** solution is approximately

  A 8   B 7   C 6   D 5.

12 Which of the following dissolves in water to give a solution of pH<7 ?

  A Potassium ethanoate
  B Sodium sulphate
  C Calcium hydroxide
  D Ammonium chloride

13 Which of the following forms an alkaline solution in water?

  A Sodium chloride
  B Potassium carbonate
  C Ammonium nitrate
  D Lithium sulphate

14 Which of the following solutions is most likely to produce hydrogen gas when magnesium is added?

  A Ammonium sulphate
  B Sodium nitrate
  C Potassium chloride
  D Sodium ethanoate

15 The grid lists various acidic solutions.

A	40 cm³ of 0.5 mol l⁻¹ sulphuric acid
B	10 cm³ of 4.0 mol l⁻¹ nitric acid
C	80 cm³ of 0.5 mol l⁻¹ hydrochloric acid
D	40 cm³ of 1.0 mol l⁻¹ ethanoic acid
E	20 cm³ of 2.0 mol l⁻¹ sulphuric acid

  a) Identify the solution which contains the least number of H⁺(aq) ions.
  b) Identify the solution(s) which would **not** produce a solution with pH = 7 when added to 40 cm³ of 1.0 mol l⁻¹ KOH.

16 For each of the following solutions, indicate
  i) the concentration of H⁺ ions
  ii) the pH of the solution.

  a) 0.001 mol l⁻¹ HCl
  b) 1.0 mol l⁻¹ NaCl
  c) 0.5 mol l⁻¹ H₂SO₄
  d) 0.1 mol l⁻¹ NaOH
  e) 0.00001 mol l⁻¹ KOH

17 The pH of aqueous solutions of various household substances were tested. The results are listed below.

Solution tested	pH
Trichlorophenol, TCP	2
Handwash	8
Cleaning fluid	11
Lemonade	4

Calculate the concentration of OH$^-$ ions in each of these substances.

18 The grid lists various pH values.

A pH 0	B pH 3	C pH 5
D pH 7	E pH 9	F pH 14

Identify the pH value of a solution which
a) has [OH$^-$] = 10^{-9} mol l^{-1}
b) has [H$^+$] = [OH$^-$]
c) is made by mixing 50 cm^3 of 4 mol l^{-1} HCl and 50 cm^3 of 2 mol l^{-1} NaOH.

19 The grid lists various solutions of salts in water.

A Potassium nitrate	B Sodium ethanoate	C Ammonium sulphate
D Lithium chloride	E Sodium sulphate	F Potassium carbonate

a) Identify the solution(s) in which [OH$^-$] > [H$^+$].
b) Identify the solution(s) in which [H$^+$] > [OH$^-$].

20 A pupil compared two solutions of acids, obtaining the following results.

	0.1 mol l^{-1} Nitric acid	0.1 mol l^{-1} Propanoic acid
Conductivity/ mA	85	15
pH	1.5	3.5

a) What result **should** have been obtained when the pH of nitric acid was tested?
b) The results show that propanoic acid is a weak acid.
   Explain what is meant by the term '*weak acid*'.
c) Excess sodium carbonate powder was added to 20 cm^3 of each acid in separate beakers.
   i) How would the rate of the two reactions compare?
   ii) When both reactions have finished, how would the total volumes of gas produced compare?

21 Two salts can be prepared when sulphurous acid reacts with sodium hydroxide solution. These salts are called sodium sulphite and sodium hydrogensulphite. Sodium sulphite dissolves in water to form an alkaline solution.

a) Write the formulae of i) sulphurous acid ii) sodium hydrogensulphite.
b) Explain clearly why sodium sulphite solution is alkaline.
c) Sodium hydrogensulphite is also soluble in water. Suggest how the pH of this solution will compare with that of sodium sulphite solution.

Redox Reactions

Oxidising and reducing agents

○ Reactions in which reduction and oxidation occur are called **redox** reactions. In a redox reaction electron transfer occurs between the reactants. One reactant is reduced while the other is oxidised.

Table 1 summarises important definitions and gives examples of ion-electron equations.

A reducing agent	An oxidising agent
loses electrons and is itself **oxidised**	gains electrons and is itself **reduced**
e.g. $Zn \rightarrow Zn^{2+} + 2e^-$	e.g. $Ag^+ + e^- \rightarrow Ag$
OXIDATION **IS** **LOSS** of electrons	**REDUCTION** **IS** **GAIN** of electrons

Table 1

Displacement reactions

○ In **displacement** reactions one metal displaces another metal from a solution of its salt. The relevant ion-electron equations can be combined to produce a balanced ionic equation for the overall redox reaction.

For example, zinc displaces silver from a solution containing silver(I) ions, e.g. $AgNO_3(aq)$. Each zinc atom loses two electrons whilst each silver ion gains only one electron. The second ion-electron equation must be doubled to balance the number of electrons lost and gained to give the redox equation.

Note that the total charge on each side of the redox equation is the same and that the redox equation does not contain electrons.

Oxidation: $Zn(s) \rightarrow Zn^{2+}(aq) + 2e^-$

Reduction:

$$Ag^+(aq) + e^- \rightarrow Ag(s) \ (\times 2)$$

Redox:

$$2Ag^+(aq) + Zn(s) \rightarrow 2Ag(s) + Zn^{2+}(aq)$$

The negative ions present have not been included since they do not take part in the reaction. It is usual practice to omit **spectator ions** from redox equations.

Redox reactions involving oxyanions

○ **Oxyanions** are negative ions which contain oxygen combined with another element. Examples include sulphite ions, SO_3^{2-}, permanganate ions, MnO_4^- and dichromate ions, $Cr_2O_7^{2-}$.

The following examples of redox reactions are given to show how to write:

i) ion-electron equations which involve oxyanions

ii) balanced redox equations for more complex reactions.

(State symbols have been omitted so as not to overload the equations with information.)

Example 1

iodine solution + sodium sulphite solution
$$I_2(aq) \qquad\qquad Na_2SO_3(aq)$$
(oxidising agent)   (reducing agent)
[spectator ions: Na^+]

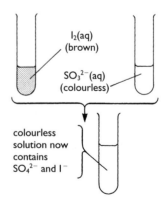

$I_2(aq)$ (brown)

$SO_3^{2-}(aq)$ (colourless)

colourless solution now contains SO_4^{2-} and I^-

Figure 1

Iodine molecules are reduced to iodide ions.

$$I_2 + 2e^- \rightarrow 2I^-$$
$$\text{brown} \qquad \text{colourless}$$

Sulphite ions are oxidised to sulphate ions.

$$SO_3^{2-} \rightarrow SO_4^{2-}$$

To complete the ion-electron equation, add H_2O to the left-hand side of the equation to obtain the oxygen atom needed and add $2H^+$ to the right-hand side to give:

$$SO_3^{2-} + H_2O \rightarrow SO_4^{2-} + 2H^+$$

Then add two electrons to the right-hand side so that the charge is the same on each side of the equation giving:

$$SO_3^{2-} + H_2O \rightarrow SO_4^{2-} + 2H^+ + 2e^-$$

The two ion-electron equations can now be combined to give the balanced redox equation:

$$I_2 + 2e^- \qquad\qquad \rightarrow 2I^-$$
$$\underline{SO_3^{2-} + H_2O \qquad \rightarrow SO_4^{2-} + 2H^+ + 2e^-}$$
$$I_2 + SO_3^{2-} + H_2O \rightarrow 2I^- + SO_4^{2-} + 2H^+$$

Example 2

Acidified potassium dichromate solution
$K_2Cr_2O_7(aq) + H^+(aq)$
(oxidising agent)

+ iron(II) sulphate solution,
$FeSO_4(aq)$
(reducing agent)

[spectator ions: K^+, SO_4^{2-}]

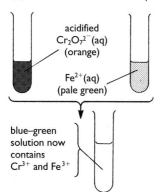

Figure 2

Iron(II) ions are oxidised to iron(III) ions.

$$Fe^{2+} \rightarrow Fe^{3+} + e^-$$

Dichromate ions are reduced to chromium(III) ions.

$$Cr_2O_7^{2-} \rightarrow 2Cr^{3+}$$
$$\text{orange} \qquad \text{blue–green}$$

The ion-electron equation can be completed in a similar way to the previous example. Only this time oxygen is being removed so that $7H_2O$ is added to the right-hand side and $14H^+$ to the left to give:

$$Cr_2O_7^{2-} + 14H^+ \rightarrow 2Cr^{3+} + 7H_2O$$

Six electrons are then added to the left-hand side to balance the charge giving:

$$Cr_2O_7^{2-} + 14H^+ + 6e^- \rightarrow 2Cr^{3+} + 7H_2O$$

This equation shows why the solution should be acidified.

The two ion-electron equations can now be combined to give the balanced redox equation. To balance the number of electrons lost and gained, the equation involving iron ions has to be multiplied by 6.

$$6Fe^{2+} \rightarrow 6Fe^{3+} + 6e^-$$
$$\underline{Cr_2O_7^{2-} + 14H^+ + 6e^- \rightarrow 2Cr^{3+} + 7H_2O}$$
$$Cr_2O_7^{2-} + 14H^+ + 6Fe^{2+} \rightarrow 2Cr^{3+} + 6Fe^{3+} + 7H_2O$$

Charges:

2–	14+	12+	6+	18+	0

$$\underline{\qquad 24+ \qquad} \qquad \underline{\qquad 24+ \qquad}$$

The total charge is the same on each side of the redox equation.

Summary

To write ion-electron equations involving oxyanions:

1 If a number of oxygen atoms have to be **added**, e.g. $SO_3^{2-} \rightarrow SO_4^{2-}$, add the same number of water molecules to the left-hand side of the equation and twice that number of hydrogen ions to the right-hand side.

OR If a number of oxygen atoms have to be **removed**, e.g. $Cr_2O_7^{2-} \rightarrow 2Cr^{3+}$, add the same number of water molecules to the right-hand side of the equation and twice that number of hydrogen ions to the left-hand side.

2 Complete the equation by adding the number of electrons needed to balance the total charge. Add the electrons to the same side of the equation as the hydrogen ions.

Using the electrochemical series

○ Most data books provide a table known as the **electrochemical series**. In this table ion-electron equations are listed as reductions i.e. each equation is written in the form:

oxidising agent + electron(s) → reducing agent

○ To use equations from this series to write a redox equation one of the equations must be reversed since an oxidising agent can only react with a reducing agent and vice versa. To decide which equation to reverse, remember that the starting materials, i.e. reactants, **must** appear on the left-hand side of the redox equation.

Example 3

Iron(III) chloride solution oxidises potassium iodide solution to form iron(II) ions and iodine. In this reaction Cl^- and K^+ are spectator ions.

The ion-electron equations obtained from the electrochemical series are:

$$I_2 + 2e^- \rightarrow 2I^-$$
$$Fe^{3+} + e^- \rightarrow Fe^{2+}$$

Since the iodide ions are oxidised the first equation must be reversed. The equation for the reduction of iron(III) ions must be doubled to balance the number of electrons transferred.

$$2I^- \rightarrow I_2 + 2e^-$$
$$2Fe^{3+} + 2e^- \rightarrow 2Fe^{2+}$$
Redox: $$2Fe^{3+} + 2I^- \rightarrow 2Fe^{2+} + I_2$$

Redox titrations

○ The concentration of a solution of a reducing agent can be determined using a solution of a suitable oxidising agent of known concentration provided that:
1 the balanced redox equation is known or can be derived from the relevant ion-electron equations
2 the volumes of the reactants are accurately measured by pipette and burette, and
3 some method of indicating the end-point of the titration is available.

Prescribed Practical Activity

To determine the mass of vitamin C in a tablet by redox titration using an iodine solution of known concentration and starch solution as indicator.

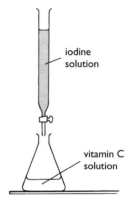

iodine solution

vitamin C solution

Figure 3

A vitamin C tablet is dissolved in deionised water (about 50 cm³) in a beaker, transferred with washings to a 250 cm³ standard flask. The flask is made up to the mark, stopped and inverted several times to ensure thorough mixing.

25 cm³ of this solution is transferred by pipette to a conical flask and a few drops of starch indicator are added. Iodine solution of known concentration is added from the burette. The iodine is decolourised at first, but the end-point is the first sign of a permanent blue-black colour. The titration is repeated, with dropwise addition of the iodine solution as the end-point is approached, to obtain concordant titres.

A specimen calculation is given in Worked Example 17.1.

○ Redox titration questions can be solved by similar calculations, if the redox equation is known, or, by using the following relationship if the separate ion-electron equations are known:

| **Concentration** × **volume** × **number of electrons** **gained per mole of** **oxidising agent** = | **Concentration** × **volume** × **no. of electrons** **lost per mole of** **reducing agent** |

Electrolysis

○ During electrolysis, **reduction occurs at the negative electrode** (or cathode).

○ Conversely **at the positive electrode** (or anode) **oxidation takes place**.

○ The total number of electrons lost and gained during electrolysis must be the same. In Table 2, the cathode reaction occurs twice as often as the anode reaction, i.e. twice as many sodium atoms as bromine molecules will be formed.

○ The quantity of electricity, i.e. quantity of electrical charge, required to produce a mole of electrode product can be found by experiment.

● Worked Example 17.1 ●

A solution of vitamin C was prepared as described above. 25 cm^3 of this solution was titrated against 0.031 mol l^{-1} iodine solution using starch indicator. The average titre was 17.6 cm^3. Calculate the mass of vitamin C (formula: $C_6H_8O_6$) in the original tablet.

The redox equation is:

$$C_6H_8O_6 \ + \ I_2 \ \rightarrow C_6H_6O_6 + 2H^+ + 2I^-$$
$$\text{1 mole} \qquad \text{1 mole}$$

Number of moles of iodine used in the titration,

$$n = C \times V = 0.031 \times \frac{17.6}{1000} = 5.456 \times 10^{-4}$$

Hence, number of moles of vitamin C in 25 cm^3 = 5.456×10^{-4}

(i.e. in the conical flask)

Number of moles of vitamin C in 250 cm^3 = 5.456×10^{-3}

(i.e. in the standard flask)

This is the number of moles of vitamin C in the original tablet.

Gram formula mass of vitamin C, $C_6H_8O_6$ = 176g

Mass of vitamin C present in the tablet = $176 \times 5.456 \times 10^{-3} = 0.960$g

	Electrolyte	Cathode reaction	Anode reaction
1	Copper(II) chloride solution $CuCl_2(aq)$	$Cu^{2+} + 2e^- \rightarrow Cu$	$2Cl^- \rightarrow Cl_2 + 2e^-$
2	Potassium iodide solution $KI(aq)$	$2H^+ + 2e^- \rightarrow H_2$	$2I^- \rightarrow I_2 + 2e^-$
3	Molten sodium bromide $NaBr(l)$	$Na^+ + e^- \rightarrow Na$	$2Br^- \rightarrow Br_2 + 2e^-$

Table 2

Prescribed Practical Activity

Dilute sulphuric acid can be electrolysed using an apparatus such as that shown in Figure 4. To determine the quantity of charge required to produced 1 mole of hydrogen the following measurements need to be made:

1 the volume of hydrogen, collected
2 the current used
3 the time during which the solution is electrolysed.

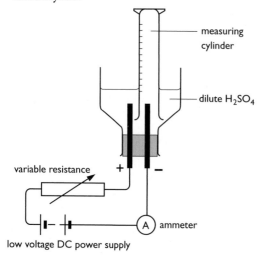

Figure 4

The quantity of electricity, **Q**, used during the experiment is calculated from the following relationship:

$$Q = I \times t,$$

where **Q** is measured in coulombs (C)
I is the current measured in amps (A), and
t is the time measured in seconds (s).

A specimen calculation is given in worked example 17.2.

Worked Example 17.2

Dilute sulphuric acid was electrolysed using a current of 0.45 A for 6 minutes 50 seconds. The volume of hydrogen collected at room temperature and pressure was 22.8 cm³. Calculate the quantity of electricity required to produce 1 mole of hydrogen.

Quantity of electricity used,
$$Q = I \times t \quad [I = 0.45 \text{ A}, t = 410 \text{ s}]$$
$$= 0.45 \times 410$$
$$= 184.5 \text{ C}$$

22.8 cm³ (i.e. 0.0228 litres) of hydrogen was produced by 184.5 C

The molar volume of a gas at room temperature and pressure is approximately 24 litres mol⁻¹.

Hence, 24 litres of hydrogen would require
$$184.5 \times \frac{24}{0.0228} = 194\,210 \text{ C}$$
$$= 1.94 \times 10^5 \text{ C}$$

An alternative to this experiment is to use an electrolyte which will deposit a metal on the negative electrode. This is cleaned and weighed before electrolysis. The time and current used during electrolysis are measured. At the end of the experiment the negative electrode is removed, rinsed, dried and reweighed to obtain the mass of metal deposited.

Table 3 below summarises the results which would be obtained with various electrolytes.

The quantity of electricity needed to produce one mole of product at the cathode is n × 96 500 C, where n is the number of electrons in the appropriate ion-electron equation. The quantity of electricity, 96 500 C,

Electrolyte	Ion-electron equation for cathode reaction	Quantity of electricity required to produce 1 mole of product
$AgNO_3(aq)$	$Ag^+ + e^- \rightarrow Ag$	96 500 C
$CuCl_2(aq)$	$Cu^{2+} + 2e^- \rightarrow Cu$	193 000 C [or 2 × 96 500 C]
$Al_2O_3(l)$	$Al^{3+} + 3e^- \rightarrow Al$	289 500 C [or 3 × 96 500 C]

is a **Faraday.** It is the quantity of electricity which is equivalent to one mole of electrons and, more precisely, has the value 96 500 C mol^{-1}.

Similar results would be obtained at the positive electrode (anode). The ion-electron equation for the reaction at the anode during the electrolysis of copper(II) chloride solution is:

$$2Cl^- \rightarrow Cl_2 + 2e^-$$

Hence, 193 000 C will be required to produce one mole of chlorine gas.

Calculations involving quantitative electrolysis

The mass of product obtained at an electrode during electrolysis can be calculated if

1 the ion-electron equation for the reaction occurring at the electrode is known, and

2 the current and time during which electrolysis occurs are both given.

◯ In other calculations the mass of product may be given so that the quantity of electricity used may be determined. Then, if the current is given, the time during which electrolysis has taken place can be calculated or *vice versa*. The following relationships should assist you.

Quantity of electricity,
in C

Current, in A Time, in s

Hence, $\mathbf{Q = I \times t}$ $\quad I = \dfrac{Q}{t}$ $\quad t = \dfrac{Q}{I}$

> ● **Worked Example 17.3** ●
>
> Molten magnesium chloride was electrolysed for 16 minutes 5 seconds using a current of 5 amps. Calculate the mass of product at each electrode.
>
> Quantity of electricity used,
> $\quad Q \;= I \times t \quad [\,I = 5\,A, t = 965\,s\,]$
> $\qquad = 5 \times 965$
> $\qquad = 4825\,C$
>
> At the **negative** electrode the product is magnesium.
>
> $\quad Mg^{2+} \;+\; 2e^- \qquad \rightarrow \qquad Mg$
> $\quad 1\,mol \quad\;\; 2\,mol$
> $\qquad\qquad 2 \times 96\,500\,C \qquad 24.3\,g$
>
> Hence, 4825 C will produce
> $\quad \dfrac{24.3}{2} \times \dfrac{4825}{96\,500}\,g = 0.61\,g$ of magnesium
>
> At the **positive** electrode the product is chlorine.
>
> $\quad 2Cl^- \rightarrow Cl_2 \;+\; 2e^-$
> $\qquad\quad\; 1\,mol \;\; 2\,mol$
> $\qquad\quad\; 71\,g \quad 2 \times 96\,500 = 193\,000\,C$
>
> Hence, 4825 C will produce
> $\quad 71 \times \dfrac{4825}{193\,000}\,g = 1.775\,g$ of chlorine

Questions

SECTION A: Redox reactions and titrations

1 Which of the following is a redox reaction?

   A $Mg + 2HCl \rightarrow MgCl_2 + H_2$

   B $KOH + HCl \rightarrow KCl + H_2O$

   C $CuO + 2HCl \rightarrow CuCl_2 + H_2O$

   D $ZnCO_3 + 2HCl \rightarrow ZnCl_2 + CO_2 + H_2O$

2 $MnO_2(s) + xH_2O(l) \rightarrow$
$$MnO_4^-(aq) + yH^+(aq) + ze^-$$
Which of the following sets of numerical values of x, y and z would balance the ion-electron equation given above?

	x	y	z
A	1	2	1
B	2	4	3
C	3	6	5
D	4	2	1

3 Copper metal can be oxidised by nitric acid. The ion-electron equations are:

$$Cu(s) \rightarrow Cu^{2+}(aq) + 2e^-$$

$$NO_3^-(aq) + 4H^+(aq) + 3e^- \rightarrow NO(g) + H_2O(l)$$

The number of moles of nitrate ions reduced by one mole of copper is

A 0.33   B 0.67   C 1.5   D 2.0

4 Which of the following is a redox reaction?

A $Pb^{2+}(aq) + 2I^-(aq) \rightarrow PbI_2(s)$

B $H^+(aq) + OH^-(aq) \rightarrow H_2O(l)$

C $Cl_2(g) + 2Br^-(aq) \rightarrow 2Cl^-(aq) + Br_2(aq)$

D $NH_3(g) + H_2O(l) \rightarrow NH_4^+(aq) + OH^-(aq)$

5 A redox reaction occurs when sodium iodide solution is added to a mixture of potassium permanganate and sulphuric acid. The grid shows the ions present in the reactants.

A $Na^+(aq)$	B $I^-(aq)$	C $K^+(aq)$
D $MnO_4^-(aq)$	E $H^+(aq)$	F $SO_4^{2-}(aq)$

a) Identify the ion which acts as a reducing agent in this reaction.
b) The ion in box **A** is a spectator ion. Identify the **two** other spectator ions.

6 Complete each of the following ion-electron equations and indicate whether the reactant is a reducing agent or an oxidising agent.
a) $Mn^{2+}(aq) \quad \rightarrow \quad MnO_2(s)$

b) $VO_3^-(aq) \quad \rightarrow \quad V^{2+}(aq)$

c) $H_2O_2(aq) \quad \rightarrow \quad O_2(g)$

d) $Ti(s) \quad \rightarrow \quad TiO^{2+}(aq)$

e) $BrO_3^-(aq) \quad \rightarrow \quad Br_2(aq)$

7 In each of the following examples,
   i)   write a balanced redox equation (with help from the SQA Data Book)
   ii) identify the spectator ion(s).
a) Bromine oxidises potassium iodide solution.
b) Iron(III) chloride solution is reduced by sodium sulphite solution.
c) Chromium metal displaces silver from silver(I) nitrate solution.
d) Potassium permanganate solution, acidified with dilute sulphuric acid, is reduced by tin(II) sulphate solution.

8 Iodine solution is decolourised by a solution containing thiosulphate ions, $S_2O_3^{2-}$. The equation for this redox reaction is:

$$I_2(aq) + 2S_2O_3^{2-}(aq) \rightarrow 2I^-(aq) + S_4O_6^{2-}(aq)$$

The following paragraph describes an experiment to find the concentration of an iodine solution using a sodium thiosulphate solution of known concentration.

20.0 cm³ of iodine solution was measured by pipette and transferred to a conical flask. 0.1 mol l⁻¹ sodium thiosulphate solution was added from a burette until the iodine had turned pale yellow. A few drops of starch indicator were added and the titration continued until the end-point was reached. The experiment was repeated twice and the three titres obtained were: 24.0 cm³, 23.4 cm³ and 23.4 cm³.

a) Work out the ion-electron equation for the reducing agent in this redox reaction.
b) What will be the colour change given by the indicator at the end-point?
c) What is the value for the average titre in the above experiment?
d) Calculate the concentration of the iodine solution.

9* For people who suffer from bronchitis, even low concentrations of ozone, O_3, irritate the lining of the throat and can cause headaches. NO_2 gas from car exhausts reacts with oxygen to form ozone as follows.

$$O_2(g) + NO_2(g) \rightleftharpoons NO(g) + O_3(g)$$

Car exhaust fumes also contain volatile organic compounds (VOCs), which can combine with NO gas.

a) Explain how a rise in VOC concentration will change the ozone concentration.

b) In an experiment to measure the ozone concentration of air in a Scottish city, 10^5 litres of air were bubbled through a solution of potassium iodide. Ozone reacts with potassium iodide solution, releasing iodine.

$$2KI(aq) + O_3(g) + H_2O(l) \rightarrow$$
$$I_2(aq) + O_2(g) + 2KOH(aq)$$

The iodine formed was titrated with $0.01 \text{ mol } l^{-1}$ sodium thiosulphate solution, $Na_2S_2O_3(aq)$, using starch indicator.

$$I_2(aq) + 2S_2O_3^{2-}(aq) \rightarrow 2I^-(aq) + S_4O_6^{2-}(aq)$$

The results of three titrations are shown in the table.

Experiment	Volume of thiosulphate/cm³
1	22.90
2	22.40
3	22.50

i) What colour change would show that the titration was complete?

ii) Why was the volume of sodium thiosulphate to be used in the calculation taken to be 22.45 cm³ although this is **not** the average of the three titres in the table?

iii) Taking the volume of sodium thiosulphate solution to be 22.45 cm³, calculate the volume of ozone in **one litre** of air. (Take the molar volume of ozone to be 24 litres mol⁻¹.)

10* The purity of iron(II) salts can be found by titration with acidified potassium permanganate solution.

Equations:

$$Fe^{2+}(aq) \rightarrow Fe^{3+}(aq) + e$$
$$MnO_4^-(aq) + 8H^+(aq) + 5e \rightarrow$$
$$Mn^{2+}(aq) + 4H_2O(l)$$

a) This reaction can be described as self-indicating. How can the end-point be detected?

b) A pupil was given 1.55 g of impure iron(II) sulphate, $FeSO_4.7H_2O$, and used this to prepare 250 cm³ of solution for the titration.
It was found that 9.5 cm³ of 0.01mol l⁻¹ acidified potassium permanganate solution was required to oxidise 25 cm³ of the iron(II) sulphate solution.

i) Use this information to show that the 250 cm³ solution contained 4.75×10^{-3} mol of iron(II) sulphate.

ii) The percentage purity of a salt can be found from the relationship:

$$\text{Percentage purity} = \frac{\text{mass of pure salt}}{\text{mass of impure salt}} \times 100$$

Calculate the mass of pure iron(II) sulphate and thus find the percentage purity of the iron(II) sulphate salt.

SECTION B: Quantitative electrolysis

1* The reduction of zinc ions during electroplating can be represented as:

$$Zn^{2+}(aq) + 2e \rightarrow Zn(s)$$

What is the quantity of electricity needed to produce 0.25 mol of zinc?

A   24 125 C   B   48 250 C
C   96 500 C   D   193 000 C

2* If a steady current of 0.4 A is passed through silver nitrate solution, concentration 1 mol l⁻¹ for 40 minutes, what amount of silver will be liberated?

A   0.001 mol   B   0.01 mol
C   0.1 mol   D   1.0 mol

3* If 96 500 C of electricity are passed through separate solutions of copper(II) chloride and nickel(II) chloride, then

A equal masses of copper and nickel will be deposited

B the same number of atoms of each metal will be deposited

C the metals will be plated on the positive electrode

D different numbers of moles of each metal will be deposited.

4 Which of the following combinations of current and time would produce 900 coulombs?

A 4 amps for 450 seconds
B 0.2 amps for 1 hour
C 0.5 amps for 30 minutes
D 2 amps for 10 minutes

5 What volume of hydrogen, in litres, would be released at room temperature and pressure if 20 000 C of electrical charge is passed through dilute hydrochloric acid?
($V_{mol} = 24$ litres mol^{-1})

A 231.6   B 25.0   C 5.0   D 2.5

6 A solution of chromium(III) sulphate is electrolysed using chromium electrodes. The passage of 96 500 C results in

A the negative electrode gaining 17.3 g
B the positive electrode gaining 17.3 g
C the negative electrode gaining 34.7 g
D the positive electrode gaining 34.7 g

7 The grid shows equations relating to changes which can occur during electrolysis.

A	$2H^+ + 2e^- \rightarrow H_2$
B	$2Br^- \rightarrow Br_2 + 2e^-$
C	$4OH^- \rightarrow O_2 + H_2O + 4e^-$
D	$Al^{3+} + 3e^- \rightarrow Al$
E	$Na^+ + e^- \rightarrow Na$
F	$Ni^{2+} + 2e^- \rightarrow Ni$

a) Identify the **two** equations in which 1 mole of ions would **not** be discharged by 96 500 C.

b) Identify the equation in which 1 mole of an element is produced by 386 000 C.

c) Identify the **two** equations representing reactions which would **not** occur during electrolysis of aqueous solutions.

8 A current of 4 A was passed for 965 seconds through 100 cm^3 of 2 mol l^{-1} copper(II) chloride solution using carbon electrodes. Identify the true statement(s) about this experiment.

A	Copper ions are reduced at the positive electrode.
B	1.27 g of copper metal is produced.
C	The electrolyte is colourless at the end of the experiment.
D	0.04 mol of chlorine gas is produced.
E	Chloride ions are oxidised at the positive elctrode.

9 Use relevant ion-electron equations from the SQA Data Book when answering the following questions.

a) Calculate the length of time required to plate a metal spoon with 0.2 g of silver when a current of 1.5 A is passed through silver(I) nitrate.

b) From the data given below calculate the current used when nickel-plating a sheet of metal. The plating solution contains nickel(II) ions.

Mass of metal sheet before plating = 198.76 g
Mass of metal sheet after plating = 200.30 g
Time taken for plating = 20 minutes

c) Calculate the mass of aluminium, in kg, produced per hour when a current of 175 000 A is passed through molten aluminium oxide.

10* Gases are produced by the electrolysis of Na_2SO_4(aq).

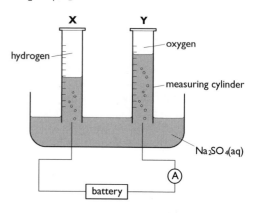

The ion-electron equations are shown.

Electrode **X**:

$$2H_2O(l) + 2e^- \rightarrow H_2(g) + 2OH^-(aq)$$

Electrode **Y**:

$$H_2O(l) \rightarrow \tfrac{1}{2}O_2(g) + 2H^+(aq) + 2e^-$$

a) Explain what happens to the pH at each electrode.
b) A current of 2 A was passed through the apparatus for 5 min and 20 s. Calculate the volume of hydrogen gas produced.
(Take the molar volume of hydrogen gas to be 24 litres mol^{-1}.)

11 In an experiment to determine the Avogadro Constant (L) by quantitative electrolysis, a steady current of 0.26 A was passed through dilute sulphuric acid, using platinum electrodes, for 15 minutes. The volume of hydrogen produced was 29.1 cm^3. The equation for the production of hydrogen is:

$$2H^+(aq) + 2e^- \rightarrow H_2(g)$$

a) Use the information given above to calculate the quantity of electric charge
  i) needed to produce 1 mole of hydrogen gas ($V_{mol} = 24$ litres mol^{-1})
  ii) equivalent to 1 mole of electrons.
b) To obtain a value for L, the charge on 1 electron is required. This is obtained by a different experiment and its value is 1.6×10^{-19} C.
Calculate L using this value and your answer to **a) ii)** above.

12

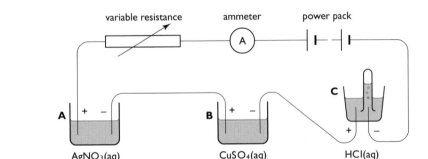

In an experiment using the apparatus shown above, 0.125 g of silver was produced in cell **A**. In answering the following questions about this experiment you should assume that
  i) the same quantity of electric charge is passed through all three cells, and
  ii) the electrodes are inert, i.e. they do not react with the electrode products.
a) With reference to the SQA Data Book, calculate
  i) the quantity of electric charge passed through each cell
  ii) the mass of copper produced in cell **B**
  iii) the volume of hydrogen produced in cell **C** ($V_{mol} = 24$ litres mol^{-1}).
b) Both hydrogen and chlorine are produced in cell **C**.
  i) Explain why the volume of each gas should be the same.
  ii) In the experiment, much less chlorine is obtained than hydrogen. Suggest a reason for this.
c) In cells **A** and **B**, the product at the positive electrode is oxygen. The relevant ion-electron equation is:

$$2H_2O(l) \rightarrow O_2(g) + 4H^+(aq) + 4e^-$$

  i) Calculate the volume of oxygen which should be produced in each cell in this experiment.
  ii) What effect, if any, does electrolysis have on the pH of the solutions in cells **A** and **B**?

13* In the Downs Process, sodium is extracted from sodium chloride (melting point 801°C) by electrolysis.

a) Suggest why calcium chloride is added to the electrolyte.

b) Is the Downs Process a batch or continuous process?
Explain your answer with reference to the diagram.

c) i) In which state of matter is the sodium collected?

ii) Explain how you arrived at your answer.

d) Write ion-electron equations for the reactions occurring during electrolysis at
i) the positive electrode
ii) the negative electrode.

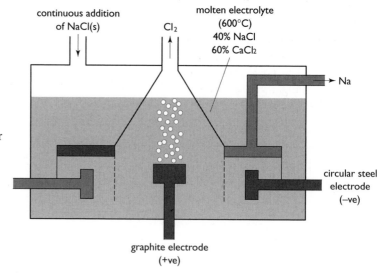

continuous addition of NaCl(s)

Cl$_2$

molten electrolyte (600°C)
40% NaCl
60% CaCl$_2$

Na

circular steel electrode (−ve)

graphite electrode (+ve)

e) In a Downs cell, a current of 20 000 A produced 16.5 kg of sodium per hour. Calculate
i) the theoretical yield of sodium
ii) the percentage yield of sodium.

(18) Nuclear chemistry

○ Radioactive elements continue to display activity in their compounds, therefore radioactivity is unaffected by changes in electron arrangement and must originate in the nucleus of atoms.

○ The stability of nuclei depends on the ratio of neutrons to protons (Figure 1).

○ Radioactive emissions change the neutron to proton ratio and at the same time release energy.

○ Radioactive emissions can be shown to be of three types by their behaviour in an electrical field:

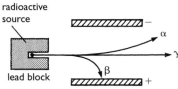

Figure 2 Radiation deflected by an electric field between charged plates

Other experiments provide the information given in Table 1.

○ Loss of an α particle causes a loss of 2 units of charge and 4 units of mass.

e.g. $^{238}_{92}U \rightarrow {}^{234}_{90}Th + {}^{4}_{2}He$

○ A β particle is an electron. It is believed to be formed by:

$$^{1}_{0}n \quad \rightarrow {}^{1}_{1}p \quad + \quad {}^{0}_{-1}e$$

neutron   proton   electron

○ Loss of a β particle causes a **gain** of 1 unit of charge and no change in mass.

e.g. $^{234}_{90}Th \rightarrow {}^{234}_{91}Pa + {}^{0}_{-1}e$

○ Radioactive isotopes can be created by bombarding stable isotopes with fast moving particles, usually neutrons, which are not repelled by the positively charged nucleus.

e.g. $^{27}_{13}Al + {}^{1}_{0}n \rightarrow {}^{24}_{11}Na + {}^{4}_{2}He$

Name	Penetration	Nature	Symbol	Charge	Mass
α (alpha)	few cm in air	He nucleus	$^{4}_{2}He$	2+	4
β (beta)	thin metal foil	electron	$^{0}_{-1}e$	1-	$\frac{1}{2000}$
γ (gamma)	great thickness of concrete	EMR	none	none	none

Table 1

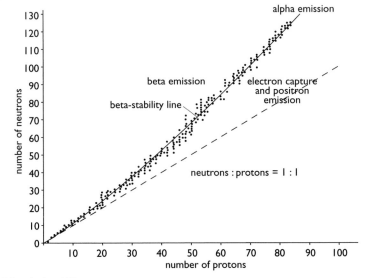

Figure 1 Band of stability

The sodium isotope produced then decays by β emission:

$$^{24}_{11}Na \rightarrow {}^{24}_{12}Mg + {}^{0}_{-1}e$$

○ In all nuclear equations, note that on each side of the equations, the sum of the mass numbers (at the top of the symbols) must be the same, and similarly the sum of the atomic numbers (below the symbols) must be the same.

○ The half-life of a radioisotope is the time taken for the mass, or activity, of the isotope to halve by radioactive decay. The half-life, $t_{1/2}$, is characteristic of the isotope.

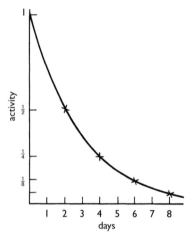

Figure 3 Change in activity with time for an isotope of half-life 2 days

○ The half-life of any isotope is independent of the mass of the sample being investigated. It is independent of temperature, pressure, concentration, presence of catalysts or chemical state of the isotope. In the half-life, half of the atoms of the isotopes decay but the process is completely random and it is not possible to predict the time of decay of any individual atom.

○ After 'n' half-lives, the fraction of the original activity which remains is given by $(1/2)^n$.

○ The quantity of radioisotope, the half-life or time elapsed can be calculated, given the other two variables.

Worked Example 18.1

Rhodium-106 has a half life of 30 seconds. What fraction of a sample's activity will remain after 3 minutes?

$t_{1/2} = 30$ seconds, so 3 minutes
$= 180$ seconds $= 6\ t_{1/2}$

Fraction of activity remaining $= (\frac{1}{2})^6 = \frac{1}{64}$

Worked Example 18.2

An archaeological sample shows a $^{14}_{6}C:^{12}_{6}C$ ratio only $\frac{1}{8}$ of that expected in a modern sample. If the half-life of $^{14}_{6}C$ is 5600 years, calculate an approximate age for the archaeological sample.

Fraction of activity remaining $= \frac{1}{8} = (\frac{1}{2})^3$

Therefore the sample has decayed through 3 half-lives i.e. 3×5600 years.

The archaeological sample is approximately 16 800 years old.

Uses of radioisotopes

Radioisotopes in medicine

The γ emitter $^{60}_{27}Co$ is used to treat deep-seated tumours.

The β emitter $^{32}_{15}P$ is used to treat skin cancer.

The short half-life β emitter $^{131}_{53}I$ is used to assess the condition of the thyroid gland which absorbs iodine. A scan shows the concentration of iodine throughout the gland.

Radioisotopes in industry

The γ emitter $^{60}_{27}Co$ is used to check the condition of welds in steel and to irradiate food to kill bacteria and fungi, so increasing 'shelf-life'.

The α emitter $^{241}_{95}Am$ is used in domestic smoke alarms.

Radioisotopes in scientific research

$^{32}_{15}P$ can be used to trace the uptake of phosphate fertilisers by plants.

$^{14}_{6}C$ with a half-life of 5600 years can be used to date archaeological specimens with an origin in living material. In living material the ratio $^{14}_{6}C : ^{12}_{6}C$ is constant. After death, the ratio decreases at a rate determined by the $t_{1/2}$ of $^{14}_{6}C$. If the present ratio is measured the approximate age of the specimen can be determined.

Radioisotopes in energy production by nuclear fission

When impact by relatively slowly moving neutrons occurs on the nucleus of $^{235}_{92}U$, the nucleus splits, or **fissions**, producing smaller nuclei and more neutrons. These neutrons can, when there is more than a critical mass of uranium, go on to split more nuclei and a self-sustaining chain reaction results. The total mass of the products of fission is slightly less than the mass of the starting materials. This mass defect is converted into a large amount of energy. An example of a fission reaction is:

$$^{235}_{92}U + ^{1}_{0}n \rightarrow ^{236}_{92}U \rightarrow ^{140}_{54}Xe + ^{94}_{38}Sr + 2^{1}_{0}n$$

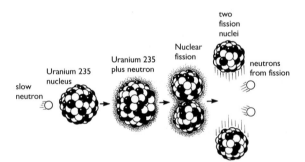

two fission nuclei

Nuclear fission

Uranium 235 plus neutron

neutrons from fission

Uranium 235 nucleus

slow neutron

Figure 4 Uranium fission

Radioisotopes in energy production by nuclear fusion

If small nuclei can be induced to **fuse** together, e.g.

$$^{2}_{1}H + ^{3}_{1}H \rightarrow ^{4}_{2}He + ^{1}_{0}n$$

then mass is 'lost' and converted into energy. So far the process has only been carried out on a large scale in a hydrogen bomb, but several major research programmes are attempting to generate energy by peaceful means by fusion.

The origin of the elements

○ In space there are large quantities of hydrogen and in the interstellar clouds this is concentrated so that fusion occurs.

e.g.
$$^{1}_{1}H + ^{2}_{1}H \rightarrow ^{3}_{2}He$$
$$^{2}_{1}H + ^{3}_{1}H \rightarrow ^{4}_{2}He + ^{1}_{0}n$$

○ The matter coalesces into stars, the energy produced by fusion initiates more fusion.

e.g.
$$3^{4}_{2}He \rightarrow ^{12}_{6}C$$
$$^{12}_{6}C + ^{4}_{2}He \rightarrow ^{16}_{8}O$$

○ By processes such as these, all the elements have been produced, essentially from hydrogen.

Advantages of nuclear power
No 'greenhouse' gases emitted
No SO_2 emitted to increase 'acid rain'
Fewer deaths and injuries in uranium mining than in coal mining
Fuel reserves will last longer than fossil fuel reserves
Power stations have less visual impact than coal or oil-fired stations or wind farms
Alternative source of energy for countries with no fossil or renewable energy sources

Disadvantages of nuclear power
Finite (but low) probability of a disastrous accident
Contribution to 'background' radiation
Difficulty of disposing of spent fuel which remains radioactive for many years
Capital cost of plant
Cost of decommissioning obsolete stations
Stations slow to respond to rapid changes in demand for power, conventional stations faster
Plutonium can be produced, possibly leading to proliferation of nuclear weapons

Questions

1* β-particles emitted by certain radioactive atoms are

   A electrons from the outer shell
   B electrons from the nucleus
   C particles consisting of 2 protons and 2 neutrons
   D electromagnetic radiations of very short wavelength.

2 A radioactive isotope of a halogen emits a β-particle. The product will be an isotope of an element in

   A Group 6   B Group 7
   C Group 0   D Group 1

3* Which particle will be formed when an atom of $^{211}_{83}Bi$ loses an α-particle and the decay product then loses a β-particle?

   A $^{210}_{79}Au$ B $^{209}_{80}Hg$

   C $^{208}_{81}Tl$ D $^{207}_{82}Pb$

4* The stability of the nucleus of an ion depends on the ratio of

   A mass : charge
   B neutrons : protons
   C neutrons : electrons
   D protons : electrons.

Questions 5 and **6** refer to the following section of a natural radioactive series.

$$^{w}X \xrightarrow{\alpha} \, ^{223}Fr \xrightarrow{\beta} \, ^{y}Z$$

5 Which of the following isotopes is ^{w}X?

   A ^{225}Ac B ^{223}Rn
   C ^{227}Pa D ^{227}Ac

6 Which of the following isotopes is ^{y}Z?

   A ^{223}Ra B ^{223}Rn
   C ^{219}At D ^{224}Ra

7 $^{238}_{92}U$ can absorb an α-particle with the emission of a neutron. What is the product of this reaction?

   A $^{241}_{93}Np$ B $^{239}_{94}Pu$
   C $^{241}_{94}Pu$ D $^{242}_{95}Am$

8* When some zinc pellets containing radioactive zinc are placed in a solution of zinc chloride, radioactivity soon appears in the solution. Compared with that of the pellets, the half-life of the radioactive solution will be

   A shorter
   B the same
   C longer
   D dependent upon how long the zinc is in contact with the solution.

9* Which of the following has an electrical charge?

   A α-particles   B X-rays
   C Neutrons   D γ-rays

10 Several isotopes of polonium appear in the two radioactive decay series on page 8 of the SQA Data Book. The mass number of the isotope of polonium with the shortest half-life is

   A 218   B 216
   C 214   D 212

11 ^{220}Rn has a half-life of 55 s. What fraction of the original number of ^{220}Rn atoms will remain after 5.5 minutes?

   A $\frac{1}{4}$ B $\frac{1}{6}$ C $\frac{1}{16}$ D $\frac{1}{64}$

12 The grid lists various outcomes for nuclear changes.

A	The atomic number increases and the mass number decreases.
B	The atomic number increases and the mass number does not change.
C	The atomic number does not change and the mass number decreases.
D	The atomic number decreases and the mass number decreases.
E	The atomic number decreases and the mass number does not change.
F	Neither the atomic number nor the mass number change.

Identify the sentence which describes what happens to an isotope when it emits
a) alpha particles
b) beta particles
c) gamma rays.

13* Nuclear transformations involve different processes.

A	alpha emission
B	beta emission
C	neutron capture
D	proton capture
E	nuclear fusion
F	nuclear fission

Identify the process taking place in each of the transformations.

a) $^{23}_{11}Na + x \rightarrow ^{24}_{11}Na$

b) $^{2}_{1}H + ^{3}_{1}H \rightarrow ^{4}_{2}He + y$

14 The following sequence shows part of a radioactive series.

$$^{235}_{92}U \xrightarrow{\beta} Q \xrightarrow{\beta} R \xrightarrow{\alpha} X \xrightarrow{\alpha} Z$$

Identify the true statement(s).

A	**Q** and **Z** are isotopes of the same element.
B	**R** has a mass number of 235.
C	Atoms of **X** have 141 neutrons.
D	**Z** is an isotope of radium.
E	Atoms of **Q** have 91 protons.
F	**X** is an isotope of uranium.

15 The following diagram shows how mass number and atomic number alters during a radioactive series.

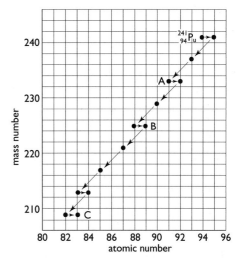

a) Write the nuclide notation for isotopes A, B and C.

b) How many **i)** α particles **ii)** β particles, are released **in total** in the series?

c) Draw a similar diagram to represent the first 6 stages of the Thorium Series given in Table 2 on page 8 of the SQA Data Book.

d) The series shown above is sometimes described as the '4n + 1 Series', while the Thorium Series is denoted the '4n Series' where 'n' is an integer. These designations are related to the mass numbers of the isotopes present in the series.
What designation should be given to the Plutonium-Uranium Series shown in Table 1 on page 8 of the SQA Data Book?

16 a) Write the appropriate symbol of the particle produced when
   i) ^{210}At loses an α particle
   ii) an astatine atom gains an electron in its outer shell.

b) Suggest why the mass number is specified in **a) i)** but not in **a) ii)**.

17 Nuclear changes which are used to produce radioactive isotopes can be summarised as follows:

$$T(x,y)P$$

when: T = target nucleus,
      P = product nucleus,
      x = bombarding particle
      y = ejected particle.

For example, the nuclear equation:

$$^{14}_{7}N + ^{4}_{2}He \rightarrow ^{17}_{8}O + ^{1}_{1}p$$

can be summarised: $^{14}_{7}N(\alpha,p)^{17}_{8}O.$

a) Write the nuclear equation for the change: $^{27}_{13}Al(n,\alpha)^{24}_{11}Na.$

b) Write the summarised form of the following nuclear equation.

$$^{32}_{16}S + ^{1}_{0}n \rightarrow ^{32}_{15}P + ^{1}_{1}p$$

18 For each of the following pairs, indicate whether or not the quantities would have
    i)   the same half-life
    ii) the same intensity of radiation.

a) 0.1 g of ^{214}Pb and 1 g of ^{214}Pb

b) 0.1 g of ^{214}Pb and 0.1 g of $^{214}PbCl_2$

c) 0.1 mol of ^{210}Pb and 0.1 mol of ^{214}Pb

d) 0.1 mol of ^{210}Pb and 0.1 mol of $^{210}PbCl_2$

19 The following paragraph describes the discovery of a new element, atomic number 111, by an international team of research scientists at the GSI heavy-ion cyclotron at Darmstadt in Germany.

'*Last month, the team detected three atoms of element 111 when they bombarded bismuth-209 with billions of atoms of nickel. The atoms had an atomic mass of 272 and decayed into two previous unknown isotopes of elements 109 and 107.*'

(from *New Scientist*, 7 Jan 1995)

(Take 'atomic mass' to mean mass number.)

a) What type of nuclear process is described in the first sentence of the paragraph?
b) What type of radiation is suggested by the information in the second sentence?
c) Predict the mass numbers of '*the previous unknown isotopes of elements 109 and 107*'.

20* Many granite rocks contain radioactive elements which decay to release radon gas. The gas is an alpha-emitter with a half-life of 55 s and contributes to background radiation.

a) Give another source of background radiation.
b) Write a balanced nuclear equation for the alpha-decay of radon-220.
c) A sample of radon had a count rate of 80 counts min⁻¹. How long would it take for the count rate to fall to 5 counts min⁻¹?
d) What effect would a temperature rise of 20°C have on the half-life of radon-220?

21* An 8 g sample of $^{24}_{11}Na$ undergoes β-decay to form a stable product as shown in the graph below:

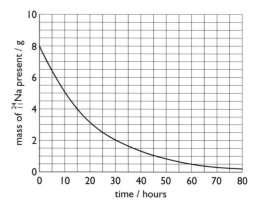

a) Write a nuclear equation for the decay of $^{24}_{11}Na.$

b) From the graph, what is the half-life of $^{24}_{11}Na?$

c) What mass of **product** would be formed from the sample after 45 hours?

22* Complete the following nuclear equations and identify **X** and **Y**.

a) $^{238}_{92}U + ^{4}_{2}He \rightarrow ^{239}_{94}Pu + 3X$

b) $^{6}_{3}Li + ^{1}_{0}n \rightarrow ^{4}_{2}He + Y$

23* The Avogadro constant (L) may be estimated in a number of ways, one of which is described below.
When a radioactive substance emits α particles, helium gas is formed by the reaction:

$$^{4}_{2}He^{2+} + 2e^{-} \rightarrow ^{4}_{2}He(g)$$

A Geiger counter is used to count the number of α particles emitted and, over a period of time, the volume of helium collected is measured. In an actual experiment, a sample of radium-226 emitted 4.4×10^{10} α particles **per second** over a period of 24 hours. The total volume of helium collected (at room temperature and pressure) was 1.50×10^{-4} cm³. (V_{mol} = 24 litres mol⁻¹.)

a) Write a nuclear equation for the radioactive decay of radium-226.
b) Use the SQA Data Book to find the value for the half-life of the radioactive **product** obtained in a).
c) How many α particles were emitted during the 24 hour period?

d) How many moles of helium are present in 1.50×10^{-4} cm^3 of the gas?

e) Use your answers to **c)** and **d)** to calculate L.

24 Fortified wine is made by adding brandy (distilled wine) to ordinary wine of the same age in order to increase the alcohol content. In a wine scandal some years ago, wine was suspected of having been fortified with ethanol made by hydrating ethene obtained from natural gas. The fraud was confirmed recently by radioactive dating techniques, using

i) $^{14}_{6}$C, half-life $= 5600$ years

ii) $^{3}_{1}$H, half-life $= 12.5$ years.

The carbon content of any fossil fuel does not include $^{14}_{6}$C.

Hydrogen-3 is present at a certain concentration in all 'new' supplies of water, including those used to make wine.

a) If the **apparent** age of the wine given by carbon-14 dating is approximately 5600 years, by what factor had the concentration of alcohol been increased by the synthesised ethanol? Explain your answer.

b) If the alcohol is distilled off from a sample of the wine, the water remaining has a $^{3}_{1}$H activity one-quarter that of fresh rainwater. How long ago was the alcohol bottled?

25 Torness Nuclear Power Station

Refer to the sketch map on page 90.
a) Suggest a reason why a relatively remote site was chosen for the power station.
b) Why are nuclear stations in the UK usually sited on the coast?
c) What other features of the surrounding area might have been useful during construction of the power station?

1 The effect of changing concentration on the rate of a reaction can be investigated using a 'clock reaction' involving aqueous solutions of hydrogen peroxide and potassium iodide.

25 cm³ of KI(aq) is mixed with sodium thiosulphate solution, dilute sulphuric acid and starch solution. A few cm³ of H_2O_2(aq) are added and the time taken for the reaction to occur is measured. The rate of reaction was obtained by calculating the reciprocal of time. The experiment is repeated four times using smaller volumes of KI(aq) but with water added, e.g. 20 cm³ KI(aq) + 5 cm³ H_2O; 15 cm³ KI(aq) + 10 cm³ H_2O etc.

The graph shows typical results from this experiment.

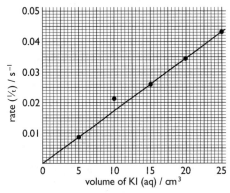

a) What variables should be kept constant for a fair comparison?
b) The method of dilution of KI(aq) described above ensures that the total volume is kept constant. Why is this important in this experiment?
c) Use information from the graph to calculate the reaction time when 20 cm³ of KI(aq) was used.
d) One of the results shown on the graph appears to be wrong.
   i) What should have been the rate for this volume of KI(aq)?
   ii) Apart from errors in timing suggest how this wrong result may have occurred.
e) What conclusion can be drawn regarding the rate of this reaction from the results shown on the graph?

2 The effect of temperature change on the rate of a reaction can be studied in the following experiment.

Potassium permanganate solution, which has been acidified with dilute sulphuric acid, is heated to about 40°C. A few cm³ of oxalic acid solution is added and the time for the reaction to reach completion is measured. The temperature is also noted. The experiment is repeated three times at higher temperatures. The table below shows typical results.

Temperature/ °C	Reaction time (t)/s	Rate ($1/t$)/s⁻¹
42	62.5	0.016
49	35.7	**X**
58	**Y**	0.052
66	11.0	0.091

a) What colour change occurs at the end-point of the reaction?
b) What variables should be kept constant in this experiment?
c) Calculate the values of **X** and **Y** to complete the table of results.
d) Draw a line graph of rate against temperature using the above data.
e) Use the graph to find
   i) the rate of reaction at 55°C
   ii) the temperature at which the rate is twice this value.

3* A page of a pupil's notebook shows instructions on how to measure the enthalpy of combustion of an alcohol.

Experimental procedure

1. Measure out 100 cm³ of water into a beaker.

2. Take steps to insulate the apparatus.

3. Read the water temperature before and after using the alcohol burner to heat it.

4. Weigh the alcohol burner before and after the experiment.

a) Draw a neat labelled diagram of the apparatus which the pupil could use to carry out this experiment.

b) Write the equation corresponding to the enthalpy of combustion of methanol.

c) The pupil found that when 0.23 g of methanol burned, the heat produced raised the temperature of 100 g of water by 9.2°C.

Using information in the SQA Data Book, calculate the enthalpy of combustion of methanol.

d) The pupil's result is well below the value in the SQA Data Book. Even with insulation, much heat is lost to the surroundings, including the apparatus. Suggest one **other** reason why the experimental result is low.

4 **P** and **Q** are carbonyl compounds which can be distinguished by using various reagents.

Test tube **1** contains a few drops of **P** added to acidified $K_2Cr_2O_7(aq)$.
Test tube **2** contains a few drops of **Q** added to $AgNO_3(aq)$ containing $NH_3(aq)$.
Water is heated as shown in the diagram until the temperature reaches about 60 °C. Test tubes **1** and **2** are placed in the hot water for several minutes.

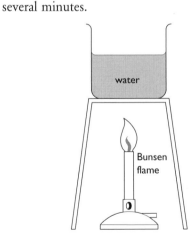

a) What precaution should be taken **before** putting the test tubes in the water?

b) In test tube **1** no colour change was observed.
What type of carbonyl compound is **P**?

c) In test tube **2** a silver 'mirror' is formed.
   i) Write an ion-electron equation to explain the formation of the 'mirror'.
   ii) What type of carbonyl compound is **Q**?

d) Supply the words which are missing from the following paragraph.

When $CH_3CH_2CH_2CHO$ reacts with acidified $K_2Cr_2O_7(aq)$, the solution changes colour from _____ to _____. The reaction produces a carbon compound called _____ .

e) Another reagent can be used to distinguish **P** and **Q**. This reagent is a blue solution which gives an orange–red precipitate with **Q**, but does not react with **P**.
   i) Name this reagent.
   ii) Name the orange–red precipitate and give its formula.

5 The diagram illustrates one way of preparing an ester.

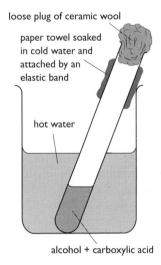

loose plug of ceramic wool

paper towel soaked in cold water and attached by an elastic band

hot water

alcohol + carboxylic acid

a) What other chemical should be present in the test tube?

b) What is the purpose of the 'paper towel soaked in cold water'?

c) After heating as shown above for several minutes, the contents of the test tube are poured into a beaker containing $NaHCO_3(aq)$.
   i) Apart from its smell, how can you tell that an ester has been formed?
   ii) Bubbles are also seen in the solution. Why does this happen?

d) An ester was prepared from methanoic acid and butan-1-ol. Write an equation showing full structural formulae for this reaction.

6

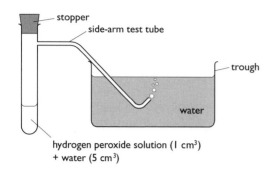

hydrogen peroxide solution (1 cm³)
+ water (5 cm³)

The diagram shows part of an apparatus which can be used when investigating the effect of temperature and pH on catalase, an enzyme which catalyses the decomposition of hydrogen peroxide solution.

a) What can be added to the test tube as the source of catalase?

b) What other pieces of equipment are needed when investigating the effect of temperature on catalase?

c) What observation enables you to judge how changing the temperature affects the catalase in this experiment?

d) It is said that an enzyme operates most effectively at an optimum temperature. How do the results of this experiment illustrate the concept of 'optimum temperature'?

e) How would the experiment be adapted to investigate the effect of pH on the ability of catalase to decompose hydrogen peroxide?

f) How would you ensure that a fair comparison was being made when altering the pH in this investigation?

7 A group of S5 pupils carried out a series of experiments to illustrate Hess's Law.

a) One pupil added 0.02 mol of KOH(s) to 50 cm³ of water in a polystyrene cup. She measured the temperature change and calculated the enthalpy change to be −52.25 kJ mol⁻¹ of KOH.

   i) Name the enthalpy change which has been obtained.

   ii) Why was a polystyrene cup used in the experiment?

   iii) Calculate the temperature rise in this experiment.

b) Another pupil carried out an experiment to determine the enthalpy of neutralisation of KOH(aq) by HCl(aq) by mixing 20 cm³ of 1.0 mol l⁻¹ KOH and 20 cm³ of 1.0 mol l⁻¹ HCl.
He obtained the following data.

Initial temperature of the alkali = 21.2 °C
Initial temperature of the acid = 20.8 °C
Highest temperature of the mixture = 27.4 °C

Calculate the enthalpy of neutralisation of KOH(aq) by HCl(aq).

c) i) Outline the experiment which a third pupil should carry out if the group are to verify Hess's Law.

   ii) Write the equation, including physical states, for this reaction.

   iii) What would be the enthalpy of this reaction if the group's results verify Hess's Law?

8

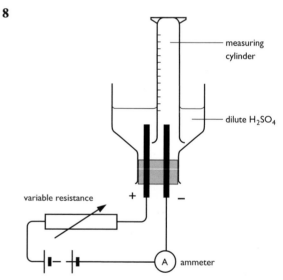

low voltage DC power supply

A prescribed practical activity was carried out using the apparatus shown above.

a) Supply the missing words in the following sentence.

The aim of this experiment is to determine the quantity of electric charge required to produce _____ by electrolysis of dilute sulphuric acid.

b) What measurements, with units, are made in the experiment to enable the quantity of electric charge to be calculated?

c) Write the ion-electron equation for the reaction occurring at the negative electrode.

d) The volume of hydrogen that is collected is measured.
What other information about hydrogen is needed to complete the calculation?

e) Some pupils obtained a result of 188 000 C from this experiment.
What is the expected result?

9 To find the mass of vitamin C in a tablet, a solution (volume: 250 cm^3) is firstly prepared and then titrated with an iodine solution of known concentration.

a) Describe in detail how the vitamin C solution is prepared.

b) Supply the words missing from the following paragraph which describes the titration.

25.0 cm^3 of a vitamin C solution was measured by _____ and transferred to a _____ . A few drops of _____ indicator were added. Iodine solution of known concentration was added from a _____ until the indicator had just turned _____ after shaking. The titration was repeated at least twice to obtain _____.

c) Calculate the mass of vitamin C present in a tablet from the following experimental results.
25.0 cm^3 of a vitamin C solution was titrated against 0.024 mol l^{-1} iodine solution. The average titre was 11.8 cm^3. The equation for the reaction is:

$$C_6H_8O_6 + I_2 \rightarrow C_6H_6O_6 + 2H^+ + 2I^-$$

End-of-course Questions

SECTION A: Grid questions

1*

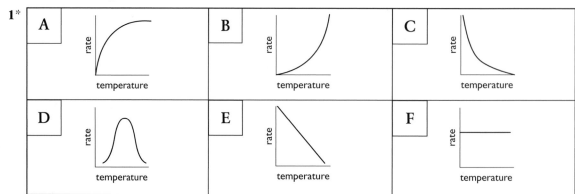

Identify the graph which shows how the rate varies with temperature in
a) the reaction between oxalic acid and acidified potassium permanganate solution
b) the fermentation of glucose
c) the radioactive decay of uranium-235.

2* An atom of X, a Group 1 element, reacts to become an ion, X^+.
Identify the **true** statement(s) about this change.

A	The diameter of the particle increases.
B	The nucleus acquires a positive charge.
C	The number of energy levels (electron shells) decreases by one.
D	The atomic number increases by one.
E	An electron is emitted from the nucleus.
F	The number of neutrons does not change.

3*

A	(benzaldehyde structure: $O=C-H$ on benzene ring)	B	$HOCH_2CH_2OH$	C	(structure: $O=C(HO)-C(CH_3)(H)-N(H)(H)$)
D	(terephthalic acid structure: COOH–benzene–COOH)	E	$C_2H_5NH_2$	F	(acetophenone structure: $O=C-CH_3$ on benzene ring)

a) Identify the molecule which could be produced when a protein is hydrolysed.
b) Identify the **two** molecules which contain the carboxyl group.
c) Identify the **two** molecules which could be used to make polyester.

128

4* A vanadium(V) oxide catalyst is used in the production of sulphur trioxide.

$$SO_2(g) + \tfrac{1}{2}O_2(g) \rightleftharpoons SO_3(g)$$

The potential energy diagram for the uncatalysed reaction is shown.

Identify the **true** statement(s) in the grid.

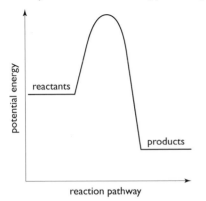

A	The enthalpy change for the forward reaction is positive.
B	At equilibrium, the energy of activation for the forward reaction is equal to the energy of activation for the reverse reaction.
C	The catalyst decreases the enthalpy change of the reaction.
D	Increasing the pressure increases the yield of sulphur trioxide.
E	The catalyst increases the rate of the reverse reaction.

5* The grid shows the concentration of solutions, in mol l^{-1}.

A 2×10^{-1}	**B** 1×10^{-1}	**C** 1×10^{-2}	**D** 1×10^{-3}	**E** 2×10^{-12}	**F** 1×10^{-12}

a) Identify the concentration of hydrogen ions in a solution which has a pH of 2.
b) A solution is made by pipetting 10.0 cm³ of 0.10 mol l^{-1} sodium hydroxide solution into a 100 cm³ standard flask and making up to the mark with distilled water.
   Identify the concentration of hydrogen ions in the solution.

6* The grid shows quantities of five different gases.

A 7 g CO	**B** 32 g CH_4	**C** 4 g H_2	**D** 32 g SO_2	**E** 17 g NH_3

a) Identify the **two** gases which occupy the same volume.
   (Assume all measurements are made under the same conditions of temperature and pressure.)
b) Identify the **two** gases which contain the same number of atoms.

7* Many factors influence the rates of reactions.

A particle size of reactants	**B** temperature	**C** surface area available for reaction
D activation energy	**E** concentration	**F** average kinetic energy of reactant molecules

a) Identify the factor which, if increased, causes an increase in the factor shown in box **F**.
b) Identify the factor(s) which, if increased, would make a reaction slower.

8*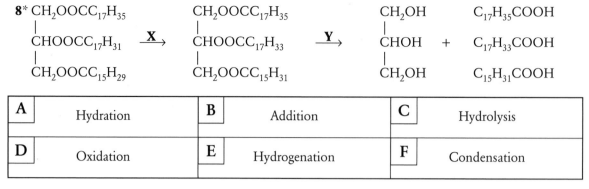

A	Hydration	B	Addition	C	Hydrolysis
D	Oxidation	E	Hydrogenation	F	Condensation

a) Identify the name which could be applied to reaction **Y**.

b) Identify the name(s) which could be applied to reaction **X**.

SECTION B: Extended answer questions

1 An ester can be prepared from butan-1-ol and propanoic acid. The equation for the reaction is shown below.

$$C_4H_9OH + C_2H_5COOH \rightleftharpoons$$
$$C_2H_5COOC_4H_9 + H_2O$$

In one method of preparation, anhydrous zinc(II) chloride, a dehydrating agent, is added to the mixture of reactants. Zinc chloride is a salt formed from a weak base (zinc hydroxide) and a strong acid.

a) Name the ester prepared in this reaction.

b) Suggest the likely pH of a solution of zinc chloride and explain your choice.

c) What would be the effect of zinc chloride on the yield of ester?

d) In an experiment 7.4 g of butan-1-ol were reacted with 9.0 g of propanoic acid.
   i) Show by calculation that the acid is present in excess.
   ii) Calculate the mass of ester produced if the percentage yield is 75%.

2 Hydrogen combines with metals at low temperatures to produce solid hydrides. These hydrides decompose at much higher temperatures. If placed in cylinders, a hydride could be used as a means of storing hydrogen for use as fuel in cars.

a) From what part of the car might heat be obtained to decompose the hydride?

b) Is the formation of the hydride an endothermic or exothermic reaction? Explain your choice with reference to the information given above.

c) Suggest **one** possible advantage of using hydrogen from a solid hydride as opposed to compressed or liquid hydrogen for motor fuel.

d) Lithium hydride, LiH, conducts electricity when molten producing hydrogen gas at the positive electrode.
   What does this tell you about
   i) the type of bonding in LiH
   ii) the charge on the hydrogen particle present?

3 The equation for the complete combustion of ethane is as follows.

$$2C_2H_6(g) + 7O_2(g) \rightarrow 4CO_2(g) + 6H_2O(l)$$

All gas volumes are measured at room temperature and pressure $(V_{mol} = 24$ litres mol$^{-1})$.

What volume of oxygen gas would be required for the complete combustion of
a) 1 mole of ethane
b) 1 litre of ethane
c) 1 g of ethane?

4* Air bags in cars are intended to prevent injuries in a car crash. They contain sodium azide, NaN_3, which produces nitrogen if an impact is detected.
The reaction which generates nitrogen is:

$$2NaN_3(s) \rightarrow 3N_2(g) + 2Na(s)$$

a) Other chemicals are present in air bags. These chemicals take part in further reactions. Suggest why these reactions are necessary.

b) Calculate the mass of sodium azide required to produce 75 litres of nitrogen. (Take the molar volume to be 24 litre mol^{-1}.)

c) In order to provide protection, the gas must be generated very rapidly. The graph shows how the volume of nitrogen produced changes over a period of time.

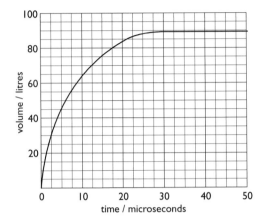

Calculate the average rate of nitrogen production, in litres per microsecond, over the first 20 microseconds.

5* Soda water is made by dissolving carbon dioxide in water, under pressure.

$$CO_2(g) + aq \rightleftharpoons CO_2(aq)$$

a) When the stopper is taken off a bottle of soda water, the carbon dioxide gas escapes. Explain why the drink eventually goes **completely** flat.

b) This graph shows the solubility of carbon dioxide in water at different temperatures.

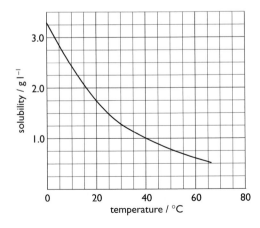

What does the graph indicate about the enthalpy of solution of carbon dioxide in water?

c) When all of the carbon dioxide is removed from one litre of soda water at 0°C, the gas is found to occupy 1.7 litres.
Use information in the graph to calculate the molar volume of carbon dioxide at this temperature.

6* In the Birkeland-Eyde Process, nitrogen and oxygen combine on sparking to produce nitrogen monoxide.

$$\tfrac{1}{2}N_2(g) + \tfrac{1}{2}O_2(g) \rightleftharpoons NO(g)$$
$$\Delta H_f = +100 \text{ kJ mol}^{-1}$$

The activation energy for this reaction is 1200 kJ mol^{-1}.

a) Copy and complete the energy-diagram for the industrial process.

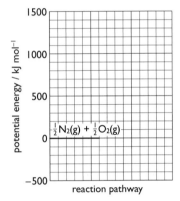

b) i) Suggest a feedstock for the Birkeland-Eyde Process.

ii) Explain how an increase in temperature would affect the yield of nitrogen monoxide.

7* Urea is a substance found in human urine. The enzyme urease catalyses the hydrolysis of urea.

$$CO(NH_2)_2 + H_2O \xrightarrow{\text{urease enzyme}} CO_2 + 2NH_3$$

urea

The concentration of urea in a sample can be estimated using an indicator as shown in the diagram.

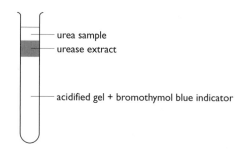

- urea sample
- urease extract
- acidified gel + bromothymol blue indicator

The bromothymol blue indicator is yellow below pH 6 and blue above pH 8.3.

a) Draw the full structural formula for urea.
b) The initial yellow colour of the indicator changed to blue as the experiment proceeded. Explain **fully** the colours observed.
c) The pH of the gel after one completed experiment was found to be 11. Calculate the concentration of hydroxide ions.
d) The graph shows the potential energy diagram for a urease catalysis of urea.

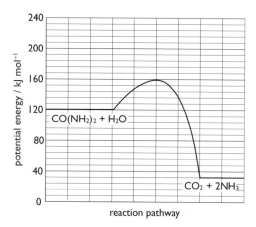

i) What is the enthalpy change for the reaction?
ii) Acid is a **less** effective catalyst than urease for this reaction. Add a curve to the potential energy diagram to show the hydrolysis when acid is used as the catalyst.

8* Diamond and graphite are forms of carbon with very different properties.
Graphite can mark paper, is a lubricant and is a conductor of electricity.
Diamond has none of these properties.

a) Draw a diagram to show the structure of diamond.
b) Why is graphite an effective lubricant?

c) A pupil uses a graphite pencil to write her signature 100 times on a piece of weighed paper.

Results	Number of signatures	= 100
	Mass of blank paper	= 4.895 g
	Mass of paper + 100 signatures	= 4.905 g

Use her results to calculate the number of carbon atoms present in one signature.

d) Boron nitride can form a similar structure to graphite. The boron and nitrogen atoms alternate throughout the structure as shown.

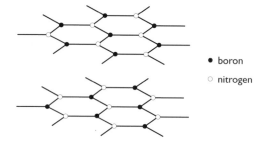

● boron
○ nitrogen

i) Why is this substance a non-conductor, while graphite is a conductor?
ii) Suggest why the bonds between the layers in boron nitride are stronger than the bonds between the layers in graphite.

9* Prefixes can be used to indicate the number of atoms in a molecule.

Term	Number of atoms in the molecule	Example
diatomic	2	hydrogen chloride
triatomic	3	carbon dioxide
tetra-atomic	4	sulphur trioxide
penta-atomic	5	tetrachloromethane
hexa-atomic	6	phosphorus pentachloride

a) What term is used to describe the following molecule?

$$H - \overset{\displaystyle H}{\underset{\displaystyle }{B}} \diagdown H$$

b) Name a hexa-atomic molecule, containing carbon, which will decolourise bromine water rapidly.

c) Write the formula for a carbon compound consisting of penta-atomic molecules with a molecular mass of 85.

10* Calcite is a very pure form of calcium carbonate which reacts with nitric acid as follows.

$$CaCO_3(s) + 2HNO_3(aq) \rightarrow$$
$$Ca(NO_3)_2(aq) + H_2O(l) + CO_2(g)$$

A 2.14 g piece of calcite was added to 50.0 cm^3 of 0.200 mol l^{-1} nitric acid in a beaker.

a) Calculate the mass of calcite, in grams, left unreacted.

b) Describe what could be done to check the result obtained in **a)**.

11* a) The graph shows how the intensity of radiation from a sample of a radioactive isotope decreased with time.

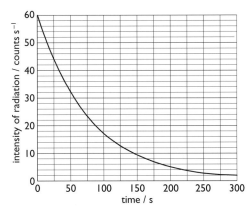

i) Calculate the half-life, in seconds, of the radioactive isotope.

ii) Starting from the same initial intensity of radiation, add a curve to the graph to show how the intensity of radiation for an isotope with a half-life of 25 s would decrease over a period of 100 s.

b) Nuclear reactions can be carried out by scientists. For example, lawrencium-257 has been made by bombarding californium-252 with atoms of an isotope of a lighter element. Each successful collision was accompanied by the release of six neutrons.
Write a nuclear equation for this reaction.

c) An example of a nuclear reaction which happens in nature is:

$$^{12}_{6}C + ^{4}_{2}He \rightarrow ^{16}_{8}O$$

What name is given to reactions of this type?

12* In 1996, the scientists Robert Curl, Harold Kroto and Richard Smalley won the Nobel Prize in Chemistry for their contribution to the discovery of new forms of carbon called fullerenes.

a) In what way does the structure of fullerenes differ from the other forms of carbon, diamond and graphite?

b) One form of fullerene, C_{60}, forms a superconducting crystalline compound with potassium. Its formula can be represented as K_3C_{60}. A sample of this compound was found to contain 2.88 g of carbon.

   i) Calculate the number of moles of fullerene used to make this compound.

   ii) Calculate the mass of potassium, in grams, in the sample.

13* Some rockets have a propellant system which combines dinitrogen tetroxide with methylhydrazine.

$$5N_2O_4 + 4CH_3NHNH_2 \rightarrow$$
$$\mathbf{x}N_2 + \mathbf{y}H_2O + \mathbf{z}CO_2$$

a) State the values of **x**, **y** and **z** required to balance the above equation.

b) Draw the full structural formula for methylhydrazine.

c) Methylhydrazine burns acccording to the following equation.

$$CH_3NHNH_2(l) + 2\tfrac{1}{2}O_2(g) \rightarrow$$
$$CO_2(g) + 3H_2O(l) + N_2(g)$$
$$\Delta H = -1305 \text{ kJ mol}^{-1}$$

Use this information, together with information from the SQA Data Book to calculate the enthalpy change for the following reaction.

$$C(s) + N_2(g) + 3H_2(g) \rightarrow CH_3NHNH_2(l)$$

14*

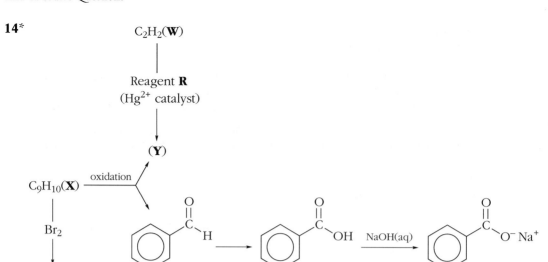

Oxidation of compound **X** produces compounds **Y** and **Z**, **both of which give a positive Benedict's (or Fehling's) test**.

a) From its reaction with bromine, which functional group must compound **X** contain?
b) Name compound **W**.
c) How many moles of bromine are required to saturate 1 mole of compound **W**?
d) To which class of organic compounds does **Y** belong?
e) Compounds **W** and **Y** contain the same number of carbon atoms.
   Work out the formula of reagent **R**.
f) Draw the full structural formula for compound **X**.
g) Name a reagent capable of converting compound **Z** to benzoic acid.
h) Benzoic acid is a weak acid.
   Explain why the pH of sodium benzoate solution is alkaline (pH > 7).
i) The benzene ring can be drawn in two ways:

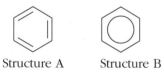

   Structure A   Structure B

Give **two** reasons why structure B is considered to be the better representation of the benzene ring.

15* The reaction scheme shows a number of common reactions.

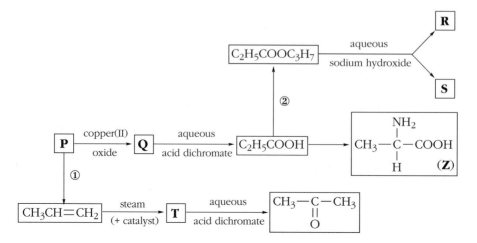

a) Name compounds **P**, **Q**, **R** and **S**.
b) State the types of chemical reaction occuring at ① and ②.
c) Write a structural formula for compound **T**.
d) Describe a chemical test you could use to distinguish between compound **Q** and propanone.
e) Name the class of compounds to which compound **Z** belongs.
f) Assuming 80% efficiency, what mass of propanone would be formed from 84 kg of propene?

16* The idea of **oxidation number** leads to a systematic method of naming inorganic compounds. The systematic name of $KClO_3$ is potassium chlorate(V) where the Roman numeral in brackets represents the oxidation number of the chlorine atom.
Simplified rules for working out oxidation numbers are:
- all Group 1 metals have an oxidation number of +1
- oxygen has an oxidation number of –2
- the sum of the oxidation numbers of all atoms in the formula of a compound is zero.

a) Copy and complete the table below.

Formula	Oxidation number of non-oxygen atom in the negative ion	Systematic name	Charge on the negative ion
$KClO_3$	+5	potassium chlorate(V)	–1
Na_2SO_4	+6		–2
	+7	potassium iodate(VII)	–1
Na_3PO_4			

b) In acid solution, potassium chlorate(V), $KClO_3(aq)$, oxidises sodium iodide.
  i) Write an ion-electron equation for the oxidation reaction.
  ii) During the reaction, chlorate(V) ions are reduced to form chlorine.

$$ClO_3^- \rightarrow Cl_2$$

Copy and complete the above to form the ion-electron equation.

17* Perfumes normally contain three groups of components called the **top note**, the **middle note** and the **end note**.
a) The **top note** components of a perfume form vapours most easily. Two compounds found in **top note** components are:

p-cresyl acetate   geranyl acetate

  i) With reference to the structure of these compounds, why are they likely to have pleasant smells?
  ii) Describe a chemical test which would distinguish between these two compounds and give the result of the test.

b) The **middle note** compounds form vapours less readily than the **top note** compounds. A typical compound of the **middle note** is:

2-phenylethanol

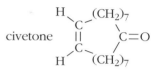

Due to hydrogen bonding 2-phenylethanol forms a vapour less readily than *p*-cresyl acetate. Draw two molecules of 2-phenylethanol and use a dotted line to show where a hydrogen bond exists between the two molecules.

c) The **end note** of a perfume has a long lasting odour which stays with the user

An example of an **end note** compound is:

civetone

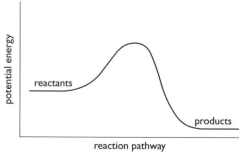

Draw the structure of the alcohol which would be formed by the reduction of civetone.

18* The first twenty elements of the Periodic Table are as follows.

H							He
Li	Be	B	C	N	O	F	Ne
Na	Mg	Al	Si	P	S	Cl	Ar
K	Ca						

a) From the first twenty elements of the Periodic Table, give **one** example of a covalent molecular solid at room temperature.

b) Which **two** elements, from the first twenty elements in the Periodic Table, form a compound with the highest degree of ionic character?

c) i) Name the type of structure in silicon.
　　ii) Why do elements with this type of structure have high melting points?

d) Sodium and magnesium both contain metallic bonding. Why is the bonding in magnesium stronger than that in sodium?

19* Methanoic acid, HCOOH, can break down to carbon monoxide and water by two different routes, **A** and **B**.

Reaction A (catalysed)　$HCOOH(aq) + H^+(aq) \longrightarrow CO(g) + H_2O(l) + H^+(aq)$

Reaction B (uncatalysed)　$HCOOH(aq) \xrightarrow{\text{heat}} CO(g) + H_2O(l)$

a) i) What is the evidence in the equation for Reaction **A** that the $H^+(aq)$ ion acts as a catalyst?
　　ii) Explain whether Reaction **A** is an example of heterogeneous or homogeneous catalysis.

b) The energy diagram for the **catalysed** reaction is:

Copy the diagram and draw a line to show the reaction pathway for the **uncatalysed** reaction.